THE PHILLIPS GUIDE TO
TOMORROW'S
ANTIQUES

Text ©	Peter Johnson
Illustration ©	Phillips Fine Art Auctioneers
	Dunestyle Publishing Ltd.
Edited by	Peter Rea
Assistant Editor	Megra Mitchell
Art Director	John Strange
Devised by	Dunestyle Publishing Ltd.
Production	Zivia Desai, Hugh Allan
Produced by	Multimedia Books Ltd.
Copyright ©	Dunestyle Publishing Ltd.
	and Multimedia Books Ltd. 1987, 1993
Designed by	Strange Design Associates

This book was devised by Dunestyle Publishing Ltd. and produced by Multimedia Books Ltd.

This edition published 1993 in the United Kingdom by MMB, an imprint of Multimedia Books Limited, 32 - 34 Gordon House Road, London NW5 1LP

Exclusive distribution in the USA by Smithmark Publishers Inc. 16 East 32nd Street, New York, NY10016

ISBN 1 85375 128 6

Colour separation by J. Film Process Co. Ltd., Bangkok, Thailand.
Typesetting by BWS Graphics, London.
Printed and bound in the Czech Republic by Imago.

Title page. An Edwardian compendium of games.

Contents. A German lithographed paper toy of the nineteenth century, The Fashion Shop.

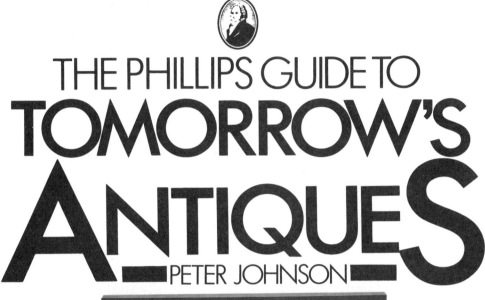

THE PHILLIPS GUIDE TO
TOMORROW'S
ANTIQUES

PETER JOHNSON

MMB

6	ACKNOWLEDGEMENTS
8	INTRODUCTION
16	ADVERTISING
20	AIRMAILS
26	AUTOGRAPHS
30	AUTOMOBILIA
34	AVIATION
38	BADGES AND MEDALS
42	BAR AND PUB
46	BOOKS
50	BOTTLES AND CORKSCREWS
54	BUSTED BONDS
58	CARTOONS
60	CATS AND DOGS
64	CHRISTMAS AND GREETINGS
68	CIGARETTE CARDS
74	CINEMANIA
78	COMICS, MAGAZINES AND ANNUALS
82	COMMEMORATIVES
86	CRESTED CHINA
88	CYCLING
92	DISNEY
96	DOLLS
100·	DOLLS HOUSES AND CONTENTS
104	FAIRGROUND
108	GAMES

GRAMOPHONES	112
ILLUSTRATORS	116
MODEL TRAINS	120
PAPER MONEY	124
PHOTOGRAPHY	126
POP AND ROCK	130
POSTCARDS	134
POSTERS	138
RAILWAY	142
SHIPPING	146
SMOKING	150
SPORT	154
TEDDY BEARS	158
THEATRE	162
TILES	166
TINS	168
TIN TOYS	172
TOY SOLDIERS OLD	178
TOY SOLDIERS NEW	184
TOY TOWN AND COUNTRY	188
TOY VEHICLES	192
VALENTINES	196
WAR EPHEMERA	200
WAR HARDWARE	204
WILD WEST	208
THE WORLD AROUND US	212

ACKNOWLEDGEMENTS

The overwhelming majority of illustrations in this book have been provided by Phillips, the international fine art auctioneers. My gratitude goes to the Phillips staff who have given freely of their knowledge and patiently answered my questions, not only during the preparation of this book, but over nearly two decades of happy association. Especially, I acknowledge the professional assistance and invaluable support given during the book's research, compilation and writing by Noelle Anton, my colleague in the public relations department. Elsewhere at Phillips, my thanks are due to: Christopher Weston and Christopher Hawkings, who have built up the corps of specialists whose expertise I have tapped; Andrew Hilton and his enthusiastic team in the Collectors' Centre, London; the New York saleroom staff, headed by Bob Frye, and in particular Eric Alberta, Mary Hansen and Henry I. Kurtz; my friends at a score of Phillips branches throughout the United Kingdom; Christopher Halton for his talents seen in so many of the fine photographs.

I have had privileged, 'inside' access to the fabulous collections of *Forbes* magazine of America, and I express gratitude to Malcolm Forbes and his sons, Robert and Christopher, for the opportunity to study these collections at close hand over the period of a long relationship; my thanks go also to Margaret Kelly, *Forbes* curator in New York, and her staff for the efficient and helpful way in which they have met my requests for photographs. I am grateful for permission to publish photographs provided by Alfred Dunhill of London (cigarette lighters) and the Yu-Chee Chong and Vanessa Devereux galleries of London (cinema design).

The idea and genesis of this book came to me from John Strange of Dunestyle Publishing and Strange Design Associates. His enthusiasm has been catching, his design an inspiration, his support unstinting. I also acknowledge the important contribution made by his colleague, Megra Mitchell. Finally, my thanks go to the numbers of collectors and dealers I have known over the years, the writers and lecturers on collecting, whose views have gone into the making of this book.

Peter Johnson

Peter Johnson, London

Phillips, 7 Blenheim Street, New Bond Street, London W1Y OAS, England.
Telephone 01 629 6602
Phillips, 406 East 79th Street, New York, NY 10021, USA.
Telephone 212 570 4830

Phillips

FINE ART AUCTIONEERS & VALUERS SINCE 1796.

It is 11 a.m. on the day of the wedding of Charles, Prince of Wales, and Lady Diana Spencer – and the secret of the princess and the parasol can be revealed. Among those sworn to secrecy in the planning of the bride's wedding ensemble has been Anne-Marie Benson, head of lace and textiles at Phillips, the fine art auctioneers, in London. Emanuel, the designers of the wedding dress, have been in confidential consultation with her for months on types of lace, and through her specialized knowledge she has provided a Victorian parasol which, remodelled and re-covered, forms part of the princess's ensemble. Not even Anne-Marie's closest colleagues know about it until an official Buckingham Palace announcement is made as Diana arrives at St Paul's Cathedral, and her wedding dress is displayed to the world.

Phillips, founded in 1796 (and, incidentally, the only auction firm to hold a sale inside Buckingham Palace – in 1836 when the contents of various royal apartments came under the hammer), has a reputation for specialization. Its specialists, whose resources of expertise and experience have contributed to this book, handle fine art, antiques and collectors' items under more than sixty departmental headings – a huge spectrum of art and artefacts that ranges from Old Masters to cigarette cards. There is a day-to-day operation of identification, valuation, research, cataloguing and the organization of 1,300 sales a year.

The Collectors' Centre, in the heart of a large Art Deco-fronted headquarters in Mayfair, London, is constantly recognizing, defining and catering for new trends in collecting. It answers hundreds of queries a day from collectors, museums, dealers and the public at large. The shelves of its cataloguing halls are packed with a medley of wonderful, weird and sometimes whimsical treasures – toys, photographic material, uniforms, musical machines, radios, tins, china, trophies, memorabilia of the movies and of pop, motoring, nautical and aviation mementoes, ephemera on a bewildering variety of topics, and much, much more. There are antiques in profusion, and also many of the treasures to be found in this book – the antiques of tomorrow. To continue to be successful, a great auction house must be a dynamic, constantly questing operation, charting new trends, feeding new enthusiasms, extending the boundaries of collecting.

To varying extents, the scene in London is repeated at a score of Phillips salerooms elsewhere in Britain and throughout the world. The firm has developed the largest network of United Kingdom regional salerooms, each one of which can draw on the international expertise of specialists based in London or the company's New York salerooms. The Phillips team in Manhattan has its own specializations: there have been many landmark sales of Americana, illustrators' works, posters, photographs, carousel collectables, comic and cinema art, and American toys.

The firm's founder, Harry Phillips, an ebullient entrepreneur with a lively style when conducting an auction, would have approved of the way his professional heirs go out to discover and explore new areas of collectables. When he conducted his first sale under his own name – at the vendor's residence in Crown Street, Westminster – George III was on the throne and Harry wielded the gavel over many splendid pieces of contemporary furniture and decorations: antiques of tomorrow, all.

INTRODUCTION

Right. Biscuit blandishment. A stunning example of biscuit-tin art is represented in this design of 1920/30 for a pastilleria bar in Palermo, Sicily. Art Deco style is translated with Italian panache. A collectors' item to be treasured in the years ahead.

Far right. Fairground fancy. This magnificent carved wooden carousel horse is a prancing leader in a new American collecting vogue. Carousel art has become a specialization of Phillips in New York, and some of the rarest animals are heading towards six figures.

Early Coca-Cola bottles are the real thing to American collectors. Clockwork robots of instant mashed-potato fame have climbed out of British television commercials, passed through the toy stores, and are croaking with glee in the antique markets. The postcard on which a transatlantic passenger wrote, 'Dear Bill, We are alright up to now and having a jolly time', just before the departure of the *Titanic*, has come under the hammer. Medals won in Vietnam and the Falkland Islands have been bartered. History is being collected as fast as it is made.

Where do we start looking for tomorrow's antiques? A broad answer in terms of a dateline would be: any time after the threshold of the 1890s – if only for the reason that any collectable dating from before that time, give or take a year or two, comes within the technical classification of 'antique'. While the majority of the many hundreds of items described and illustrated in this book fall on our side of this sketchily drawn dateline, there can be no simple formula for identifying tomorrow's antiques, the objects and ephemera of our age that will stand the test of time in collectors' esteem. There are tracts of hitherto uncharted ground, and they must be explored and signposted, subject by subject. A list of rules learned for toys may have to be discarded and a whole new set

of standards applied when dealing with, say, crested china or autographs.

Defining future collecting subjects, and exploiting new potential in those already established (some of which may even embrace a proportion of true antiques), *can* lead to profit. Much more important, however, in this game of discovery is the fun of it. Three happenings of recent years illustrate the factors – sometimes predictable, often unexpected, always fascinating – that go into the enjoyment of pursuing tomorrow's antiques.

In the late 1970s an immense outdated stock of tinplate key-wind playthings went on to the market from the warehouses of Marx, the American toy firm. The event triggered some of the most unusual auctions ever seen in the salerooms of New York and London. 'Lot 80 – what am I bid for Uncle Wiggley and the Popeye Eccentric Airplane?' ... the Acrobatic Marvel jumped for bids and the Whee-Whiz Auto Racer whirled giddily. The bulk of this tinplate juvenilia dated from the Fifties and Sixties, and there was such an enormous mass of material that much of it went at bargain prices. The Marx Merrymakers, a group of Mickey Mouse-like automata around a piano, were an exception: being of earlier vintage, they established a four-figure base

around which they have since fluctuated, but they remain one of the most desirable examples of clockwork 'Disneyana'. Wise collectors and dealers, however, flocked in from Los Angeles, Chicago, Philadelphia and Boston to stock up on the bargain mountain, judging rightly that 1950s tin would turn into gold.

In October 1984, Malcolm Forbes, multi-millionaire owner of the American *Forbes* magazine, and collector-extraordinary, despatched one of his lieutenants from New York to an out-of-town auction to buy china. Up for sale was the tableware from the former liner *United States*, a ship that had shared the fate of many a great transatlantic giant. It seemed to Mr Forbes an appropriate nautical conclusion that the china, crested and marked with the great ship's great name, should once more sail the high seas in his new luxury yacht, then being fitted out in the shipyard. The Forbes bidder brought home the china.

The spring of 1985 saw the chandeliered salerooms of London's fine-art 'golden mile' pulsing to the beat of rock and peopled by clientele not normally seen around these august purlieus. Potential buyers viewed lots through reflector shades. 'Sold to the gentleman with the purple hair' became a catchphrase backstage among the auctioneers' staffs. What

had Bond Street come to? The answer was – pop. Rock 'n' roll memorabilia of the Sixties was climbing the saleroom charts and fetching prices to equal those of Old Masters. Regular pop auctions have been held since.

Obsoleteness is a factor that links all three of these collecting phenomena. Tinplate toys are especially interesting when weighing this factor. After a leading and respected company such as Marx has come to the end of production of a series of lines, those products assume a cachet for collectors. A clockwork motorcyclist, made by Arnold in West Germany in the Fifties, was clocking up nearly £270/$400 within three decades. Many Japanese toys of the mid-1960s – such as Charley Weaver Bartender and Travelling Sam, both battery-operated – have risen above a tide of contemporary trash and entered auction catalogues and collectors' hearts. Similarly, obsoleteness enhances the crested tableware of the transatlantic liners. (For that matter, scale models of the great ships, which used to grace the shipping companies' metropolitan ticket-office windows, vanished into the wealthiest collectors' harbours even as the famous vessels themselves were pensioned off or scrapped.) And pop? Not every genre of popular music would necessarily leave a collectors' heritage, but the Sixties meant the Beatles, and the Beatles meant a mass of original and manufactured memorabilia, from the autographs of the Fab Four to their motor cars. The pop artefacts of the Sixties, being largely Beatle-based, were ensured of collector esteem within a very short time.

The end-of-a-line syndrome happened dramatically to the lead soldiers of William Britain when that company went over entirely to plastic and diecast in the mid-1960s. There had been for many years a small band of serious collectors of the multifarious lines of this premier, and British, toy-soldier maker. Obsoleteness immediately heightened interest, and the great collecting boom that followed (and is still going strong) diversified to embrace the toy armies of other countries, ranging from old Mignots in France to the long under-estimated dimestore 'cheapies' of the United States. The making of tomorrow's antiques is an evolving process, however: the very plastic that replaced the last of the lead soldiers is steadily appreciating in the case of some early, now discontinued lines.

The toy industry is a prolific source of tomorrow's antiques. It caters for a fickle market, with wildly veering fads and fancies, so that lines come and – more importantly – go. The onrush of technology makes yesterday's favourite out of date today. Tin and wooden toys, dolls, teddy bears rise in fashion, then fall: a collecting vogue is born. The second half of the 1980s has seen an enormous saleroom boom in teddy bears, fuelled largely by American interest, in which some octogenarian growlers have climbed well into four figures. But post-war teddy bears have joined the picnic, too. And a recent international touring exhibition of American dolls enshrined modern Barbie and Cindy among the rag and wooden veterans.

Far right. Hearts and flowers at the turn of the century: a stand-up Valentine which gives a three-dimensional appearance, a big-selling novelty of its time and popular today among the growing ranks of Valentine collectors.

Far left. The furniture around us contains examples that will become the antiques of tomorrow. Twentieth century elegance is provided by this black-lacquered table, attributed to the school of Josef Hoffmann on stylistic grounds.

Below. Brash, cheerful, colourful: modern tinplate toys have an appeal of their own. The Japanese, in particular, have produced many that will stand the collecting test of time. These battery-driven floor-runners hoot, flash lights, and change direction when they come to an obstacle.

Tomorrow's antiques are all around us. In Britain, Robert Opie's museum collection of everyday packaging and related advertising matter (see the chapter on Advertising on page 16) demonstrates that collectables – and history – are to be found sometimes in the most ephemeral of materials. It also serves to remind us of the importance of the original packaging: the existence of the original box in good condition can add a large percentage to the value of, say, a tinplate vehicle or a set of toy soldiers.

The ordinary becomes the unusual when it is no longer in ready and universal supply: some of the Lalique-designed glass perfume bottles that have made five figures at auction in New York in recent years were once – say, in grandmother's day – no more than the routine, if elegantly fashioned, containers of the scents themselves.

There are a number of key questions the potential collector should ask when attempting to decide whether an object will become one of tomorrow's antiques:

● Is it attractive? In the USA there is a dedicated band of collectors of barbed wire (a commodity which, should you be interested, comes in a multitude of forms), but a strand of triple-barb, high-tensile ranch fencing is not everybody's notion of the ideal decoration. On the other hand, the humble beer mat and the pub ashtray may qualify.

● Is it obsolete? If the answer is Yes, there is a supplementary question. Is the type of object in existence in sufficient quantity to provide a collector with a reasonable hope of fulfilment, sufficient to sustain collecting interest, with all the fun of exchanges, trading and pooling of information? At the same time, any collecting field must have its ultra-rarities to

stimulate the chase. There must be the spur of availability at base level, coupled with the incentive to seek the almost-unattainable.

● Is it of good quality? Many of the trashy toys of today will never emulate the record of products from blue-chip Bing, Joumet, Ives, Meccano, Britain's, Märklin and the like.

● Will it appreciate in value? The question must be asked critically about the modern plethora of commercial limited editions of so-called 'heirlooms', even the ones which may have a certain intrinsic value in their material. On the basis of saleroom experience, many a specialist will tell you that the majority of these 'limited-edition heirlooms' barely keep pace with inflation. Moreover, buying newly produced limited editions can hardly be called *collecting*. Where is the hunt? Where is the joy of the unexpected discovery? Where is the exhilaration of the bargain purchase? On the other hand, the categories of tomorrow's antiques examined in this book will satisfy the true collector requirements; furthermore, given time, most of them will probably appreciate in real value, albeit only modestly in some cases.

● Am I in it only for the money? If the answer is Yes, forget it. That is not what collecting is about. On the other hand, one of the pleasures of spotting trends in and playing the collector market is watching one's investment of time and cash appreciate in monetary terms.

● Am I in it for the fun? If the answer is Yes, then you are a true collector. If your collection notably increases in value, look on that as a bonus on top of the enjoyment it has given

Below. Hornby meant trains to several generations of British boys (and those of other nationalities). This gouache of the King George V thundering along the coast was commissioned from Bryan de Grineau for the 1938-39 Hornby catalogue. A classic piece of railwayana.

you. Many dedicated collectors use the profits from resale of items to refine their collections.

Finally, a hoard is not a collection. Be selective. Choose a theme and stick to it until you have mapped out the byways that will enable you to branch out from, and enlarge on, that theme. Collecting tomorrow's antiques is, above all, about exploration.

How to use this book

Tomorrow's antiques are examined under 50 category and chapter headings. The first 49 chapters deal with the subjects alphabetically, from 'Advertising' to 'Wild West'; the final chapter, 'The World Around Us', takes a general look at the field and ranges in subject matter from furniture to fountain pens. The vast majority of the illustrations come from the current and past archives of Phillips, the international fine art auctioneers. I have also been able to draw on the resources of expertise and experience and the records of some 130 Phillips specialists based in Britain, the United States and Continental Europe. However, aware that collecting – and, particularly, collecting tomorrow's antiques – is far from being an exact science, I must emphasize that any assessments or judgments formed as to the future market performance of collectables or trends in collecting are essentially my personal opinion.

A starting mark of circa 1890, as already explained, is, to all intents and purposes, where we begin our exploring for tomorrow's antiques. It would be unrealistic, however, to

Below. A quaint survivor from the pre-World War I era. It is a clockwork, hand-painted 'electric tramcar' with hinged roof, of a type that was popular in the United States. Scratched, well-played with, it nevertheless made nearly £2,000/$3,000 at auction in the 1980s.

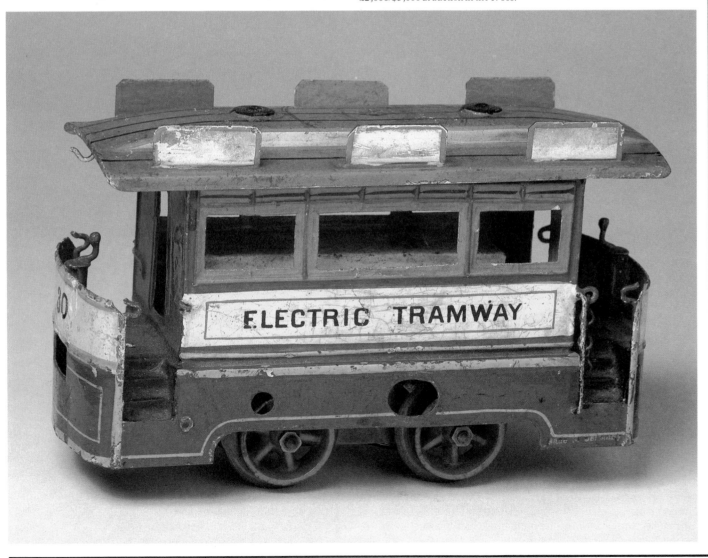

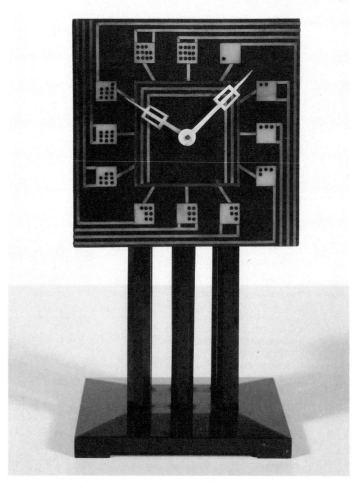

Above. Art Nouveau time. The Domino mantel clock was designed in 1917 by the celebrated Charles Rennie Mackintosh as a wedding present for two friends, Alec Sturrock and Mary Newbery. It measures 10 inches, (25cm) in height.

Right. One of a set of nine painted wooden panels, 'English Garden Delights', commissioned from Edward Bawden in 1947 for a lounge of the British liner *Orcades*. The panels became collectors' items after the ship was broken up in 1973.

delineate this frontier too boldly: to take only one example, it would be difficult and mistaken to try to separate the crested china of the 1880s from that of 1914.

Prices and values are generally given in both £ sterling and $ US, using an exchange rate, simplified for convenience, of $1.50 to the £. The values of certain items are higher in the USA than in Europe, and this factor is often taken into account, which will help to explain some apparent discrepancies in conversion. This book does not pretend to be a price guide, but it does make an attempt to give the reader an idea of values, projected into the 1990s on readings of price-performance records (both current and immediate-past) available to one of the world's great auction houses.

After dealing with each category of tomorrow's antiques, I present my table of Collector Rating, hopefully to add to the fun as well as the reader's knowledge of collecting:

● Scope and Variety. This rating is assessed on a scale of points from 1 to 10. Shipping collectables, for example, score the maximum number of points, 10, thanks not only to the wide range of artefacts and ephemera available, but also

because the subject embraces such a large variety of media and offers exceptionally abundant opportunities to the collector. The category of collectables relating to Cats and Dogs is a similar high-scorer.

● Investment Potential. This is judged on a scale descending from A to E, the A rating being awarded to those categories which, in the my opinion, stand the best chance of increasing in value over a period of 5-10 years. As a general rule, this exercise has most relevance when applied to the items which are of the highest quality in any given category.

● Price Range. Beginners may want to know: What is it going to cost me to start collecting? Any encapsulated guide can be in only the broadest terms. As a general principle, the prices quoted have been 'weighted' to take the collector forward into the 1990s. Chapter by chapter, category by category, the picture that emerges is that the antiques of tomorrow hold collecting opportunities to suit all pockets.

Peter Johnson, London

Above. No other branch of tomorrow's antiques has had such a speedy advance in the past two decades as the lead figures of William Britain, the toy-soldier maker. This foxhunting set of 'The Meet' is of post-war vintage, but it is already enshrined in collections and museums.

ADVERTISING

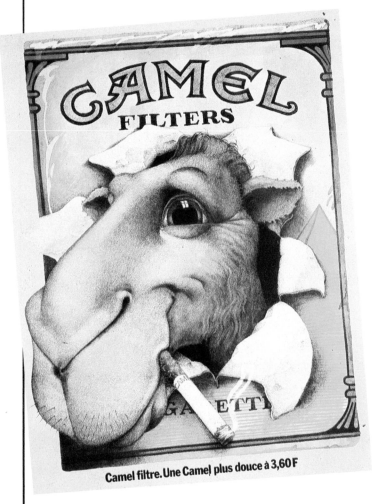

Camel filtre. Une Camel plus douce à 3,60 F

Below and overleaf. Enamel advertising signs that have been called jewels of the street – bold, expressive, clear in their message. The 1940s generally saw the end of this sort of advertising. Around and after that time, the signs began to come down and disappear into collectors' hoards. Size and range are enormous. The good news is that fakes would probably be too expensive to produce.

Above. This 1975 tobacco poster by Nick Price fell foul of French law which decreed that nobody, not even a camel, could be depicted smoking a cigarette. A long legal battle set alight collector interest.

The 1975 poster of a smiling camel, bursting through a packet, cigarette in mouth, might have been regarded as just another graphically brilliant work of Nick Price, an international advertising artist. While that in itself would have been sufficient to make it collector material, there was an additional factor that has enhanced the price on the head of this cheeky camel.

Designed to publicize Camel filter cigarettes in France, the image ran foul of French law which decreed that nobody – not even a camel – may be depicted actually smoking a cigarette. A legal battle trailed on into the Eighties over 'the camel with the laughing eye' who had been seen on hoardings and in print all over France, 'smoking with relish'. The tobacco company and the head of its advertising agency were fined, but still the legal fight went on. As the lawyers argued, however, the poster's collector value rose. An original example of the poster, 5ft (1.5m) tall, has sold for well into four figures at auction in New York. Such is the stuff of collecting!

Advertising ephemera, by its very nature, is one of the most readily available commodities in collecting. Enormous amounts are produced daily in the Western world, and advertising material, more than anything else, epitomizes the essence of the disposable society. Today's advertising campaign is merely a memory tomorrow. But, by the same token, an outstanding campaign can become a collectors' 'Classic' within the space of months. Therefore, we see the situation of collectors fighting with each other in the saleroom to bid for framed and glazed posters of successful Heineken or Budweiser beer onslaughts before the companies have even had time to change agencies. And the really dedicated collector is busy recording that most ephemeral of all advertising, the television or radio commercial, putting on to cassette the most interesting, dramatic or controversial 30-60 second fragments of, say, a US Presidential campaign or the launch of a share issue for British Gas.

Outdoor advertisements for commercial products or events can be traced back at least to Ancient Greek times. The development of printing in Europe in the fifteenth century gave a fillip to advertising. As the consumer society expanded simultaneously with the start of the industrial revolution in the eighteenth century, so there was more growth in advertising and it became fashionable to disparage it as 'puffing'. The nineteenth century – particularly the decades following 1870 – saw an explosion in advertising. In London alone there were an estimated 200 or more bill posters working in 1870. The proliferation of street announcements led to newspaper criticsm of 'the horror of the walls', but Oscar Wilde felt that street advertising 'brought colour into the drab monotony of English streets'. Indeed, when in 1979 a major exhibition of 100 years of enamel advertising signs was staged at the Geffrye Museum in London, it was entitled 'Street Jewellery' in tribute to the decorative qualities of this genre of advertising.

Metal signs are at the forefront of collecting. They are, however, a thing of the past. The 1940s probably saw the last production of this 'street jewellery', and the days when examples could be picked up for nothing or next to nothing at demolition sites have gone. The size as well as the range of signs is enormous, from 3 inch (7.5cm) wide door finger-plates to 8ft (2.5m) spreads intended to adorn gable-ends. There is very little left for today's collector unless he thinks of spending a minimum of £100/$150 per item, and the really rare pieces can easily climb into four figures.

Left. Rare ceramic tile for British biscuits, from the late nineteenth century (8 inches, 20cm). Once a salesman's giveaway on his round of retailers, now it is a treasured collectors' item.

Below left. Alphonse Mucha poster for a French spray perfume, 1896 (18 inches, 46cm high). Mucha's work seldom costs less than four figures.

Posters remain a less expensive way of forming a collection of advertising ephemera. Many of the big agencies are happy to meet private requests for small posters, examples of aspects of current campaigns, and this is a free way of starting a collection of antiques of tomorrow as far as advertising is concerned. Whether your freely acquired poster collection will appreciate in value is problematical – but it will be fun. On the other hand, collecting original examples from the great era of the poster – which extended from the Gay Nineties to the 1930s, and is dealt with in detail in the chapter on posters – can be an expensive business, with commensurately high rewards in the investment stakes for the shrewd buyer.

Objects are a part of any comprehensive collection of advertising material. The aristocrats among them would be the old shop signs with which traders advertised their premises. Perhaps the most readily recognized is the red-and-white striped barber's pole, signifying the blood and bandages of his traditional double role as surgeon or bloodletter.

An American cigar store Indian – or in Britain a life-sized carved wooden Scotsman to advertise a tobacco and snuff shop – is a saleroom flyer costing several thousands. A fashionable hairdresser might have put a carved wooden periwig over his doorway, a perfumier a wooden or stuffed civet cat (the source of musk), an optician a pair of gilded eye-glasses, a horse butcher a gilded tin outline of a horse's head, a chimney sweep a broom; a grocer would traditionally place large, japanned tea caddies in his window, and the pawnbroker, of course, resorted to three brass balls (originally blue, these are said to have come from the coat of arms of the Dukes of Medici, from whose states many bankers originated).

Advertisers continue to turn out a mass of promotional objects to publicize their wares. Some of them are undoubtedly destined to be valued as images of their time in the years ahead. Robert Vince, a British advertising executive, has built up an impressive collection of objects and ephemera, no doubt helped by the

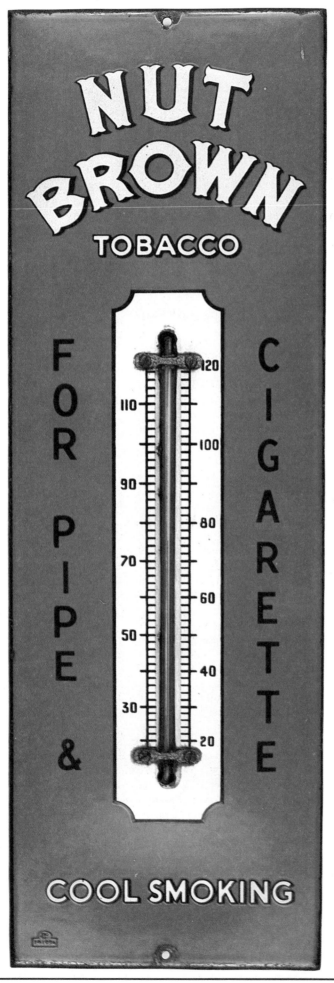

connections he established when he once owned three antique shops in Surrey. When interviewed by a collectors' magazine, he admitted that he suffered from a well-known problem; he wouldn't throw anything away, and he wouldn't sell items, other than to refine his growing collection. The only thing he had disposed of which he regretted was a 7ft (2.1m) Guinness bottle, which went to a New York restaurant. 'It broke my heart to see it go,' said Mr. Vince. 'but I simply had nowhere to put it.'

Many advertising give-aways have become specialized branches of collecting, notably toys. In the United States there is great allegiance to collecting radio premiums of the 1930s, '40s and '50s – cheap toys and other knick-knacks that were showered in millions to boost shows on the air. A precedent had been the inclusion of collectable cards in cigarette packets (see Cigarette Cards on Page 68), and radio premiums are considered to have begun with 'Little Orphan Annie' in 1931.

Jim Harmon, a writer, broadcaster and collector, has observed in Richard Brien's excellent guide *Collecting Toys:* 'The plucky little waif from the Sunday comics first gave away sheet music of her theme song ("Who's that pretty chatterbox with the pretty auburn locks?") and her own photo but, very shortly, she offered a drinking mug that could be used to shake up Ovaltine powder with milk to make something resembling a soda fountain milk shake. The first significant radio premium, it was the only successful one that encouraged further use of the sponsor's product.'

Many different models of the shake-up mug were offered by Annie, and later by Captain Midnight (on both radio and TV). So successful were the offers that the mugs are among the most common premiums available to collectors today. 'It took two more years after Annie came to radio,' wrote Harmon, 'for the fledgling medium to develop its really classic adventure heroes. There appeared the Lone Ranger, Tom Mix and Jack Armstrong. Unlike Annie, the two Westerners and the All-American Boy were still around until the 1950s, when television began driving out all radio drama. In those nearly 20 years, these shows offered hundreds of give-away toys, which inspired similar premiums on dozens of different shows. Any small toy that could be manufactured inexpensively enough might turn up as a premium. Those concerned with the great outdoors were popular. We had compasses, pedometers, telescopes, flashlights, pocket-knives, signal mirrors, and portable telegraph sets.'

A rare paper item was the Lone Ranger Frontier Town, offered about 1947. To complete this model of a Western settlement, one had to get four different envelopes by mail, then augment this by buying several packages of Cheerios in order to cut out the model buildings from the packs. Collectors reckon that a complete set would fetch well over £660/$1,000 on the market. Other premiums – such as a Captain Hawk Sky Patrol propeller badge of the late 1930s or an Indian chief tiny tin badge for Post Raisin Bran of the 1950s – is in the under-£13/$20 range. Who can deny that today's give-aways in breakfast cereal packets or at filling stations will become the collected material of tomorrow?

In Britain, children of the Thirties could collect about 15 different cut-out backs from packs of Quaker breakfast foods to make up the buildings, parks, factories, aerodrome and port of Quakerville, a town rich in period architecture. Another classic promotion of the time was the Cococub collection of some 25 lead-alloy animals which Cadbury launched to push its sales of cocoa. They were made especially for Cadbury by the toy soldier firm of Britain's. Cococubs can be worth between £5 and £12, $7.50 and $18 each, depending on rarity of type, at London auctions today.

Packaging, an essential advertising vehicle, forms a limitless branch of this field of collecting. Its strongest devotee is Robert Opie, who crammed his London home with 250,000 packets, tins, bottles, advertisements and posters, and was in danger of being buried by his obsession until he opened his own Museum of Advertising and Packaging at Gloucester in 1984. His unique collection, augmented daily, gained the accolade of an exhibition, entitled 'The Pack Age', at the Victoria and Albert Museum in 1975.

He explains that in 1964 at the age of 17, 'I bought a packet of Munchies from a vending machine, and it was literally while I was consuming the Munchies with their wrapper in my hand that the thought came to me: here is this wrapper that I am about to throw away, and yet it is a part of our social history.' He says he can pick out ten or more different ways of looking at an item. 'How it has been printed; the technical aspects of the packet; how it changed over a 10-year period; what it was used for; what the competition was for the particular product; how it was advertised; the design; the social interest; the lady who appears on the packet; the distribution…you can go on and on. And that is why I don't just stick to packaging and advertising. I also go into social ephemera so that at the end of the day one will be able to pick a year and ask what it was like living at that particular moment of time.'

Advertising: Collector rating

Scope and variety	10
Investment potential	D
Price range	Nil to five figures for rare posters

AIRMAILS

Right. Happy returns for a balloon postcard among many showered from the skies over Kent for the 1902 coronation of Edward VII. It depicts his six King Edward predecessors, and brought 'love to all from Hilda and Chris'.

Below. In the early 1980s this was the world's most expensive airmail, at £1,150/$1,700 – a card dropped by balloon for Edward VII's coronation. It was the only known example of this card to survive the drop.

Three o'clock in the morning was not the ideal time to be attempting a landing after a transatlantic flight, given the state of aviation technology in 1933. But Jim and Amy Mollison, Britain's celebrated man-and-wife flying team, had no other option as they arrived in their tiny machine Seafarer, over Bridgeport, 55 miles/80km short of New York City, on 24 July that year. They were near the end of the 420 gallons of fuel which they had taken aboard at their British lift-off field in South Wales. In the event, they nearly crashed on touchdown, but both crew and plane made it – to enter another statistic into the annals of aviation.

The Mollisons were so exhausted after their flight that they forgot – until 14 August – to mail four souvenir letters they were carrying, treasure for future collectors of airmails. One of the envelopes, colourfully decorated with portraits of the pilots, their signatures and a map (showing that they planned a return flight via Iraq), has gone into postal history as a collector item in the £330/$500 class, after being mailed by the Mollisons to a Mr Goldschmidt at 603 State Street, Larned, Kansas.

Airmails belong to the future like no other branch of tomorrow's antiques. The vast international industry of transporting letters and cards by air daily produces copious amounts of source material for collectors in first-day covers, new stamp issues, and memorabilia relating to inaugural flights, celebratory anniversaries, conventions, trade exhibitions, national landmark events, aviation development and a host of other land-based and airborne happenings. And, as in any other field of collectables, the key to the future is in the past.

Pioneer powered flight was a hair-raising, highly competitive business peopled by daring aviators who stayed airborne more on will than engine performance. Those magnificent men and their flying machines have gone, but they have left a tangible and colourful legacy in the souvenir envelopes and cards, the first airmails, that they carried for a spellbound public. Some of those letters and cards, franked and inexpensively stamped, change

hands today at many hundreds of dollars or pounds apiece. But it is more than a hoard of expensive paper; it is the living story of how mail grew wings.

The covers that have been handed down to us are as colourful as those pioneers who piloted the 'string-and-cardboard' contraptions in the early part of this century. They reflect the fact that once those men and women managed to get and stay airborne they frequently subsidized the cost of their flying machines by transporting mail.

Engrossed as they were with the paramount problem of getting airborne, the Wright brothers were not concerned with carrying souvenir mail on their momentous hop at Kitty Hawk, North Carolina, in 1903 in the Flyer. Had they done so, however, you can rest assured that Flyer's load of 'airmail' would now be enshrined in collector esteem as probably the most desirable and most expensive example of aviation postal history.

Not that it would have been the first such example by any means. Intrepid balloonists were there, long before the Wright brothers and their contemporaries, building up a stock of airmail ephemera for present-day collectors. Indeed, the very year of the Wrights' first flight produced a rare but exceedingly well known postcard 'from the clouds' which brings four figures at auction. It is a coloured postcard (illustrated and described in the chapter on Postcards on page 134), sold to raise funds in the north of England for lifeboats and issued to be dropped from a balloon in a stunt over Manchester.

There are earlier examples of British postal balloon history – notably postcards carried aloft during the 1902 celebrations of King Edward VII's coronation. One flown from Beckenham, Kent, in the south of England, has soared at auction to more than £1,000/$1,500. Another from the same event bore the handwritten message, 'Much love from Hilda and Chris'; it lay undiscovered for three months after it came to rest until it was picked up and popped into a mailing box.

Even earlier in date are rare examples of mail history from the

Top. Souvenir of an Atlantic flight completed by the British team of Amy and Jim Mollison in 1933. Some time after their arrival in New York, they mailed this decorated envelope to Kansas, a very personal piece of aviation history.

Above. Sent from Britain to Spain's Canary Islands in the Spanish Civil War of 1936-9, this envelope bears coveted German Zeppelin mail cachets and has the added attraction of a Spanish military censor's stamp.

far-flung Great Barrier Islands, 65 miles/100km northwest of Auckland, New Zealand. A company with the splendid name of Great Barrier Pigeongram Service established a mail system by homing carrier pigeons between Auckland and the islands in 1897 and special stamps were issued a year later. Postal history records refer to small sheets of these stamps which have survived, among the rarest-of-the-rare collectors' items. Pigeon mail, it must be noted, had been effectively used in the Franco-Prussian war of 1870 when a combination of balloons and pigeons maintained a tenuous connection between besieged Paris and the outside world.

It was, however, the coming of powered flight that gave the main impetus to the carrying of airmails. The golden era was in the years prior to the outbreak of World War One, when daring young aviators in the USA, Britain, France, Italy and Germany, hopping from town to town by navigating along highways, railroads and rivers, subsidized their flights by carrying postcards and letters. Airmails at this time were unofficial and little more than stunts: the correspondence carried by the wing-and-prayer machines still had to be mailed by normal means once the aviator had touched down (as it still does today, of course).

But public interest in aviation was at fever-pitch, fuelled by newspaper magnates like Hearst in the USA and Lord Northcliffe in Britain. Northcliffe's *Daily Mail* took a leading part in a great flying circus over the English countryside which created a highly-publicized network of souvenir flights and competitive events. Every happening was accompanied by its quota of souvenir mail as thousands flocked to send 'greetings by wing' to friends and relatives in distant towns and villages. Freelance airmen, working for publicity-conscious organizations, flea-hopped from sports field to racetrack, from Exeter to Barnstaple, from Hendon in London to Northampton, from Hull to Halifax, navigating their loads of 'airmail' barely above the treetops. On the eastern seaboards of the USA, the air was similarly buzzing with a new breed of gnats. 'The decade before 1914 was a phenomenal era,' says a leading airmail collector. 'The ordinary person's interest in aviation was fantastic. Huge crowds turned out to see the air events on both sides of the Atlantic. Think of it – the London *Daily Mail* offered the first airman to fly between London and Manchester (a distance of 184 miles) £10,000/$15,000, a staggering amount of money in those far-off days.'

But postmasters-general throughout the Western world were slow to give official sanction to the new method of mail carrying. Britain was one of the first off the ground: by 1911 the head of the Post Office had to admit, albeit tentatively, that there was a future for airmails. The first 'official' aerial mail had his approval when souvenir covers were flown between Hendon in London and Windsor (the royal seat, 18 miles away) to celebrate King George V's coronation that year. Privilege reigned in the skies as well as on the ground in those days. Violet coloured postcards for the Windsor flights were strictly for the use of members of the organizing committee and distinguished senders; lesser groundlings had to make do with greys, green and browns (the type of categorization that is a delight to collectors, of course, with enthusiasts willing to pay twice as much for a 'violet' as for a 'grey').

The official programme for the Hendon 1911 coronation event – itself a collectors' piece worth about £300/$450 – solemnly proclaimed: 'Immediately the first "mail" is "off" the Union Jack will be run up at the flagstaff, the band will play the National Anthem, and a megaphone will call upon the crowds present to give three cheers for the King and Queen.' Marvellous stuff for collectors, who are partly in the game for the nostalgia

Below. The first 'official' airmail to win government approval was a flying stunt between Hendon in north London and Windsor to celebrate George V's coronation in 1911. This souvenir programme called for three cheers for the monarch and Queen Mary.

Bottom. One of the violet-coloured souvenir envelopes issued only for the use of important persons sending mail by air in the Hendon-Windsor celebrations. Ordinary groundlings made do with greys, greens, browns.

Above. In April 1914, on the eve of war, this envelope marked an air rally from eight national destinations in Europe to Monte Carlo on the Mediterranean. A few months later the European powers were blasting each other from the air.

Left. Sponsored by correspondence schools as a publicity stunt, pilot Robert Slack flew signed postcards such as this around Britain. Primitive flying machines like Slack's hopped from field to field in Europe and America, navigating by rail, road and water routes on a wing and a prayer.

evoked by this sort of complementary documentation.

These flights remained gimmicks, however. Although Hendon, in 1911, had established an early coup for Britain in the matter of an official sanction, a real airmail service had to wait until 1919, when rattling de Havilland biplanes, little removed in design and performance from their wartime bomber antecedents and piloted by redundant war aces, started to carry letters from London to Paris. Forced landings in the backyards of astonished French farmers were common. Cross-Channel flying hadn't changed much from pre-war days, which have left collectors with a colourful postcard carried by one Paul Verrier, England's sole entrant in a 1914 air rally to Monaco in the south of France. He was turned back by fog, damaged his machine in a forced landing in northern France, and hit a tree further south;

but he made it – in two weeks. And he won a consolation prize, long after everybody else had packed up and gone home.

Meanwhile, what was happening in the United States? In 1910 Glenn Curtiss had flown airmail unofficially, but that year Congress rejected the first legislative proposal for an experimental mail route. In September 1911 Earle Ovington, flying from an aviation meet at Garden City, Long Island, carried mail on a 6 mile (10km) round trip with official blessing: a pouch was dropped into a field from his Blériot monoplane, Dragonfly (so named because it looked like one). Still there was no solid enthusiasm in the establishment, though a seed of hope was planted when the US postmaster-general, Frank Hitchcock, went up for a spin at Garden City and was elated by the experience. Congress stalled: it was unimpressed by two facts –

Above right. 31 July 1939 – a souvenir cover of the first airmail to the remote Orkney Outer Isles from the north of Scotland. The route was flown by Scottish Airways. Throughout the world, hundreds of similar pioneering flights of the 1930s provide exciting collecting ground for enthusiasts.

Right. 'Fluvial Aero-mail' – down the River Thames, up the River Seine to Paris by Hispano-Suiza amphibian. This card commemorates the inaugural flight in 1925. The journey with the mails meant many an unscheduled touchdown for repairs and adjustments.

the top speed of Ovington's Dragonfly was, at 59 miles (95km) an hour, less than an express train, and the amount of mail that could be carried in a flimsy plane was limited. The breakthrough was to come in May 1918, when an official experimental airmail run between Washington DC and New York was accomplished under the aegis of the second assistant postmaster-general, Otto Praeger. It was a giant step in the air. As Praeger put it, America now had a 'Pony Express with wings'.

The 'pony' sometimes went astray. On this inaugural flight, one pilot who was supposed to follow the railtracks north from Washington took the wrong rail route and crashed 25 miles south of the capital. After repairs, however, he completed his mission and a cover from the flight has climbed into the £400-£660/$600-$1,000 altitude.

Airmail ephemera from these and many more early events in American aviation is eagerly collected. Highly esteemed is that relating to the pioneer aviator Charles Lindbergh, such as the mail that came unscathed through his plane crash in fog near Chicago in September 1926, when he parachuted safely from a machine that had run out of gas. One year later he stunned the world with his 33½ hour Atlantic flight – and left collectors with fresh material to cherish. Similarly, a single commemorative

cover of Howard Hughes's round-the-world flight in 1938 is treading the frontiers of £130/$200.

In two world wars the idea of airmail was extended to propaganda, and the target wasn't always the enemy. The mass appeal of communication from the skies was exploited in World War One by the British government, which 'leaflet-raided' English cities with exhortations to buy war bonds. Uncle Sam used the same techniques from 1917. A collector's item is a London *Daily Express* 'aeroplane post' leaflet proclaiming the signing of peace which was scattered from planes over seaside resorts. On the Western Front facsimiles of letters home from German prisoners of war in Britain were dropped over enemy lines by the Royal Flying Corps. They were carefully chosen to indicate humane treatment in British prison camps. and were meant as an inducement to desert the muddy hell of Flanders. 'I am sending you a new picture…standing in our competitive flower garden which again this year has won the camp first prize,' prisoner Karl Topf wrote cosily to his mother from the Isle of Man in 1917. The message was clear: you are far better off in a prison camp.

Crash mail, rescued from disasters, is another branch of collecting. So, too, is Zeppelin and other airship correspond-

Below. This envelope was aboard the east-bound flying-boat City of Khartoum when it crashed at Alexandria, Egypt, in 1935. The mail, soaked and stained, was salvaged and later laid out to dry on the lawns of Bombay post office in India. Wear and tear can be a bonus with crash mail.

ence, which reached its peak in the late 1930s. Mail commemorating historic flights, such as those between Britain and Australasia, as well as the transatlantic crossings of the 1920s and '30s, postwar Comet, 747 and Concorde maiden passenger flights, and inaugural route-runs are all grist to the collector's mill.

As the frontiers of flight are constantly being extended it is obvious that airmails are the true antiques of the future. In stepping into this exciting field, the collector is advised to choose a theme. Terry Marvin, a postal history enthusiast from Britain, has built an international reputation as a collector by concentrating on British airmails, covering any aerial post which originated or terminated in the British Isles. His collection therefore has wide scope, including, for example, such colourful periods as the German obsession with airship flights (via the United Kingdom to North and South America during the inter-war era). He is an example to other collectors in the way he amassed relative but peripheral material on his collector items, such as a fascinating hoard of information, documentation and photographs of World War One prisoner Topf.

Visionary collectors should set their sights on 'aero-philately' of the space age, taking advantage of the mass of contemporary documentation on terrestial and spatial flight. It has, after all, been a short haul in years from the days when postcards were showered from the clouds, even if methods of flight then and now seem to be worlds apart. Comparatively speaking, it may not be in the too far distant future that 'Much love from Hilda and Chris' comes courtesy of airmail on the first pay-flight of passengers into space.

Airmails: Collector rating

Scope and variety	8
Investment potential	B
Price range	£5 to £5,000/$7 to $7,500

AUTOGRAPHS

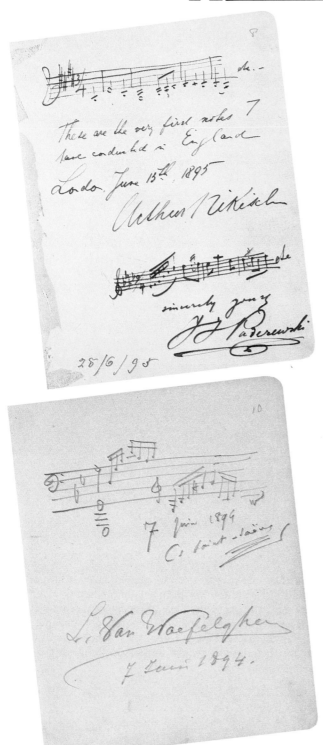

What is an autograph? The late Ray Rawlins, a British collector who amassed 14,000 letters and documents over 40 years, learned the answer in disconcerting circumstances at the age of 15. When he asked the then Duke of Devonshire for his autograph, the duke wrote in the proffered book: 'You are a nuisance.' Rawlins reminded the duke that he had failed to sign it, whereupon the duke appended 'Devonshire', remarking that he had been asked for his autograph, rather than his signature. Rawlins realized that Devonshire was drawing the distinction between autograph and signature, and henceforth never forgot the golden rule in this collecting field that every signature is an autograph but not every autograph is a signature.

Some autographs are obviously more valuable than others, depending on the subject matter. A Thomas Jefferson signature – no more – on a cheque is enough to lift it into the £2,000/$3,000 class, while his signing of, and association with, an eighteenth-century bottle of claret has on one occasion priced the wine at £100,000/$150,000. On the other hand, a letter from President Harry S Truman, thanking his hostess for dinner, is a fraction of the worth of Truman's famous letter in which he threatens to knock out the music critic Paul Hume for panning his daughter Margaret's concert.

Truman's bitter missive is in the Forbes magazine's collection of US Presidential manuscripts and related historical documents and memorabilia in New York. It contains such items as Lincoln's last address (and the top hat and opera glasses he carried on the night of his assassination), but there are also important autographs of the twentieth century. The Enola Gay log, a chilling account of the atomic bombing of Hiroshima by the aircraft crew, is here, and the collection was recently augmented by the purchase (for over £133,330/$200,000) of a letter from Albert Einstein to President F.D. Roosevelt which stimulated the building of The Bomb. The collection has more than 2,500 items, a far cry from the days when Malcolm Forbes, as a boy, snipped signatures of luminaries from his father's correspondence.

Autograph-hunting, however, is a pursuit for everybody, rich or poor. It was a craze during the latter half of the nineteenth century among young and old alike. Then, in the twentieth century, the interest waned. It has been only in the last 30-35 years that collecting has become widespread again, not only as a hobby but as big business attracting the investment-conscious. Some autographs of the twentieth century show an interesting 10-year growth rate. A Winston Churchill letter once priced at £120/$180 would have risen in value to £750/$1,125, an Einstein from £75/$112 to £750/£1,125. A signed studio photograph of Ronald Reagan from his Hollywood days has climbed into the £65/$100 class, and higher if accompanied by an autographed message. The value of Richard Nixon's signature trebled the day he resigned as President.

Some famous personalities were such prolific writers that they have undercut their own value in the autograph market: Churchill and George Bernard Shaw would be achieving even higher prices for their autographs if they had not been so active with the pen. Occasionally a successful motion picture can stimulate interest: Charlton Heston's epic *Khartoum* gave a temporary fillip to the autographs of the Victorian hero, General Gordon, and *Lawrence of Arabia* quickened the existing interest in letters from the World War One desert adventurer. Ray Rawlins acquired a snippet in which T.E. Lawrence replies to an

Top. For many years to the 1920s, a music lover kept an album in which were collected musicians' autographs at performances all over the world. Paderewski signed boldly with a few bars of music.

Above. A lively performance of the pen was contributed by Saint-Saëns with a spirited snatch of music. An inscription, such as these examples of musical accompaniment, adds to a signature's value.

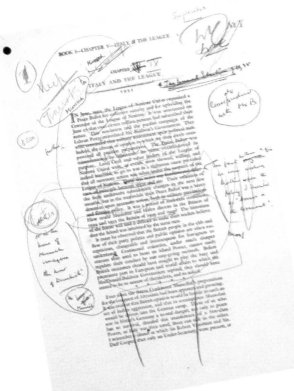

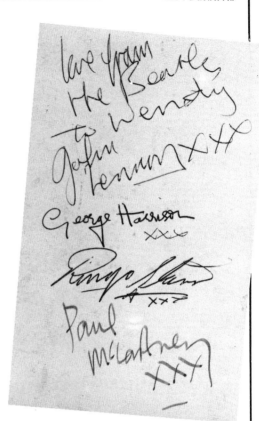

Left. These treasured collectors' items are the galley proofs of the book, *The Second World War*, marked with autograph corrections by Winston Churchill, and a signed photograph of the young Churchill showing him in the uniform of the 4th Hussars at Cairo in 1898 (below).

Below. Names of the twentieth century. Among the signatures are those of Edward Prince of Wales (later King Edward VIII, and Duke of Windsor) and Queen Elizabeth II. The Beatles were prolific signers in the 1960s.

Adolf Hitler's characteristic signature, seen for real here, was appended to thousands of official documents in World War Two – so many, in fact, that he resorted to the use of a machine that would reproduce his handwriting from a matrix. The leader of the Third Reich features in a contemporary wartime snap (right).

enquiry from the Army and Navy Stores in London concerning private circulation of his most famous book, which is unfortunately referred to as *The Seven Pillows of Wisdom*. Lawrence has ignored or missed the typist's error. Such an aberration (like a philatelic error) can double the price of an autograph in some circumstances.

The full meaning of autograph mania can only be appreciated when stories come to light like that behind a collection the nucleus of which was sold by Phillips in New York in May 1983. A waiter identified simply as Ernest had died at the age of 75, leaving behind the evidence of a lifelong obsession: 7,000 autograph items stacked in closets and cardboard boxes in his small Upper West Side apartment in Manhattan. There was an extraordinary collection of autograph letters and signed photographs from leading personalities of the twentieth century, which was formed by a man who most likely never met any of his correspondents. Ernest left missives from John F. Kennedy, John Steinbeck, Marilyn Monroe, James Dean, Gloria Swanson, Aldous Huxley, Duke Ellington and many others.

His method of collecting was simple but painstaking. He daily clipped and filed every newspaper article which mentioned a person of talent or distinction. Locating addresses through various sources, he then sent a handwritten 'formula' letter which professed admiration for the person's work, personality or skill and requested an autograph or a signed photograph. When he received a response, he inscribed the back of the envelope in pencil with the person's name, category of fame and date of receipt. Ernest often wrote to people at the beginning of their careers, on the first mention of their names in print. In this way

he obtained many authentic signatures from struggling (and flattered) talents who would later shun autograph seekers. In 1960 Woody Allen wrote to him: 'As I am a new act, I do not as yet have professional photos. In fact, it was only recently that I acquired an autograph.'

Ernest followed a basic rule of collecting in that he documented each item as he acquired it. A collection of autographs without documentation is just a hoard of paper. There are some other guidelines to note when embarking on an autograph collection. It is advisable to buy autographs from a reputable dealer or auction house – but do not miss browsing in bric-a-brac shops where bargains such as signed theatre programmes can sometimes be found. Pay attention to condition, as foxing (brownish damp marks), discolouration and tears can undermine value. Do not repair tears with adhesive tape. Never paste autograph letters into albums, but enclose them in transparently-fronted and paper-backed envelopes.

And, finally, remember the example of Ernest; he conducted his hobby at little more cost than his time, patience and mailing. Autograph hunting need not mean an ominous collection of letters from your bank manager.

Autographs: Collector rating	
Scope and variety	8
Investment potential	A
Price range	Nil to six figures

Left. Jean Harlow signed for a fan. But did she? After her death it was revealed that the Hollywood star employed her mother to sign a great number of the letters, notes and photographs which she sent to fans. Harlow scholars have considerable difficulty in distinguishing the real signature from the imitation.

Above. The Hollywood actor who became the President signs his name. Collectors apply a very critical scrutiny to Reagan signatures emamating from the White House, where, they suspect, the mechanical writer has been put to frequent use.

Left. Hollywood's irrepressible comedy team of Laurel and Hardy signed this picture for a Yorkshire fan while they were on a British tour. Stan Laurel, in particular, was generous with words when answering fan mail, giving autograph collectors good value.

AUTOMOBILIA

Pull over, park the car and read this:

'Somewhere west of Laramie there's a bronco-busting, steer-roping girl who knows what I'm talking about. She can tell what a sassy pony – that's a cross between greased lightning and the place where it hits – can do with eleven hundred pounds of steel and action when he's going high, wide and handsome. The truth is – the Playboy was built for her. Built for the lass whose face is brown with the sun when the day is done of revel and pomp and race. She loves the cross of the wild and the tame… Step into the Playboy when the hour grows dull with things gone dead and stale. Then start for the land of real living with the spirit of the lass who rides, lean and rangy, into the red horizon of a Wyoming twilight.'

The year was 1923 and Ned Jordan was advertising his Playboy car in the Saturday Evening Post. Jordan cars, sadly, did not survive the Depression, but this classic, chromium-plated piece of advertising copywriting earned a place in Madison Avenue annals; no budding copy-writer allowed himself or herself to forget it, and the Ogilvy and Mather agency made all its executives learn it by heart. Present day collectors of automobilia enshrine the ad in their hearts, along with everything else associated with motoring – 'If it's to do with wheels, collect it.'

Original art work for motoring promotions is obviously at a premium, but posters (even replicas), brochures, shop or trade cards and magazines that recall the advertising of pioneer motor cars are all valid collectables.

French motoring artists revered by collectors include Montaut (who designed the celebrated art nouveau tiles on the Michelin building in London), René Vincent, Pierre Simmar, Leon Facret, Pierre Louys, Jean Routier and many others. In Britain, the leaders included R.O. Nockolds and F. Gordon Crosby, who also produced many memorable covers of Autocar, and cartoonists such as John Hassal, who also designed humorous radiator mascots. In the United States, the incomparable Norman Rockwell (see Illustrators on page 116) contributed to motoring commercial art, as did Peter Helck. Italy gave us G. Carpenetto, Balleria, P. Codognatto and, in later years, the multi-talented Annigone; Germany, Von Loewe and Ludwig Hohlwein. Sometimes these artists linked their four-wheeled subjects to the engrossing theme of flight, sometimes they chose nautical settings, at other times patriotism – even blatant jingoism – would be the theme. Occasionally there was controversy, although the cause would appear tame to modern car enthusiasts who are used to seeing fleets of nubile nudes at international motor shows: in 1934, for example, an advertisement for Fiat invoked the Vatican's disapproval because it was said to have illustrated too explicitly the line of a female buttock.

Most auctions of automobilia (now regular offerings at the

Right. High style in 1932. The Delahaye car is coming straight at the viewer in this poster by Roger Pérot, who grabs extra effect by parallel positioning of type to horizon line.

major salerooms of London and New York) include sections of motoring books and magazines. Books range from tomes of snooty advice passed on from the aristocratic perches of early autocarists such as Max Pemberton, to annuals and lavishly illustrated volumes for children. The thrills, glamour, excitement and adventure of motoring are embodied in these children's books of the inter-war periods: they have titles such as *Buck Gordon's Speed-Track Avengers*, and *Look Out! Here comes the Crasher!* – both from a popular library series. At Christmas, a lucky child would find *The Wonder Book of Motoring* at the foot of the bed. Examples of these highly-collectable children's motoring books can still be picked up at swap-meets, rummage sales and antique fairs for a few pounds or dollars apiece.

The array of motor accessories on view at auctions would appear, at a glance, to be only for the technically minded – bits of engines, valves, lighting-parts, the nuts and bolts of motoring romance. But what have we here? An Imperial Communicator: a sort of motoring ship's telegraph by means of which an Edwardian passenger in the back seat conveyed his instructions to the chauffeur; the lever on the dial may be pointed, at will, to Turn, Faster, Right, Stop, Straight, Left, Slower and Home. A fearsome boa-constrictor horn of polished brass would honk its brazen warnings to the pedestrian – a snip these days at several hundred pounds or dollars. And who could resist the luxury of

DELAHAYE

Above. An Automobile Association car badge, presented to a member. Badges such as this are at the forefront of automobilia collecting.

Left. The essence of motoring in the inter-war years: speed, power, colour and raising the dust. This spirited promotion for Renault cars is in lithographic poster form (54 inches, 139cm wide), and has climbed into the four-figure price bracket on the collector market.

Right. Tin toy motoring. A post-war Gama 300 friction Cadillac with its original box, from West Germany. Once in the spearhead of West German toy production (the box is pencilled with a price of 42 shillings – £2.10, or about $3-$4), it sold at auction in 1986 for £600/$900.

Above. Adolphe Mouron Cassandre's 1936 poster announces that the new Simca 5 costs only 9,900 francs, a bargain (63 inches, 160cm wide). Cassandre produced stunning work on vehicles and ships.

Right. Related to the car mascot, this Hispano-Suiza desk piece of a stork is nickel-plated bronze, signed F. Bazin, on a calchite base (overall height 7 inches, 18cm).

Below. A 1927 Rolls Royce Phantom One open tourer represents the enormous range of choice available in the veteran, vintage and classic car field.

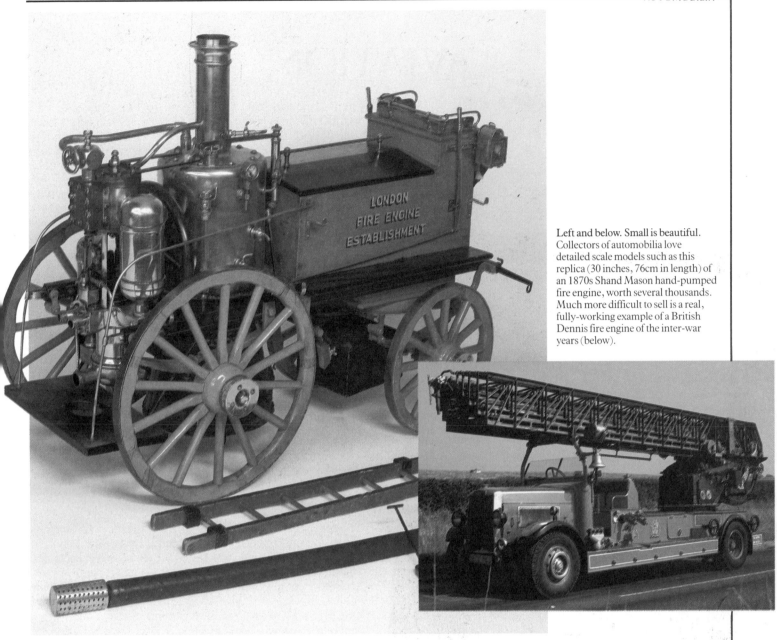

Left and below. Small is beautiful. Collectors of automobilia love detailed scale models such as this replica (30 inches, 76cm in length) of an 1870s Shand Mason hand-pumped fire engine, worth several thousands. Much more difficult to sell is a real, fully-working example of a British Dennis fire engine of the inter-war years (below).

an Edwardian car picnic trunk with all fittings?

Collectors have a huge choice of lighting, tools and garage equipment, technical books, radiator and club badges, trade gifts such as ashtrays and lighters, and a wealth of household items including teapots and cruets in the form of motor cars, not forgetting toys.

Perhaps the most fiercely contested area of automobilia collecting, however, is that of radiator mascots. A skier, a rabbit, a policeman, a huntress, a leaping deer, a streamlined heron, in brass, steel, chrome, bronze and glass; they all compete for the collector's attention, and none more so than the fabulous mascots of René Lalique who has given his glass 'jewellery' to the world in so many delectable forms. Lalique's first car mascots appeared in the late 1920s, and by 1932 there were 46 designs in the catalogue. They are variously in clear crystal and coloured, polished and frosted glass or mixtures of the same, works of art worth up to several thousand pounds or dollars each and far too treasured to be entrusted to the fronts of motor cars any more. Greyhounds, eagles, nudes, goddesses, spirits, dragonflies, horses, cockerels, swallows – Lalique mascots have become graceful and elegant aristocrats among the antiques of tomorrow.

And what of the cars themselves? A typical sale of automobilia includes a wide selection of transports of delight from Rolls Royces to veteran bone-shaker bikes. It might have a pedal-car de luxe for the kid who has everything, a horse-drawn phaeton of the Gay Nineties, or a sheik's custom-built Cadillac facing redundancy because of dwindling oil dollars. The author has seen a Norfolk dog cart of 1912 rubbing flanks with a bullet-proof limousine presented to Franco by Mussolini. There was the *grande-dame's* tourer which, out of fuel, once sailed on spread bedsheets, like a galleon, across the Gobi desert ... but, then, cars need a book to themselves. Just look around you – the streets are full of tomorrow's antiques.

Automobilia: Collector rating

Scope and variety	8
Investment potential	B
Price range	£5/$10 to no limit

AVIATION

The Red Barons had come to town. In New York City, on a bright October morning in 1984, a severe attack of aeronautical fever gripped the occupants of Phillips auction rooms on East 79th Street. A former Korean war ace was enthusing over the contents of an aircraft tool kit, 1918 vintage; a grandfather in his seventies measured the cockpit of a monoplane pedal 'car'; two sun-bronzed members of the Confederate Air Force were arguing over the rarity value of a giant World War Two poster, 'Keep us flying! Buy war bonds'; a Marine Corps veteran aimed a Japanese gun-camera at his buddy and shouted: 'Gotcha!' The most spectacular saleroom flying circus of the decade was airborne.

Being auctioned was the lifetime collection of an American aviation enthusiast, Donald Z. Sokol, an ear, nose and throat surgeon of Pottstown, Pennsylvania, who decided to sell on joining the US Air Force as a Lieutenant-Colonel. Dr Sokol referred to himself as 'the Red Baron of Pottsdown', after his penchant for wearing flying helmet, goggles and white silk scarf in emulation of the German World War One ace, Baron Manfred von Richtofen. The latter earned his nickname – irreverently purloined in cartoon lore by Snoopy dog – while leading a squadron of scarlet-painted Fokker triplanes against the Allies. Sokol, too, flew in vintage style – in his own biplane, similarly painted. His Red Baron sobriquet was a bit of fun, but his dedication to his hobby was serious as well as being practically all-embracing. The Sokol hoard of some 800 treasures represents a comprehensive cross-section of what is available to the growing band of enthusiasts in the field of aviation collectables.

A collection, might include ephemera such as posters, or advertising material on air themes. Indeed, anyone without the funds to set their sights on the more expensive collectables, ranging up to the ceiling of actual aircraft, might devote themselves entirely to posters thus keeping their outlay per item within a bracket of £20-£200/$30-£300 – bearing in mind that some rare posters on aerial themes can fly to four figures.

First, the two world wars have provided a mass of colourful poster material. A famous World War Two exhortation to the public to 'help Britain finish the job' by artist W. Dotton, depicts a Spitfire downing a German Heinkel bomber and a similar work by another artist shows a Royal Air Force Hurricane co-operating with Russian fighter planes. 'He can't fix the guns in the air. Build 'em right!' is the message to munition workers in an American poster of 1942, dramatically depicting the frustation of a pilot whose armament fails to function. And who could resist the appeal of a 1918 effort for the US Victory Loan Flyers, illustrating a flight of biplanes soaring over a speeding locomotive, with the call, 'Watch for the Airplane Special'. These posters, mostly some 30×20 inches (76×50cm) in size, are more than nostalgic evocations of the spirit of their time; they are works of art.

Peacetime aviation ephemera is even more richly varied than that born out of conflict, and is just as representative of its age. Posters are a rewarding field and appear to be a continuing and basically sound investment. 'Airplane Rides' of 1930 advertises 50-cent flips in Boeing Clippers operated by the Inman Brothers' Flying Circus which traveled America. Then there are posters for Britain's Imperial Airways to publicize its routes to India via Egypt, some being art deco gems of the Thirties depicting tri-motor airliners flying over silhouetted Arabs,

Above. Lineage of the air: no aviation collection is complete without the inclusion of some aspect of ballooning. A true antique is this English nineteenth-century cased model of a balloon ascent, believed to be by 'Mr. Gale at Raby Castle in County Durham', an echo of an age of elegance.

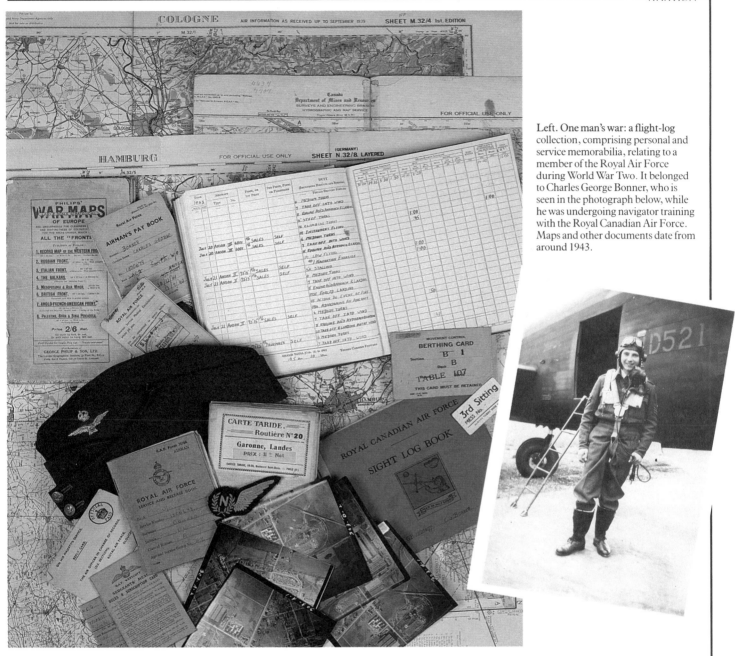

Left. One man's war: a flight-log collection, comprising personal and service memorabilia, relating to a member of the Royal Air Force during World War Two. It belonged to Charles George Bonner, who is seen in the photograph below, while he was undergoing navigator training with the Royal Canadian Air Force. Maps and other documents date from around 1943.

camels and palm trees. Even as early as 1915, the subject of aviation drew crowds to the movie houses of America and one lithograph that has survived, a collector's treasure, blurbs a six-part documentary serial, 'Panama and the Canal from an Aeroplane'; it shows two intrepid aviators with a giant box-like movie camera dominating the cockpit of their flimsy aircraft.

Advertisers in general were keen to get on the bandwagon of the air. A charming relic is a 1928 broadside advertising a model construction kit of Lindbergh's 'Spirit of St Louis'. The message was clear to anyone who bought the flour products of the advertiser, Voigt Milling Company of Grand Rapids, Michigan: 'Your boy may be greater than Lindbergh.' A French balloon advertisement of 1890 boosted a liquor distillery; Dick Tracy in 1937 is shown apparently plunging to his doom in the cockpit, a dramatic poster for a cliff-hanging Republican serial; White Flyer Armour Laundry Soap proclaimed that it 'makes dirt fly'... the catalogue of aviation advertising material is endless.

Other ephemera embraces books, prints, photographs, ticket material, log-books and aircraft operational documents, as well as airmails which are dealt with in a separate chapter (see Page 20). Autographs abound in this collecting field. Following the

Above. From the squadrons of British Dinky Toys aircraft, this post-war Avro Vulcan delta-wing bomber is a rare model. The auction catalogue warned: 'resprayed, tail-fin repaired, new transfers', yet a collector still paid £420/$630 for it in the mid-1980s.

Left. Zeppelin memorabilia is at a premium, even the ephemeral items like this Graf Zeppelin baggage label of the 1930s, showing the route from Friedrichshafen in Germany to Buenos Aires.

Below left. Real planes are the ultimate in collecting. Britain's oldest surviving transport aircraft, a 1934 De Havilland Dragon, was bought for £28,000/$42,000 in 1983 by the Science Museum.

Left. Zeppelin memorabilia is at a premium, even the ephemeral items like this Graf Zeppelin baggage label of the 1930s, showing the route from Friedrichshafen in Germany to Buenos Aires.

Below left. Real planes are the ultimate in collecting. Britain's oldest surviving transport aircraft, a 1934 De Havilland Dragon, was bought for £28,000/$42,000 in 1983 by the Science Museum.

price-setting at the Sokol sale, some US astronaut signatures have been changing hands around the £30/$50 mark and an important letter written by Wilbur Wright has been valued at more than £1,330/$2,000.

In London, an autograph book bought for ninepence in 1940 which measures only 4 inches (10cm) square has caused a saleroom battle royal. The purchaser was a young boy who lodged his autograph book with a friend, a Royal Air Force barman in the officers' mess at Martlesham Heath fighter base in Suffolk during the Battle of Britain. The book was crammed with more than 100 autographs of fighter pilots, including the legless ace Douglas Bader. On a visit to the base, Winston Churchill saw the remarkable roll-call of pilots and later wrote to Bader: 'Douglas, God forbid the book should ever be lost. It is not a book of names, but a book of heroes.' It was, indeed, preserved for posterity, and a patriotic Briton paid £16,000/$24,000 for it at auction, with the intention of putting it on public display. Moral for the collector: apart from works of art and examples of intrinsic worth, objects are valued not so much for what they are as for what they represent – in this case an episode in the history of the free world.

So much for the 'software' of aviation collecting. The hardware comes in huge variety and ranges in size from Lindbergh lapel pins to real, airworthy Flying Fortress bombers.

Many serious enthusiasts like to include at least one aircraft propeller in their collection. This sort of item need not be expensive – the price at a specialized auction of aeronautica is likely to be between £100 and £200/$150 and £300 for a World War Two example, although a connection with a well known aviator will put a premium on the value. Similarly, other aircraft components will rise in price when they derive from a famous machine or a historic event such as the crash of the Hindenburg Zeppelin in 1937. Indeed, one macabre branch of collecting is devoted to crash memorabilia. Some airmails come under this heading, of course, with crash mail – or 'interrupted' mail, as American collectors like to call it – being eagerly sought. On occasion, damage to the mails has a somewhat lighter side, with two notable items cherished in the annals of collecting for the postal clerks' inscriptions on mail covers: 'Caution, damaged by rodents', endorsed on a 1945 letter from Argentina, and 'Destruction by Tom Tits' on a British envelope of 1957.

Zeppelin memorabilia is highly regarded. Glass candy containers, chocolate moulds, china souvenirs, pipes, ashtrays, cigarette lighters, cocktail shakers, children's night-lights, biscuit tins and toys of every description were all made in the form of dirigible airships during their great era of the 1930s, when the Germans in particular were stunning the world with the exploits of these flying dinosaurs. A 25 inch (63cm) mechanical model of Britain's ill-fated R101 has topped £1,330/$2,000 at auction in the United States.

Balloon artefacts have a special place in collectors' hearts. These interests are epitomized in a spectacular ballooning museum which Malcolm Forbes, owner of the American business magazine *Forbes*, has established in the Château de Balleroy in Normandy, northern France. It contains several balloon gondolas from the various eras of ballooning – ranging from baskets like big picnic hampers to silvery space-age

AVIATION

Left. In superb condition and in their original boxes, pre World War Two model aircraft from the French factory of Dinky Toys represent types of planes long vanished from the skies. Mint sets are showing signs of soaring to the £3,500/$5,000 level in the 1990s.

Right. A Phil May wartime watercolour of a Mustang fighter in combat with a German adversary in the closing stages of the struggle in Europe.

capsules – dioramas of famous events such as the use of balloons in the American Civil War, painting, prints, ceramics, glass, clothing, commemorative stamps and covers, books, letters, photographs, magazines, tapes, documentary films and other memorabilia.

Owing to its unique status as part of the Forbes organization, however, this is not just an isolated, sealed-off collection that only harks back to the past in artefacts, records and memories. It is seen by many thousands of visitors every year and it is linked to the present and future because ballooning is a living thing for the Forbes family. A squadron of Forbes balloons flies regularly. The Forbeses would not have become the successful businessmen that they are if they did not capitalize on these soaring advertising hoardings, so their balloons are labelled with company enterprises, and banners on the ground promote the magazine with slogans such as 'For High Ups in Business'. All the time, the science of ballooning – as any other branch of flight – is creating antiques of the future.

Some enthusiasts will collect practically anything associated with flight, from airline baggage tickets to money-guzzling flying machines. At a Phillips auction in London in 1985 a World War Two buff paid £650/$1,000 to put the commander of the Luftwaffe into his collection – a life-size figure of Hermann Goering, complete with uniform and replica decorations. For those with the resources, however, the ultimate in aviation collecting is to own their own aircraft.

Some experts argue that the original frame and covering of the machine is far more important than the engine; very few old engines, in any case, are airworthy without massive reconditioning or replacement of key parts. The thrill of restoration is a major part of the attraction for the mechanically skilled. At aircraft meets, collectors enthusiastically gossip over feats of restoration such as that needed to get a 1946 veteran into flying trim after it had rotted for years in the corner of an English country airfield, at the mercy of the weather and local children. At the start of the operation there was deep water in the cockpit and mushrooms growing there. After more than a year's solid work by an amateur and his friends, the 'mushroom flyer' took wing. When already in airworthy state, a splendid example of a World War Two fighter – say, a Spitfire, Mustang or Zero – can make a big hole in a million dollars. Aircraft of World War One – rarer than genuine Stradivarius violins in saleroom circles – are no less expensive. It can take a lot of money to be a Red Baron.

Aviation: Collector rating

Scope and variety	8
Investment potential	B
Price range	£20/$30, to the limits of the sky

BADGES & MEDALS

Collecting badges is an obsessive game which anyone at almost any age can join at little expense. At the age of 11, the author's son had amassed a mountain of tin badges and lapel buttons, ranging from minor-military to McDonald's. When *Blue Peter*, the BBC children's television programme, appealed for badges to auction in aid of a charity, he was persuaded through parental cunning to do his bit by donating his metal hoard to the good cause. Three large cardboard boxes of badges duly went off to the BBC. The philanthropic donor attended the auction with his pocket money – and returned home in triumph with three large cartons of badges, different badges but equally numerous and equally space-consuming.

Anyone could, theoretically, amass huge quantities of modern badges as they are produced, and eventually find that some had become a modestly valuable investment. But storage space costs money and, anyway, a hoard is not a collection. The discerning collector must go a little further back in time, without necessarily leaving the confines of this century.

At a sale of war memorabilia in London in 1985, an eye-catching lot was a framed display of some two dozen designs for the hand-painted squadron patches worn by America's Flying Tigers of World War Two China fame: ruby-eyed snarling tigers, explosive flashes, blonde bombshells, black clouds bearing retributive lightning, vivid examples of wartime pop art. They were nothing more than facsimiles but nevertheless realized £200/$300. Had they been the real thing, the price would have been ten or twenty times as much.

British Army cap badges are an example of a rewarding field of collecting. Because of the reorganizations and disbandments which the Army has undergone since the turn of the century, older items are bound to appreciate in value. The Cardwell reforms of 1881 discontinued the system of numbering infantry regiments and linked them to specific counties or areas, thus underwriting future collector appeal.

By the end of the century khaki had been established for some time as the active service dress, the only obvious unit identification being the distinguishing badge worn in the cap, so this period – around the time of the Boer War – is an appropriate starting point for a collection. Mostly, officers wore a bronze badge and other ranks a badge of cheaper brass or white metal. The next important reference milestone for collectors came about 1922, with the disbandment of some Irish regiments, certain cavalry amalgamations and the adoption by some specialist corps of the prefix 'Royal' in recognition of their part in the 1914-18 war. Simultaneously, the Territorial Army (the nearest equivalent to the National Guard in the United States), formed in 1908, was developing on parallel lines and creating interesting badge lore for collectors.

World War Two saw the birth of several new corps; and the badges of some special service units, since disbanded, have become collector fodder. Then the post-war years produced a major upheaval, mainly affecting the infantry, in which dozens of famous regimental names were consigned into limbo, to make way for new 'large' regiments. Thus collector interest has been focused in retrospect on the two 'golden eras' of cap badges: the Boer War to 1922, and the subsequent period up to the end of World War Two.

Regular cleaning of badges causes wear, no matter how carefully it is done. When displaying them, therefore, it is advisable to coat the items with clear lacquer before mounting

Below. James Brindley Nicolson who was awarded the Battle of Britain's only Victoria Cross. He shot down a German Messerschmitt although his own Hurricane was blazing. His medals are shown, with the VC on the right of the group.

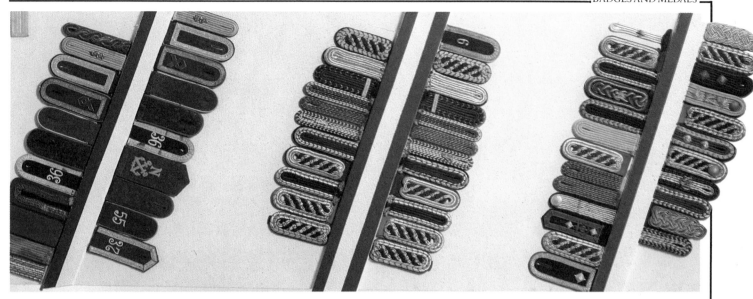

them. They are best shown off against a matt, dark background. Most medal dealers keep a stock of badges, and finds can sometimes be made at antique fairs or in the 'forgotten' corners of a general dealer's shop.

Medals, orders and decorations have been showing, generally, a tenfold increase in value over ten-year periods since the late 1960s. The field has attracted investment money and there has been keen museum buying at international auctions, triggered no doubt by the subject matter's undeniable claim to be a valuable part of the national heritage. Leading dealers say that there is a relative shortage of goods on the market, and this will ensure higher prices. While the military badges discussed above would be hitting absolute top price in the lower hundreds of pounds or dollars, the sky is the limit for medals.

A world record auction price for a Victoria Cross was set in the 1980s at £110,000/$165,000, more than twice the original estimate of the auctioneers, Glendining's of London. This stratospheric price classically reflects the factors that place the worth of one particular medal over that of another. But first, the medal and the man. The VC was awarded in 1944 to Flight Lieutenant James Brindley Nicolson of the Royal Air Force for bravery in his first combat action, at the age of 23. In the Battle of Britain he shot down a German Messerschmitt 110 although he was badly wounded and his Hurricane was on fire. Parachuting down to a Hampshire field, he was further wounded when an excitable Home Guard volunteer, thinking he was a German, drew a bead on him with a shotgun. Nicolson was killed five years later on active service in the Burma theatre of war. After a saleroom tussle, his group of medals was saved for the nation by a bid from the RAF Museum at Hendon, London.

How, precisely, did James Nicolson's VC meet the scale of value criteria for medals? First, rarity. The value of a medal, bar or decoration, of which only a few have been issued or awarded, is greater than where a large number are involved. The Victoria Cross, in relative terms, falls into this class. The scarcity of particular medals to particular regiments or service groupings is also taken into consideration. Nicolson's VC was the only one awarded to Fighter Command in the whole of World War Two.

Historic interest can influence price to the extent that it may overtake the absolute rarity aspect. The VC was also unique in that it was the only one from the Battle of Britain, a crucial milestone in Britain's wartime fortunes. The age of a medal is, in itself, of relatively little or no importance. Many modern campaign medals are worth considerably more than common issues a century old.

Above. Badges and insignia of the Third Reich are big business. German shoulder and collar insignia of World War Two demonstrate the enormous variety.

Below. Part of one man's dedication to the British Royal West Kent Regiment: the regimental cap badge and part of a large medal collection.

Left: A close-up of the Nicolson Victoria Cross, Britain's premier award for bravery in action. This was the only one awarded in World War Two to Fighter Command.

Right. Hand-signed by Adolf Hitler, a citation for the Knight's Cross of the Iron Cross honours Hans-Ulrich Rudel, Germany's Stuka pilot hero of World War Two. Rudel destroyed 500 tanks on the Russian front, was shot down 30 times, lost a leg and continued to fly. At Phillips in the mid-1980s the citation sold for £22,000/$33,000 after a bidding battle in which Rudel's widow failed to obtain the memento.

Far right. Colourful shoulder and arm flashes of the United States fighting services and related organizations and units, a specialized branch of badge-collecting.

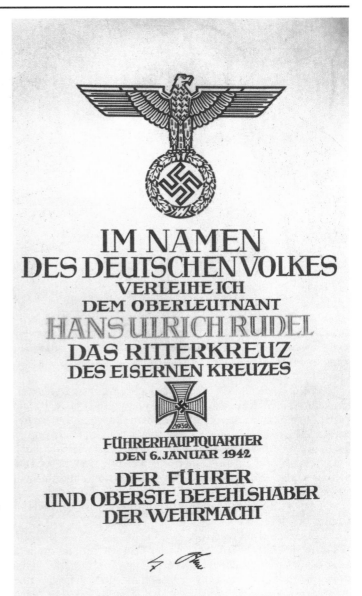

IM NAMEN DES DEUTSCHEN VOLKES VERLEIHE ICH DEM OBERLEUTNANT HANS ULRICH RUDEL DAS RITTERKREUZ DES EISERNEN KREUZES

FÜHRERHAUPTQUARTIER DEN 6. JANUAR 1942

DER FÜHRER UND OBERSTE BEFEHLSHABER DER WEHRMACHT

Sometimes the value of a group of medals is considerably greater than the value of the constituent parts. This may not necessarily have been the case with Nicolson's VC but, as it happened, it was sold in a group which included his other important decorations and campaign medals, together with archive material, his flying jacket and partly burned uniform.

Unlike coins, the condition of medals used to be of little importance. In recent years, however, collectors have begun to demand good condition and are willing to pay a premium for those in very fine order. Nicolson's VC had been carefully preserved by his family, latterly in a bank vault.

Finally, flying high among present-day collectors' favourites are medals awarded to air forces.

Growing collector interest is now devoted to souvenir commemorative medals, a once neglected area. Medals were made to mark all kinds of events and achievements in the Victorian age in Britain, and similarly in the United States and many European countries. Souvenir medals continue to be struck today – to mark space achievements, for example – and these form collector material for tomorrow. In Britain, anything from Queen Victoria's jubilees to a child's attendance at Sunday school would be commemorated in medals of a silvery-looking alloy known as white metal. Some of the smaller ones were sold by the batch for as little as twopence each. The survivors can still be acquired inexpensively as they have no intrinsic value.

Daniel Fearon, head of Glendining's coin and medal auctioneers, offers some advice for newcomers to commemorative-medal collecting: 'Always try and buy medals in good condition, for white metal corrodes easily. Dirty medals can be cleaned with washing-up liquid and a little water, but they must be thoroughly dried. Moisture is again a problem if medals are kept in plastic display envelopes, and many medals have survived 100 years or more in perfect condition only to be ruined by being kept in a plastic album.'

Fearon passes on a tale which illustrates the motivation and dedication of a true medal collector. In 1986 he auctioned a remarkable collection of five hundred items relating exclusively to the Royal West Kent Regiment, a British record of gallantry and service stretching from the Napoleonic wars to beyond World War Two. The story of the collection goes back to 1945 when a young Royal Air Force man, John Etkins, on leave in London bought on impulse two old campaign medals for £1 – 'which was rather more than my day's pay of fifteen shillings as a pilot officer'. 'I became hooked,' said Etkins, looking back at the age of 60 when he put his collection of medals and decorations on the market.

After ten years of spasmodic collecting, Etkins 'took on' the Royal West Kents in 1954 when, he says, 'I married into the regiment.' His bride's father and three brothers were officers of the regiment. He set out to try and collect the best possible

example of every decoration, medal and clasp ever awarded to a West Kent soldier. The collecting went on even after Etkins moved to Australia. Why, then, did he dispose of his collection? 'Within my family, my collection has always been known as my "pension fund", for I soon realized that under this heading my conscience took fewer knocks when it came to over-stressing my purse. However, while this ruse worked well, now that I am approaching my retirement "the fund" is being called to account.'

Along with the Etkins 'fund' of medals came meticulously kept notes, research material and documentation, the true mark of a collector. He discovered that one Indian Mutiny medallist subsequently suffered fifty lashes for a 'crime'. He traced the

commissary records of an 1867 Abyssinia veteran who had to feed an unusual unit – nineteen elephants. The family tree of a Sudan campaigner took him several months to work out and spread across paper 10ft (3m) wide. 'All collectors,' says John Etkins, 'must be slightly mad'.

Badges and medals: Collector rating

Scope and variety	8
Investment potential	B
Price range	£5/$8 to six figures

BAR & PUB

'The trouble with the world,' Humphrey Bogart once said in an interview with *Esquire* magazine, 'is that everybody in it is three drinks behind.'

Collectors of bar and pub memorabilia might be forgiven for feeling similar sentiments. In that post-war era of pub revisionism, when the brewery overlords decided that the brave new world had no place for splendidly furbished saloons and gin palaces, much mayhem took place before collectors were really aware of it. Juke-box furnishing and noise took over the dignified Victorian and Edwardian temples to barley, malt and conviviality, and many fine fittings were sent to the scrap heap before people woke up to their value.

Now it is perhaps too late: genuine old artefacts are soaring in price as more and more collectors, restaurateurs and interior designers realize the decorative potential of public-house and bar 'antiques'. The bitter irony is that the companies who own the drinking establishments have themselves detected the whiff of nostalgia, and places that had their traditional interiors ripped from them two or three decades ago are now being dolled out seemingly much as they used to be, but in replica.

From yesterday's pubs, tiled panels and etched glass are classed among decorative items of substantial importance in the fine art salerooms. Reproduction glass panels, for doors or windows, abound. But the real thing is wildly expensive – when it can be found. An interior decorator would have to start

thinking in terms of four figures to buy a double-door set of Edwardian glass panels, etched with scenes or patterns. Oddly enough, some of the beneficiaries of the post-war brewery blitz have been so-called 'English pubs' which have mushroomed across the world from California to the Costa del Sol. Into this heritage drain have gone casks and barrels, beer and wine racks of venerable oak, ceramic-handled beer pumps, bar tops made of slate, zinc and mahogany, entire wood and glass-panelled rooms, and pewter tankards by the ton.

Promotional giveaways such as Guinness tableware and wall plaques, advertising ephemera related to drinks, and bar 'furniture' such as bottles and jugs are fairly accessible areas of pub collecting (see also Advertising, Bottles and Posters). The author once used to be the unofficial and unpaid spotter of new British bottled and canned beers for a New Jersey enthusiast who not only collected medals and toy soldiers but tried to gather together every known modern example of beer can and bottle in the United States and United Kingdom. Some people even find their thrills in beer mats!

One happy side effect of brewery mergers is that collectors have found tavern signs a little more plentiful on the market. Reappraisals of policy and fresh approaches to corporate design often mean more frequent replacement of pub signs in these days. Thus, an alert collector privy to information straight from the landlord's mouth may snap up a discarded sign for a

Above. An unusual Guinness hanging sign of a type that would be highly regarded by a collector of pub memorabilia. The company's advertising has appeared in many varieties through the years.

Above left. The famous symbol of the toucan stands guard over a representative collection of promotional and sales material for Guinness, the brewing giant. Values for this highly collectable material vary from a few pounds to several hundred pounds an item. This group includes chinaware, salt and pepper containers disguised as glasses of Guinness, and routine bar-top and pub 'furniture'.

Above right. In their attempt to create a corporate identity immediately recognisable by the customer, British brewers have spent vast amounts of money on 'labelling' their pubs and other outlets. This is a ceramic plaque distributed in quantity by one popular brewery.

reasonable amount. The sign would, of course, be a modern artefact painted by a modern artist, but it is almost certain that the subject matter, the pub's name, is steeped in tradition.

English hostels and inns started as resting places for pilgrims and displayed religious motifs. Many of these name-signs are still with us. The Star at Alfreston in Sussex is the Star of Bethlehem. The Crossed Keys at Stratford-on-Avon is the insignia of St Peter. Crusaders back from the Holy Land gave us the Saracen's Head and the Turk's Head; at Nottingham is to be found the Trip to Jerusalem. Royalty received homage in many names: the Red Lion was called after John of Gaunt's insignia, the Rose and Crown for Henry VII. After the accession of George I the White Horse of Hanover was included in the royal arms and became a popular name for pubs.

Many London pubs have names derived from ancient trades: the Three Compasses is the insignia of the Company of Carpenters, the Painter's Arms is self-explanatory, and the Wheatsheaf is part of the arms of the Company of Bakers. Similarly, country pubs are called the Jolly Blacksmith, or the Jolly Farmer – even the Jovial Foresters. Ale-houses and taverns were used by the community as venues for sport and meets for the local hunt: hence the Fox and Hounds, the Fighting Cocks, the Falcon, and many more.

The Green Man appears often, in town and country. Some authorities trace it to legends of Robin Hood and his Merry

Bottom. Original watercolour design by Donald McGill, master of the English seaside saucy postcard, who often found inspiration in the pub scene: 'Poor Bill went home last night and found his wife in bed with peritonitis.' 'Wot! D'yer mean that dam old ice-cream man round the corner?'

Below. As a poster (here 45 inches, 114cm wide), the bowler-hatted Dubonnet-drinking man became one of the most familiar graphic images in France during the 1930s. It was displayed in huge versions on walls and hoardings, and in smaller sizes around the Metro and other advertising sites. The masterpiece was created in 1932 by Adolphe Mouron Cassandre, king of posterists.

Men, who dressed in their famous Lincoln green. Others argue that it was traditionally the dress of any woodman. This latter view is partly espoused by a manuscript of 1610 which explains the appearances of the Green Man thus:

'They are called woudmen or wildmen thou at thes days in ye signe call them Green Men, covered with grene boughs: and are used for signes by stillers of strong watters and if I mistake not are ye supporters of ye King of Denmarks armes at thes day; and I am apt to beleve that ye Daynes learned us hear in England the use of those intosticating licker which berefts them of their sences.'

In 1986, Phillips in London played a part in promoting the pub antiques of tomorrow when it put up for auction a piece of sporting memorabilia which introduced the controversial cricketer Geoffrey Boycott to saleroom exposure. A metal pub sign of the Cricketers Arms, bearing the celebrity's portrait, was sent for sale by Mike Dewar, the landlord of the 140-year-old pub of that name at Bedford. Dewar commissioned the sign from an artist friend when a redecoration was imminent, but the brewery which owned the pub did not approve of it, despite a local petition in its favour. It was hoped that the sale of the sign would cover the landlord's expenses in commissioning it, but in the end there was not a successful bid. Sometimes, tomorrow's antiques may be just a step too far ahead of their time.

Bar and pub collectables: Collector rating

Scope and variety:	7
Investment potential	Lesser items E, top quality A
Price range	Nil to many thousands of pounds or dollars

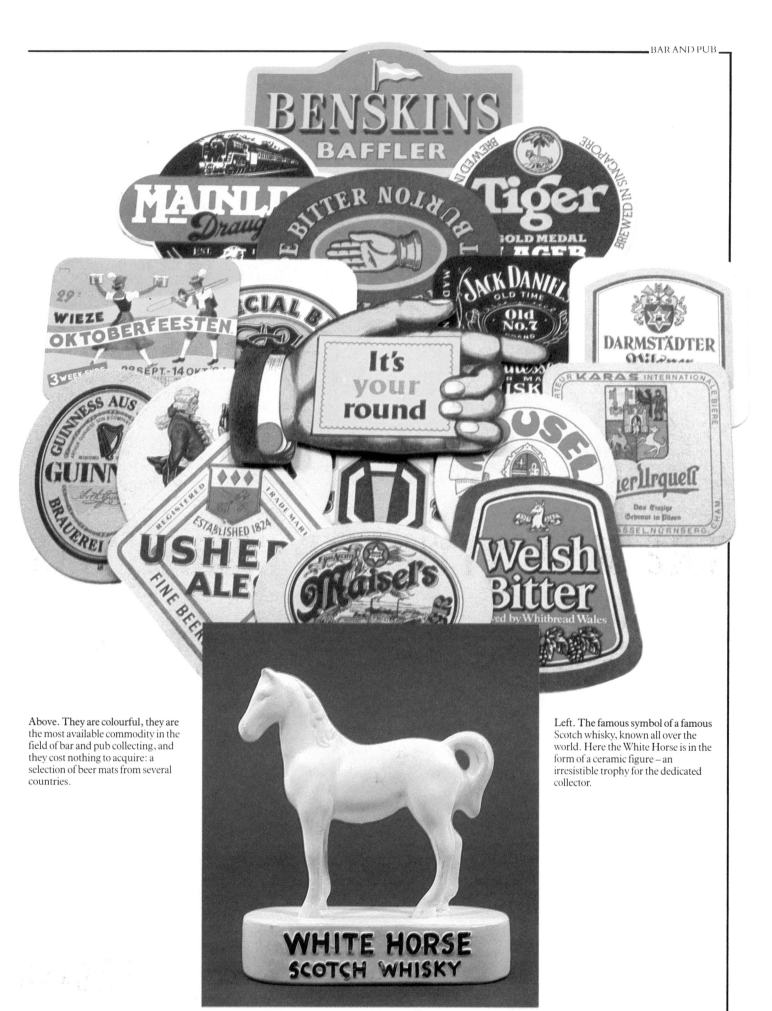

Above. They are colourful, they are the most available commodity in the field of bar and pub collecting, and they cost nothing to acquire: a selection of beer mats from several countries.

Left. The famous symbol of a famous Scotch whisky, known all over the world. Here the White Horse is in the form of a ceramic figure – an irresistible trophy for the dedicated collector.

BOOKS

A first edition. The phrase is usually delivered with some awe, certainly respect. To nail a common misapprehension, however, most books found on the collecting trail are first editions because nobody ever wanted to reprint them. It is essential that the collector knows which first editions are desirable before the hunt will begin to pay off.

There is a simple rule of thumb that may help someone setting out into modern first editions for pleasure and hope of profit. Let us assume that the beginner has grasped the importance of at least some degree of specialization (children's literature, crime, travel, one author, the Twenties, American, and so on ad infinitum), and let us take children's books. The plan is to establish which children's books out of the annual avalanche have been regularly reprinted over the last decade or two – in effect, those that may be on their way to becoming classics. Then start looking for the first editions.

But where? Modern first editions regularly have their place in antiquarian book sales at the major auction houses, and if you are prepared to buy a smallish multiple lot, the cost may work out at not more than £30/$45 per item. The book buyer, however, has a much better than average chance of finding the quarry in unexpected circumstances. A good book of any vintage may change hands half a dozen times before reaching the rare book end of the market and the alert individual can intercept it at any stage in its progress. It is still possible to make an exciting find at a rummage sale, where the chances of coming across fine porcelain or furniture in the same way is almost nil.

Nevertheless, the old bookstores for browsers are dying as specialization extends its frontiers. The beginner should get a feel of the market by spending some time at auction views, comparing estimates with prices subsequently achieved, visiting as many bookshops as possible, and arranging to receive booksellers' mailing lists. Book Auction Records, published annually in Britain and the United States, can help on prices.

Modern first editions are the fastest-growing area of book collecting, according to leading lights in the trade. How the book has been cared for is important in placing it in the scale of values.

First of all, it must have its dust jacket, known as dustwrapper in the trade. Even the early paperbacks had them. They are analogous to antiquarian books' 'original boards', are intended as a temporary protection, and must be expected to have a shorter life than the book itself. Nevertheless, most collectors regard them as an essential feature of a modern first edition. Their absence can reduce the value of a book dramatically – much to the surprise of literary-minded book lovers.

Dust jacket worship was highlighted in an incident regarded as a classic nugget of bibliographical lore. In a US sale of 1977 a copy of Kenneth Grahame's *Wind in the Willows* with its dust jacket in perfect condition was auctioned for seven times the price realized for a comparable copy without the dust jacket.

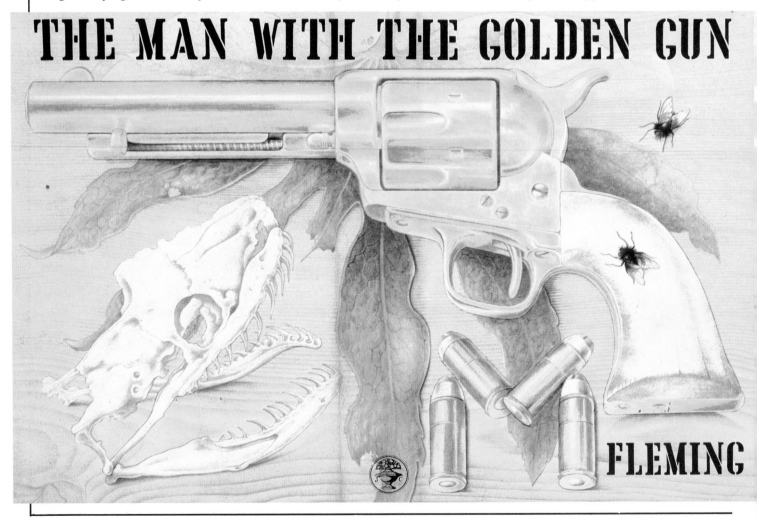

THE MAN WITH THE GOLDEN GUN

FLEMING

The full extent of the absurdity became apparent when the market realized that, in theory, it had valued the book at around £330/$500 and the dust jacket at £2,000/$3,000.

Books with broken spines and turned-down pages, and those which feel 'loose' when shaken, are rejected. Battered library copies stand little chance. Foxed (damp-marked) illustrations, grubby fingerprints and notes and doodles in the margins can all bring down the value. The author's signature or more extensive autograph can add a premium to the price, however.

The very nature of the books that sell well in the modern first edition market means that anyone could have a few desirable examples on their bookshelves. Just William stories by Richmal Crompton, volume after volume of dark-crimson bindings, are popular, as are early copies of *Watership Down* by Richard Adams. Some bibliophiles concentrate on mystery works by such authors as Raymond Chandler and P.D. James. A survey of readers to find out who were the most collected authors in Britain, conducted in the mid-1980s by Book and Magazine Collector, revealed that P.G. Wodehouse was the leader. His Bertie Wooster novels had been fetching £200/$300 apiece, and some of his works involving earlier characters as much as £400/$600. Ian Fleming's James Bond books were second in popularity. *Casino Royale*, published in 1953, has been steadily heading towards £1,000/$1,500 in absolutely pristine first-edition condition. Doing equally well, it seems, is *The Mysterious*

Far left. The dust jacket for a first edition of Ian Fleming's *The Man with the Golden Gun*, featuring James Bond, 1965. The collecting value of a first edition can drop catastrophically if the dust jacket is tattered or stained, and may be nil if the book does not have its dust jacket.

Left. When the British publisher Penguin celebrated the 50th anniversary of its paperback books in 1986, artist Beryl Cook designed this special logo – and the original artwork became a collectors' item through a charity auction.

Affair at Styles, Agatha Christie's first book (although a first-edition copy of the same book by Penguin, which made it number six in its lists in 1935, languishes around the £30/$40 mark). First editions of children's books, such as *Tom Sawyer*, *Winnie the Pooh* and *The Flopsy Bunnies*, are doing nicely, showing that the juvenile field could well be one of the best for future investment.

Watch out for the works of G.A. Henty, journalist and story-writer, who died in 1901. Writing in boys' magazines, he had an enormous turnover of words. (In the department of output, however, he could not match Edgar Wallace, thriller and racing writer: at the height of *his* career *Punch* carried a cartoon of a man asking a bookseller, 'Have you got the midday Wallace, please?'). Henty produced 31 books, which sold 150,000 copies each. They do not have a niche in literary fame, but they represent a genre of boys' adventure writing and have boldly designed, embossed covers that few schoolboys of yesterday or collectors of today could or can resist.

One admirer, borrowing Victorian vernacular, has written: 'If you want to know how deal with a mad dog, rescue a girl from drowning, escape from any number of prisons, dye yourself dark brown or yellow, stalk caribou, plait a pigtail, or trip up, knock down or generally thwart every brand of frog-eating Frenchie, wily Chinaman or treacherous Turk, Henty will give you the essential information.' To this should now be added the words, 'At a price'. Henty books were published by Blackie who employed illustrators of the calibre of Frank Dadd, Gordon Browne and Solomon Solomon. They could be picked up for a few shillings in the late 1960s. Now, even a well-thumbed copy would be in the £20/$30 class, and appreciating steadily.

Together with others of his ilk, such as R.M.Ballantyne and Harry Collingwood, Henty has a bright future among collectors.

The boys do not have it all their own way. Angela Brazil, born in 1869, was still writing strongly in 1939 (she died in 1947). She sold three million copies to young ladies eager to read of *The Girls of St Cyprians* or *The Luckiest Girl in the School*. Her quintessentially English girl heroines said things like, 'Jubilate! You're right, old sport! Scooterons-nous this very sec! What a chubby idea!' Whether she reflected or moulded schoolgirl vernacular is hard to tell. She was in the habit of sending to any schoolgirl correspondent a personal letter and a highly romantic and flattering photograph of herself. One recipient wrote back to say: 'So pleased to know you aren't *old* and mouldy looking.' Will Angela make it? You can bet she will. With works of her genre ascending, it might be a chubby idea to invest in her first editions now.

If the rules of first editions appear to be relatively simple, beware: the market (where a first-folio Shakespeare can run up to £20,000/$30,000) has some strange anomalies. An early *Pickwick*, in parts with wrappers, at £2,000/$3,000 may puzzle the uninitiated when, as has happened, eight 'first editions' of Dickens including *Pickwick* sell in an auction lot for £100/$150. The explanation is that the lot was made up of early Dickens editions published as printed books, a different proposition from the collected part-works of Dickens' stories as they were initially issued.

In such a field, first-edition spotting is very complicated. Of the parts of *Pickwick* which preceded the introduction of Sam Weller only 400 copies were printed. Then the increase in popularity and circulation became phenomenal. The older

Far left. The original artwork, now in a collector's hoard, for the dust jacket of *The St Trinian's Story*, with some work by Ronald Searle.

Below. William Heath Robinson, the designer of fantasy contraptions, turned his talents to the Great Western Railway in this illustrated book of 1935, a minor but attractive collectors' item.

Above. First editions, between 1903 and 1912, of works by Beatrix Potter, in small format. Beatrix Potter material is avidly collected, not only her books and ephemera associated with them, but china, lead and bronze models of her animal characters. These first editions averaged about £100/$150 in the late-1980s.

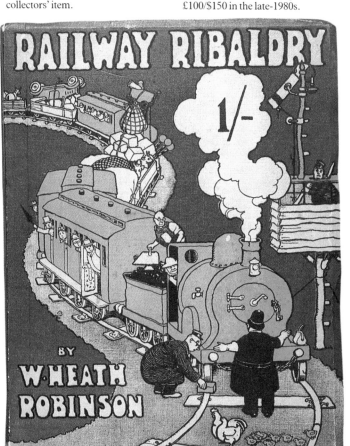

plates had to be re-etched hurriedly to stand the wear and tear of increased press work. There was a mixing of old and new plates. Advertisements were thrown out and others substituted. A little way through the series, the artist shot his brains out and the man employed in his place failed to please Dickens. Two plates of the short-lived artist's work were cancelled and another artist was appointed to start afresh.

One collectors' authority, laying down the number of basic recognition points which constitute 'a perfect first edition' of *Pickwick*, lists no fewer than 11 stipulations, detailing minute differences in wording and design between parts 1 and 20.

The 50th anniversary of Penguin books in 1985 placed the spotlight of attention on the appreciation rate of paperbacks. The very first Penguin of 1935, a sixpenny edition of *Ariel* by André Maurois, realized £120/$180 at a birthday auction. But on the whole, early Penguins were selling at not more than a few pounds or dollars each. It means that it is still possible to buy into an interesting collecting field without large expenditure.

Penguin enthusiasts talk in mega-statistics. At the time of the anniversary the company's public relations department was busy informing journalists that its warehouse annually despatches enough books to stretch from London to Moscow, and that the paper involved is equivalent to the weight of 900 London buses. Many of the Penguin collectors set themselves the target of collecting the first 100, 200 or even 1,000 editions. One man had all the first 1,500, except one. He hunted for it for years, until Penguin told him that by some quirk that number had never been published.

Books: Collector rating

Scope and variety	10
Investment potential	C
Price range	Minimal to £2,000/$3,000 for modern editions

BOTTLES & CORKSCREWS

From the early part of the century, this mineral-water bottle is collector material thanks to the glass-marble stopper fitment in the neck. There are believed to be about 200,000 bottle collectors in the USA.

If you hear talk of Codds, torpedoes, Radam's Microbe Killers, Daffy's Elixirs and Doctor Steer's Opodeldocs, you will know you are among bottle collectors. They are the names of types of bottle, in some cases based on the original contents. Bottle collecting takes many forms and spans time from the seventeenth century, or even earlier, right up to the present day. It embraces such contrasting themes as rare old wine receptacles, ball-stopper inventions of the soda-pop era, foot-warmers for cold beds, a £26,700/$40,000 perfume phial for a lady's dressing table, liquor flasks, and containers for medicine, ink and all manner of beverages, brews and poisons.

Old wine bottles have an expensive niche in collecting because of their rarity. In England, for example, it was illegal for many years to sell wine by the bottle and there was a punitive tax on glass. Theoretically, therefore, imbibing was the privilege of rich people, although their lessers, if they could afford it, would happily indulge themselves by the jugful straight from the cask in alehouse and tavern. Wine was ordered by the barrel and decanted for home-drinking into personally owned bottles. That is why the most highly collected wine bottles have seals bearing the initials, crest or name of the owner and, sometimes, dates. A rare seventeenth-century example can reach four figures.

Pop, or soda, bottles span the era from the closing decades of the last century to the 1930s, and prices range in Britain from a pound or two for a common type to £100/$150 for a very rare stoneware or extremely unusual marble-in-the-neck example. There are corresponding values in America, with its rich soda-bottle heritage. Aquamarine, dark green, cobalt blue, amber, brown, these bottles make an attractive shelf display, even if the collector is only in the most inexpensive bottle class. That is the beauty of bottle collecting: it is for everybody.

The greenish colour in a bottle, the makers discovered, was due to the presence of iron oxide in the constituent sand. For a deeper green, they added more iron oxide. Still more would produce a fine brown glass. Charcoal or coal added to the melt resulted in near-black glass. The deep blue found in many medicine bottles (originally a 'colour warning' device for a largely illiterate population) was produced by introducing cobalt; copper oxide resulted in a light blue. Ruby red, extremely rare, required the addition of real gold, though latterly selenium was used to produce a similar effect much more cheaply. Selenium in glass can react with strong sunlight to change colour. Sun-coloured bottles, of yellow or amethyst, are less common in Britain than in sunnier parts of the world. American collectors are well-off for sun-coloured bottles but short of the quintessentially British stone ginger-beer variety; therefore a healthy two-way transatlantic exchange has developed.

Digging for bottles on the sites of old rubbish dumps has become a popular pastime. One leading British collector reckons that a Victorian rubbish tip could contain as many as 10,000 bottles. He believes there are at least 20,000 'serious' bottle collectors in the United Kingdom, and possibly 10 times as many in the United States and Canada. To these figures must be added thousands of 'amateurs' who dig up the occasional old bottle and add it to their modest collections.

The international fraternity has drawn up a scale of value levels, ranging from 1 to 6 for exhumed bottles: 1, widespread in dumps of several countries; 2, widespread in dumps of at least one country; 3, an interesting item worth collecting; 4, a select

A delightful array of late nineteenth-century scent bottles. Features such as silver and silver-gilt tops and floral decoration on the coloured glass bodies put some of these tiny phials into the four-figure category of value. The most desirable piece is the rare swan's head type with a silver-gilt top.

collector's item, difficult to find; 5, a very rare find; 6, fewer than 50 items recorded. Cash value on this scale ranges from nearly nothing to a few hundred pounds or dollars if two dedicated collectors were to fight it out at a bottle auction or swap-meet.

Modern bottle collectors worship at the shrine of one Hiram Codd, who in 1875 invented his internationally famous marble-stoppered bottle. A glass ball was trapped just below the neck and forced against a rubber ring when the fizzy drink was in and the pressure was high. Thus it acted as a stopper. By means of a wooden cap/plunger, the drinker was able to displace the glass ball which was then trapped behind two lugs, allowing the contents to flow freely. Codds, as these designs are known, were universally pirated and are among the most collected in the world today, their values ranging widely, depending on rarity and condition.

Medicine bottles are in a class of their own, with a poison at a premium. There is a vast variety. One nineteenth-century manufacturer even issued a bottle in the shape of a coffin. Bottle swap-meets see fierce bargaining over the relative merits of, say,

a Turlington's Balsam of Life and a Dr Soule's Hop Bitters. Gems of the late nineteenth-century American market are Warner's 'Safe' Cures, some of which near the three-figure bracket. Warner was a quack who was eventually jailed for selling coloured water, claiming it could cure anything from rheumatism to diabetes. His bottles are smoke-green or dark brown with the word 'Safe' deeply embossed on the glass.

Ink bottles are among the cheapest to collect. They seldom cost more than a couple of pounds or dollars, and have to be hunted for in the top-shelf stock of general antiques dealers, in junk shops or at rummage sales. Do not be put off by the rough, sometimes very jagged tops. It was traditionally considered unnecessary to apply smooth lips to ink bottles.

Setting aside the prototypes of masters such as Lalique and Gallé, and some of their limited-number 'first editions', perfume bottles fall into three types for collectors. First there are the craftsman-made 'specials' whose purpose was to hold the perfumes dispensed from larger containers; often made of or mounted in precious metals, they can be four-figure value.

Right. An early twentieth-century British bottle from the Coventry Mineral Water Company which incorporates a cycling motif into its design. The inclusion of a special feature such as this immediately adds a cachet to its collecting attractions; it might be sought as keenly by a cycling enthusiast as by a bottle collector.

Far right. No bottle collection would be complete without there being represented in it a selection of old soda syphons. This one was made for E. Spooner & Sons, British Syphon Company.

Second came the quantity-produced scent bottles for dressing table sets, sometimes silver-mounted, with prices ranging into the hundreds. Last and least in price are the more modern, commercially produced bottles.

Scent-bottle price history was made as the 1980s opened when the result of René Lalique's first attempt at making pure crystal glass – a 4 inch (10cm) teardrop-shaped phial – was sold for nearly £26,670/$40,000 at Phillips in New York. While Lalique was making his scent bottle in 1895 by cooking his glass mixture on the kitchen stove, he was so engrossed in the experiment that he failed to notice that he had set his apartment ablaze. The furious landlord evicted Lalique, but the artist moved to new lodgings in triumph: he had rescued the teardrop flask that set alight his career as a glassmaker.

Corkscrews have existed as long as corks have been used to seal bottles, but any dating from before the middle of the eighteenth century are very rare indeed. Our collector span is from the late nineteenth century to post-Prohibition time in the United States. In this period manufacturers applied their full ingenuity to developing mechanical effectiveness and decorating their corkscrews. Collectors have the choice of single and double levers, lattice levers, ratchets and other devices to facilitate the

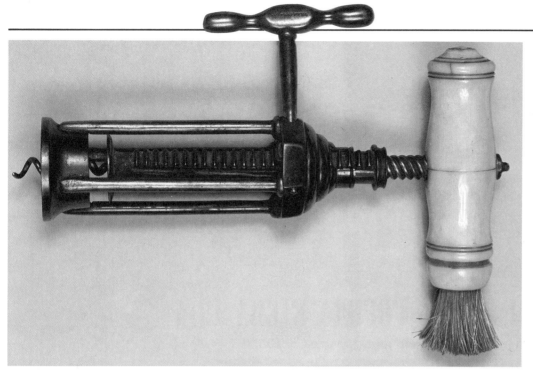

Left. A narrow side-rack corkscrew with a brush (for dusting away particles from the lip of the bottle) incorporated into the handle. It was made in the late nineteenth century by the firm of Holzapffel, based in St James's, London.

Left. Gay Nineties corkscrew from Germany, a saucy variety which was universally known as 'Lady's Legs'. The legs are some three inches long (7.5cm) and the corkscrew, when folded, would fit easily into a gentleman's waistcoat pocket.

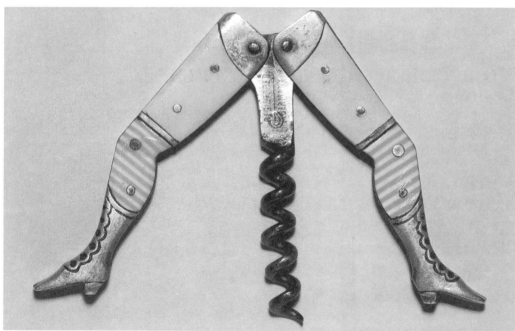

withdrawal of the cork. Travelling corkscrews are popular, folding or screwing into a cover which, when removed, forms the handle. One example screws into a hollow steel cellar door-key, and has a loop to hang on the butler's key-ring. Handles were as varied as the many types of corkscrew. At the other end of the size scale from travelling corkscrews are large, brass-barrelled contraptions designed to sit on bars.

Collectors recognize several value points in a corkscrew. First comes the degree of complexity or novelty. Second, a maker's name or that of an advertiser such as a distillery or a wine-shipper can add a premium to value. Third, attention is paid to the material of the handle: wooden handles patently have less value than those of silver, ivory or bone.

Corkscrew collecting fever is found at its most virulent in the United States, where devotees compete avidly to possess the mechanical wonders of their own country, Britain and Germany. It is not extraordinary for a collector to pay more than £670/$1,000 for a rare item at a special auction. Interest ranges from the ponderously serious business of an R.B.Gilchrist 'Yankee Number 7' bar-top model of 1913 to the frivolity of a German 'lady's legs' in which the folding handle is shaped as such and decked out in saucy striped hose.

Bottles: Collector rating	
Scope and variety	9
Investment potential	C
Price range	Nil to many thousands for a rare scent bottle

Corkscrews	
Scope and variety	8
Investment potential	B
Price range	In the USA where interest is highest, £27/$40-£670/$1,000

BUSTED BONDS

The collector market in busted bonds did some hard self-reappraisal in the summer of 1986 when Eduard Sheverdnaze, the Soviet foreign minister, roared out of London with his police motor-cycle escort after a visit for talks with Sir Geoffrey Howe, his British opposite number. In the never-never land of the Russian Poland Land Banking Company, the Kokund-Namangan Railway, the Russian Tobacco Company and others, Mr Sheverdnaze had left a time-bomb ticking. It was about to blow those cobwebbed, defunct Tsarist enterprises of commerce back into the twentieth century.

The Soviet Union had agreed to unfreeze some £46/$69 million-worth of assets held in Britain for the benefits of claimants who lost their investments after the Russian Revolution of 1917. Tsarist bonds, which their owners had come to regard – like American Confederate or any other long-dead bonds – as nothing more than colourful collector material to be framed and hung on the wall, now appeared in a new light as redeemable properties. The Russian writing on the wall was plain, however: with some £267/$400 million-worth of British claims already outstanding against the modern heirs of the Tsars, the payout could be only a small percentage of the total compensation claimed. Bond holders were resigned to the fact that their collections would pay out no more than 10 per cent of face value at the most, and in the event probably much less, if they were to cash in their paper chips through these newly opened official channels.

It was an interesting interlude, which served to highlight the collecting phenomenon of busted bonds, or scripophily as it has been called. The net result, in collecting terms, was probably to increase the value of Russian material and busted bonds

generally; not because of the new-found but negligible redemption value of Tsarist certificates, but as a result of nationwide publicity. For bond holders the message was clear: the auction room pays more than the Kremlin.

Busted bonds were an almost unknown branch of collecting until the close of the 1970s. The market peaked in 1979-81 and then slumped dramatically when they began to appear from everywhere and several speculators pulled out. A rare bond for which someone might have paid £1,500/$2,250 in 1980 fell in the next five years to about one tenth of that figure. The second half of the 1980s, however, has seen the prices recover somewhat, thanks to increased American interest. Specialist shops and auctioneers began trading in bonds because people like them for their decorative appearance; many are beautifully coloured and lettered, nicely illustrated and adorned with scrollwork.

Countries involved include the USA, Britain, Russia, China, Central and South American states, South Africa, Australia, France, Spain, Germany, Scandinavia and Egypt. Collectors go for the bonds of Imperial China (the Imperial Gold Loan, the Tientsin-Pakow and Hukuang railways, and their like), a whole paperchase of long-defunct British canal, rail and coal-mining companies, and snippets of history such as the 1927 Free City of Danzig loan. Russian bonds cover a multitude of capitalistic enterprises ranging from the Cities of Moscow and St Petersburg loans to flotations for obscure settlements fringing the Trans-Siberian rail route.

America is represented not only by the attractive Confederate states bonds – some of which can be picked up for less than £7/$10 each – but by a host of corporations across the Union. A dip into a recent auction catalogue reveals the ghosts of Utica and

Left. Russian bonds, like this certificate for a £20, or 189-rouble, share in the City of Kieff (Kiev) loan of 1914, appear in large numbers in the West. This one is worth only a few pounds, but others peaked at about £1,500/$2,250 in the busted-bond boom of 1979-81.

Right. A £100 share in a 1917 pioneering aerospace company of Britain, Whitehead Aviation. There is a specialization in old transport shares and bonds, especially those which combine industrial history with attractive typographical and pictorial design.

Schenectady Railroad's 1870 share issue, an 1880 bond of the New York, Pennsylvania and Ohio Railroad, the Indiana Coal Company's flotation of 1881 and an American Express Company's certificate of 1850 showing a vignette of a locomotive. Like other countries' bonds, American certificates range in size from 8×6 inches to 25×15 inches (20×15cm to 63×38cm).

The collector new to bonds is advised to choose a specialization – common enough advice in any branch of collecting. But choice of specialization should be related to

Above. This sterling-funded loan was floated in 1871 on behalf of the State of South Carolina. It was payable in 1890 at 6 per cent. Related, but dating from an earlier period, are the dramatically decorated busted bonds of the Confederate States of America.

Far right. The colourful residue of Tsarist Russia: a bearer-bond certificate for a City of Moscow loan of 1908. When the Russian Revolution came in 1917 bonds such as this became just so much waste paper overnight. Now, collectors have found that they make attractive wall decoration.

market values, in case the collection ever has to be sold. The market for collections of early Egyptian cotton companies may be so limited as to make resale impossible. Similarly, a person may pick as a theme the share certificates of firms of East Coast morticians in the United States, but when the time comes to sell he would be hard-pressed to find another enthusiast of mortician companies. One of the 'safest' areas, and one well served by quality and variety, is that of the railroads of America or Europe.

The busted bond is such a 'young' branch of collecting that it is comparatively little documented. Much research needs to be done. For this reason alone, the newcomer can feel that he or she is not entering an intricately-charted area where all the route maps are held by the long-term, established devotees. In scripophily the beginner will find no great crocks of investment gold, but in some cases he certainly stands to gain more than did the original holder of the busted bond.

Busted bonds: collector rating

Scope and variety:	8
Investment potential:	D
Price range:	£2/$3 to £400/$600

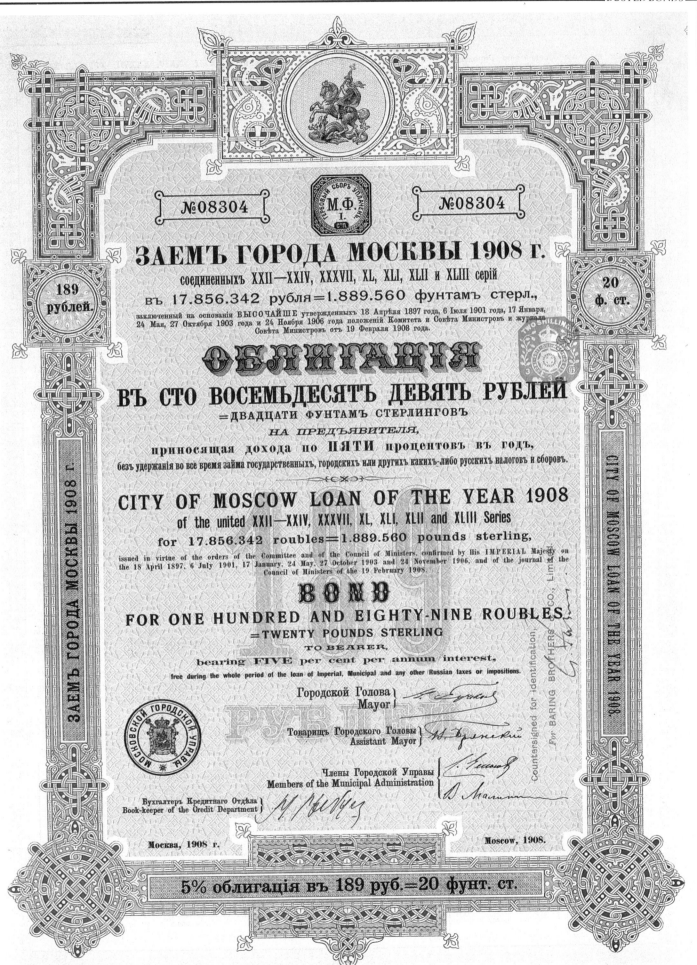

№08304   М.Ф. I. СП   №08304

189 рублей.

20 ф. ст.

ЗАЕМЪ ГОРОДА МОСКВЫ 1908 г.

соединенныхъ XXII—XXIV, XXXVII, XL, XLI, XLII и XLIII серій

въ 17.856.342 рубля=1.889.560 фунтамъ стерл.,

заключенный на основаніи ВЫСОЧАЙШЕ утвержденныхъ 18 Апрѣля 1897 года, 6 Іюля 1901 года, 17 Января, 24 Мая, 27 Октября 1903 года и 24 Ноября 1906 года положеній Комитета и Совѣта Министровъ и журнала Совѣта Министровъ отъ 19 Февраля 1908 года.

ОБЛИГАЦІЯ

ВЪ СТО ВОСЕМЬДЕСЯТЬ ДЕВЯТЬ РУБЛЕЙ

=ДВАДЦАТИ ФУНТАМЪ СТЕРЛИНГОВЪ

НА ПРЕДЪЯВИТЕЛЯ,

приносящая дохода по ПЯТИ процентовъ въ годъ,

безъ удержанія во все время займа государственныхъ, городскихъ или другихъ какихъ-либо русскихъ налоговъ и сборовъ.

CITY OF MOSCOW LOAN OF THE YEAR 1908

of the united XXII—XXIV, XXXVII, XL, XLI, XLII and XLIII Series

for 17.856.342 roubles=1.889.560 pounds sterling,

issued in virtue of the orders of the Committee and of the Council of Ministers, confirmed by His IMPERIAL Majesty on the 18 April 1897, 6 July 1901, 17 January, 24 May, 27 October 1903 and 24 November 1906, and of the journal of the Council of Ministers of the 19 February 1908.

BOND

FOR ONE HUNDRED AND EIGHTY-NINE ROUBLES

=TWENTY POUNDS STERLING

TO BEARER,

bearing FIVE per cent per annum interest,

free during the whole period of the loan of Imperial, Municipal and any other Russian taxes or impositions.

Городской Голова } Mayor }

Товарищъ Городского Головы } Assistant Mayor }

Члены Городской Управы } Members of the Municipal Administration }

Бухгалтеръ Кредитнаго Отдѣла } Book-keeper of the Credit Department }

countersigned for identification.

For BARING BROTHERS & CO., Limited.

Москва, 1908 г.

Moscow, 1908.

5% облигація въ 189 руб.=20 фунт. ст.

ЗАЕМЪ ГОРОДА МОСКВЫ 1908 г

CITY OF MOSCOW LOAN OF THE YEAR 1908.

CARTOONS

"My brother says he's on a lonely gunsite in Yorkshire—two miles from the nearest pub!"

We've often been under the weather, ol' man, but never under the hammer!

Phillips
SALE OF 2 OLD MASTERS

Top. Wartime Jon cartoon of the Western Desert: 'My brother says he's on a lonely gunsite in Yorkshire – two miles from the nearest pub!' Jon's 'Two Types' kept an army laughing through the African and Italian campaigns.

Above. After Jon's original wartime cartoons were dispersed at auction – with London's Imperial War Museum a succesful bidder – the artist produced this portrayal of the 'Two Types' on the auction block. (*Author's collection.*)

When Jon, the cartoonist, auctioned off his collection of wartime cartoons in the early 1980s the biggest single buyer at the Phillips sale was the Imperial War Museum of London. Jon (in real life William John Philpin Jones) saw the funny side of it. After returning home to civilian life at the end of World War Two, he recalled, he had little room to store the large pile of original cartoons which he had drawn for service newspapers and which recorded the hilarious adventures of the Two Types, a pair of indestructible, incorrigible desert veterans of the British Eighth Army. So Jon offered the entire collection to the Imperial War Museum, free. The insouciant response from a museum employee was: 'What would we do with cartoons – you don't happen to have a tank, do you?' Nearly 40 years later, Jon enjoyed the irony of the museum paying more than £300/$450 each for some of his drawings, all of which it could have had for nothing.

In the context of the fortunes of press cartoons as collector material, the museum's attitude in the old days is understandable. Only the past two decades have seen them rise in esteem as art to be collected – as mirrors of contemporary social and political attitudes and unique windows on history. The irreverent Two Types by Jon, an artist who subsequently followed a distinguished career cartooning for the *Daily Mail*, made an army smile in days of darkness and triumph. New Zealand's General Freyberg, VC, said they were worth a division of troops. Field Marshal Alexander tried to stop the cartoons when they first appeared because he thought they were laughing at officers. He was persuaded otherwise. The Two Types conned, scrounged, philosophized and calculated their way through thick and thin to victory. They are truly part of Allied history in World War Two.

Political cartooning is one of the foundations of democracy. In *The Cartoon History of Britain* (a work produced by Michael Wynn Jones for publisher Tom Stacey) Michael Cummings, political cartoonist of the *Daily Express* in London, writes: 'The cartoonist must remain fundamentally bloody-minded, slightly anarchistic, hold no cows sacred, and must be capable of thoughts in the worst possible taste – but being capable of keeping such thoughts under control when necessary.' And he observes: 'After all, the political cartoonist is a weapon of attack, a warmonger in pictorial aggression. To see his victim writhe ministers to his sense of power.'

Today, leading cartoonists' views on burning topics are quoted as widely as the leading articles of the newspapers which employ them. On both sides of the Atlantic professional, highly-paid cartoonists work in a tradition that goes back more than two centuries.

In the early days, however, cartooning – although it was not then known by that name – was open to anyone with a talent for drawing in the Anglo-Saxon world. It had wholly amateur origins based on a vogue for personal caricature imported by Grand Tourists who had visited Italy in the early eighteenth century. The root of the word *caricature* is the Italian *caricare* – to overload, burden or exaggerate. 'Cartoon', essentially a design for a painting, tapestry, mosaic etc, began to mean a full-page illustration in a paper or a periodical, usually comic, in the mid-nineteenth century. It was not until the turn of the century that the term was applied to any comic drawing. By that time illustrated newspapers such as *Harper's* and *Leslie's* in the United States and the *Illustrated London News* and *The Graphic* in

Below. Forebear of today's cartoonists, Thomas Rowlandson showing his talents for lampooning in pen and ink and watercolour. The target is the auction trade. What am I bid for tomorrow's antique?

Right. In World War One, Bruce Bairnsfather, soldier-artist, produced his memorable cartoon of Old Bill and young comrade in a lonely shell-hole.

"Well, if you knows of a better 'ole, go to it."

London – not to mention the venerable *Punch* – had established large circulations.

From being the province of amateurs in the early part of the eighteenth century, when men-about-town indulged in the fashion of sketching for private circulation, caricature had by mid-century become a political weapon. Its popularity was stimulated by a boom in print shops selling the works. A fashion based on anonymity became an industry, and the professionals moved into the field. In England, Thomas Rowlandson, James Gillray, Isaac Cruikshank and sons Robert and George, Robert Newton, James Sayers and William Heath all followed the great tradition of freedom of expression, a tradition of unbroken line to the cartoonists of today.

About a century ago a new phase of cartoon history dawned with the rapid advancement of newspaper techniques such as half-tone blocks, linotype and rotary presses. In the 1880s a new newspaper-reading public was sustained by progress in education in the United States and Britain. New methods of reproducing photographs sounded the knell for the special reporter-artist. But the cartoonist was to have a new lease of life, a daily opportunity to comment on the news in a mass of cheap, popular newspapers. Significantly, however, the cartoonist's role was changing. More and more, he was required to *entertain*.

Cartoon historian Michael Wynn Jones argues that the very exposure which was such a blessing to the cartoonists at the same time blunted their edge. Twentieth-century editors wanted their readers to be amused; humour rather than wit was required, explicitness rather than innuendo, pleasure rather than passion ... 'though some cartoonists managed to circumvent it, the editorial policy of the newspaper was invariably the guideline for the staff cartoonist'.

But passion there was, and is, in plenty. The rapidly-changing Sixties and Seventies laid the foundation throughout the Western world for a new breed of hard-hitting political cartoonist. 'Very occasionally, a temporary increase in heat under the collar can blast off a dynamic cartoon,' says Michael Cummings, practitioner of mordant cartoonery. 'Further, if that dynamic cartoon produces shrieks of rage from the victim or victims, the cartoonist hugs himself with malicious glee.'

Post-war original cartoons used to be hard to find, owing to publishers' reluctance to part with them. Until a few years ago, the collector's main chance of securing a cartoon was to watch out for donations of work by cartoonists to charity auctions. In latter years, however, many front-rank cartoonists employed by newspapers on both sides of the Atlantic have begun to sell their original works on request. A telephone call to the cartoonist at his office will often lead to a deal. Prices vary enormously, of course, with some cartoonists valuing a large original in the hundreds and others selling 'pocket cartoon' artwork at prices starting from about £50/$75 a time. Cartoonists' galleries, which have sprung up in some major cities, are another source of original work.

Dealers selling watercolours have, in the past decade, developed specialized departments devoted to illustrators (see page 116), and these often include cartoonists of the inter-war years. Similarly, works of this genre occasionally appear in auctions of watercolours and drawings. The art of contemporary cartoonists, in the view of saleroom experts, remains an underpriced area, and one with ample scope for investment possibilities. The latest Presidential crisis, tantrums at the Summit, the price of oil ... they now belong to the collector's wall. Cartoons are a subject as alive as today's news.

Cartoons: Collector rating

Scope and variety	9
Investment potential	B
Price range	£50/$75 to four figures

CATS & DOGS

Cats, said Ernest Hemingway, can look after themselves. In the collectors' charts there is no doubt about that. And dogs do very nicely, too.

A Chinese porcelain hound, with some two centuries of age, can make £10,000/$15,000, in the saleroom, which is twice as much as he might make were he a heron or rabbit. Even more startlingly, a 3 inch (7.5cm) painted bronze cat from Vienna, not yet 70 years old and once considered toyshop kitsch, is at home in the £300-£400/$450-$600 bracket.

In saleroom terms a top cat would be found in a Louis Wain watercolour or as a slinky, enigmatically smiling Gallé master-piece of glass. 'Cat and dog pictures, illustrated books, postcards, bronzes, porcelain and pottery sell like mad,' says a London auctioneer. 'Put "cat" or "dog" in a catalogue description, and you just know that the lot is going to bring in the bids.' Even an arched-back spitfire, thumb-nail-sized, issued as the 'spiteful cat' in the 1920s by Britain's, the lead soldier and farm maker, is now marked up well into two figures in collectors' listings.

Dogs have appeared in paintings from early times, but it was not until the nineteenth century and the development of the Industrial Revolution that attitudes towards dogs became sentimental and they started to feature prominently in works of art. Painters such as Landseer depicted them with almost human expressions and his style influenced that of many of his contemporaries. Prices for dog paintings continue to rise. Over the last few years, primitives dating from the late eighteenth and the early nineteenth centuries have proved particularly buoyant, thanks mainly to growing American interest. In this branch of collecting anything from fine art to dog collars goes. (A collar belonging to Lord Byron's dog has changed hands at more than £2,000/$3,000).

London's annual synod of dog worship, Crufts, triggers off feverish activity among the salerooms and dealers. 'Dog antiques' might include a 5 inch (13cm) high bronze by P.J. Mêne, around the £1,000/$1,500 mark, or a pair of Stafford-shire's ubiquitous porcelain spaniels, which can still be found for about £100 in Britain, perhaps $200 in the United States. Much nearer our own times and a quarter the price of the Staffordshire spaniels are comic china dogs such as Bonzo and Dismal Desmond, serving as mugs or lampholders. Doggy brooches, of base metal, porcelain, enamel, silver or gold, are fast-sellers. Walt Disney's Pluto has long since lost ground to the pushy Snoopy in cuddly fabric, china, tin and plastic.

Left. Superb work by Theophile-Alexandre Steinlen, who specialized in portraying cats. He employs his cats for a poster to advertise an 1890s exhibition of drawings and paintings in Paris.

Right. Arguably the most popular dog of all. He achieved fame in celluloid and has been celebrated in paint, print, ceramics, bronze, silver and plastic. Here, Walt Disney's Pluto appears as a pottery figure from Japan.

Far right. Modern animal art. One of a set of five bone china plaques of the Big Five of African wildlife, after paintings by David Shepherd for the Boehm porcelain factory.

Below right. Louis Wain, said H.G. Wells, 'invented a cat style, a cat society, a whole cat world'. Dogs, too. This book of 1902, with Wain's work, was published by Raphael Tuck.

Feline fever has been creeping over the collector market for many years, but its present and most serious bout can be traced back to the mid-1980s when a remarkable collection of cats came on the market en masse. It was a menagerie of 250 of the Viennese cats, ranging in height from 1-3 inches (2.5-7.5cm). The cats were cast in bronze, then brightly painted in various colours; the technique is known as 'cold-painted bronze'. Nearly all these Viennese cats are anthropomorphic, and the human activities in which they indulge are practically endless.

They had belonged to a British collector whose grandfather bought them, mostly in Austria, between 1900 and the 1920s. Anna Marrett, head of the department of dolls and related items at Phillips, had lurking fears that the appearance in the saleroom of such a large collection at one time might depress the market. But, in the event, her fears were groundless. Cat prices went crazy. The collection realized £25,000/$40,000.

First came the culinary cats. They wore their old fashioned floppy chef's hats with panache, eight of them, carrying the tools of their trade: one brandished a copper pan, one a butter tub, another a mixing bowl; they displayed joints of meat and a huge fish on platters; one held a struggling pig. There were cats playing musical instruments, joining in sports, working around the house, studying, gardening: just about anything a human does, a Viennese bronze cat can do. Kitchen cats washed dishes, churned butter and made tea. A photographer cat snapped £240/$360, and a telescope-gazer made £190/$285. The bill for the chefs was £460/$690, and a 12-piece orchestra tuned up to £700/$1,050.

There are many other fields open to cat collectors. Feline images are found in earthenware, the finest being the tin-glaze cats from Delft and Lambeth. There are aristocratic Staffordshire cats and humble animals featured in late nineteenth century fairings – the comical pottery groups given away as prizes or sold for a few pence on Victorian fairgrounds. The Continent has sent us venerable beauties from the Kaendler factory. The London factory of Chelsea produced the first English porcelain cats in the 1750s and 60s. Later, Rockingham, Derby and Worcester cats were much more realistic. By the

beginning of the nineteenth century, with the advance of techniques, porcelain cats really looked like cats; some collectors prefer the older, more naïve forms.

In France, the master Gallé produced an exquisite 12 inch (30cm)-high creature, seated and somewhat Cheshire-like in its smile, delicately enamelled in many colours, its green-glass eyes sparkling. Such a super-cat can easily soar into four figures at auction. Modern pottery and porcelain cats abound. Notably, Royal Worcester has a delightful set of six 4 inch (10cm) kittens modelled by James Alder. Some, like the set's ginger tom, sit up appealingly; the black and white rolls on its back in play.

China has left us a heritage of porcelain and bronze cat colonies. In Japan, cats were so revered that the work of keeping down mice was considered beneath their dignity. People painted cats on doors and bought cats of bronze, wood and porcelain to scare away the mice. Thus Japan was overrun with mice and

Left. Another stunning production by the 'cat artist' Theophile-Alexandre Steinlen, this time promoting a veterinary clinic in Paris in 1905. Examples of this poster have sold for £6,500-£13,500/ $10,000-£20,000 in New York.

Above right. They are small models of cats made in bronze and then painted, many of them not much more than 1.5 inches (4cm) in height. Think big in value, however: some groups cost hundreds of pounds. The source was Vienna in the first twenty years of this century.

Right. Thrift cat: this attractive china money bank dates from the period between World Wars One and Two. It would appeal not only to cat enthusiasts, but to the growing legion of money bank collectors.

stocked with a wealth of beautiful cat objects!

Cat collectors know all about cat lore, of course. Few, however, would go as far as the British artist Louis Wain who claimed that 'all people who keep cats, and are in the habit of nursing them, do not suffer from those petty little ailments which all flesh is heir to, *viz*, nervous complaints of a minor sort. Hysteria and rheumatism, too, are unknown, and all lovers of "pussy" are of the sweetest temperament'.

Wain's name is, of course, synonymous with cats among collectors. He first started drawing cats in human form in the 1880s, and at his prime in the early part of this century he was turning out 600 drawings a year for postcards and illustrations in books and magazines. His animals and those of the Viennese bronze-makers have a striking resemblance. Some not uncommon Wain cat cards easily top £10/$15 apiece today. While his original watercolours are the stuff of Bond Street and Madison Avenue galleries. His collectors are legion. But, alas, his faith in cats' ability to ward off nervous troubles in human beings was to have an ironic twist – in the end he went raving mad. Even though he was committed to an asylum, however, he still went on drawing cats.

Tribute to Wain's feline artistry was paid by the writer H.G. Wells, who observed: 'He invented a cat style, a cat society, a whole cat world. English cats that do not look like Louis Wain cats are ashamed of themselves.'

Cats and dogs: Collector rating

Scope and variety:	10
Investment potential	A
Price range	£10/$15 to the limits of fine art.

CHRISTMAS & GREETINGS

Christmas past is alive and thriving in the United States as nowhere else in the world. Collecting passion shows itself in an annual carousel of holiday antique shows, swap-meets, mail order offers and new tomes from publishers on Christmas memorabilia. American collectors have done more than any other national group to document Santa's heritage.

The Christmas card, however, has been a slow starter with collectors everywhere. In the past five years it has emerged from the rear ranks of collecting to a forward position, although it has some way to go before it shares top honours with the Valentine (see page 196). The inventiveness of twentieth-century Christmas cards will ensure them a place among the antiques of tomorrow, and the key to their fortunes lies, as so often, in yesterday.

The Victorians, be they from either side of the Atlantic, had some funny ideas about Christmas cards, which makes the field a fascinating and much varied one for collectors. Dead robins with their feet in the air and half-naked little girls unprotected from the cold are not the modern idea of a merry Christmas, but in the nineteenth century people thought such images would nudge social consciences. In the 1890s a writer on art, Gleeson White, made his protest about some of the more unusual cards: 'We need not be concerned with the large number of makers who delight in reproducing imitations of unlovely objects, luggage labels, cork soles, slices of blankets, or of bacon, burnt ends of cigars, extracted teeth and other horrors ... practical jokes of the feeblest order.'

To be fair, though, most cards of the late nineteenth century were not like that. Many were elaborate creations of layered cut-out paper decorated with tinsel. Flowers had symbolic messages for lovers: honeysuckle for bonds of affection, red rosebuds for purity and loveliness, and so on. Cards burst into pop-up bouquets, and three-dimensional Nativity scenes were also popular.

Queen Victoria (it was her beloved Albert who introduced the German tradition of the Christmas tree to Britain) was an avid sender of Christmas cards. Her poet laureate, Alfred Lord Tennyson, is said to have been offered £1,000/$1,500 by an enterprising card magnate for verses suitable for greetings. There were even women's lib cards by the first decade of this century. The suffragette movement inspired a verse which aroused fierce criticism:

'Downtrodden woman now arise,
No more let men thus tyrannize;
Let's push the tyrant from his throne,
And have a Christmas of our own.'

Controversy had also rumbled over the Christmas card which is regarded as Britain's very first commercial example. Said to have been inspired by Sir Henry Cole, the first director of the collection that was to become the Victoria and Albert Museum, it was designed in the 1840s by the artist John Calcott Horsley, known as 'Clothes-Horsley' because he campaigned against the fashion for nude paintings. It showed a family raising their glasses in a toast, and was savagely attacked by the temperance lobby. Nevertheless, although only 1,000 of these cards were printed, the hand-coloured lithographs sold like hot mince pies at one shilling each, a tidy sum in those days. Few have come up for sale in recent times, and when one does it tends to go to America, with not much change out of £670/$1,000. It is arguably the most expensive Christmas card, apart from one

Below. One example of a mass of Christmas greetings and decorations in pressed-card cut-outs, made in Britain in the early years of this century and used primarily for store display. The availability of the medium makes it a popular – and relatively inexpensive – collecting area.

BEST CHRISTMAS WISHES

May Christmas
with its pleasures
with you rest,
And bring you
of its love and joys,
the best.

which would assume a value on the strength of a desirable autograph.

Collectors of tomorrow's antiques must look closer to our own times: to the turn of the century when the fashionable wanted the very *modern* idea of their family photographs on their Christmas cards; to the huge export traffic of tinselled Santa Clauses from Germany about this time; and to later, by a decade or so, when mechanical pop-ups, moving-part cards and fold-over tricks were the rage. There were some remarkable twists of the imagination: in post-Edwardian Britain, if you were on the Lord Mayor of Birmingham's Christmas card list you might receive an ultra modern greeting showing Santa in a stringbag aeroplane, showering municipal gifts of electric lights, trams, dustcarts, baths and policemen on grateful citizens.

What of general greetings cards – birthday, wedding anniversary, get-well and the rest? They tend to be lumped into job lots at card auctions, where the devotees concentrate on Valentines and, to a lesser degree, Christmas cards. General greetings lack the cachet of a defined collecting area, although there have been signs of Easter cards taking off in a modest way. There are exceptions, of course, notably among specialized areas such as Disney or Louis Wain cat subjects. A 3-D scene of Snow White talking to the little animals in the wild wood, with cosy cottage and dwarfs in the background, is sure of bidders at any auction. In general, however, ordinary greetings seem underpriced: only time will tell.

Christmas decorations are big business in the United States. The wealth of collectables available from the not too far distant and the immediate past is illustrated on the fir tree which greets Christmas visitors to the *Forbes* Magazine Galleries on Fifth Avenue, New York. Inspired by warm memories of his childhood Christmases, Malcolm Forbes charged his curator of collections, Margaret Kelly, with assembling a glittering array of old-fashioned ornaments. Coaxed out of attics and acquired from antique dealers all over the United States, the collection of several hundred pieces encompasses paper, spun glass, tinsel, and pressed cotton, wooden and metal ornaments.

European blown-glass creations, dating from around 1870-1940, form the basis of the collection. Products of a cottage industry based primarily in Lauscha, Germany, these charming glass ornaments were first brought to the United States by immigrants and later retailed by the dime-store magnates F.W.

Above. Christmas means toys. The appearance of the teddy bear in this Christmas greeting probably dates it after the first decade of this century when the new toy craze had become firmly established.

Below. Another good quality, cut-out and free-standing Christmas display scene, made in Britain. Many such items find their way into American collections, the fever for collecting Christmas being at its highest in the USA.

Right. Turn-of-the-century sentimentalism at Christmas time – from Germany. Such cards were made in vast numbers and shipped over to Britain and America on an export tide. During World War One the German trade was, of course, interrupted, receiving a blow from which many producers never recovered.

Far right. Christmas, birthday, Valentine, general greetings: an array of good wishes prior to going under the hammer in a special auction at Phillips in London. (See also the chapter on Valentines).

Below. 'Love from Mabel', wrote the sender of this German-made card at the dawn of a new century, thus making it a 'personalized', one-off collectable. Some collectors concentrate on amassing only cards which have been signed or bear handwritten messages.

Woolworth and Samuel Kress. Early kugel balls in lustrous glass are complemented by naturalistic ornaments such as grapes, silver and gold nuts, acorns, clip-on trees and roses, frosted pine cones, and an art nouveau pansy that reveals the face of a young girl. The tree is peopled by a comic Keystone Kop, a rare Indian head, Jackie Coogan, a hand-blown Happy Hooligan, multiple images of Father Christmas, and a leprechaun huddling under a clump of mushrooms. There are dogs, cats, frogs, fish, and a bevy of birds, many with spun-glass tails. These glass fantasies are much sought after, fetching from a few dollars to several hundred.

The tree sparkles with some choice Dresden pieces. These ornaments were hand-made in Germany between 1888 and 1910 and in soft lighting appear to be silver and gold; closer inspection reveals that they are meticulously embossed cardboard. A gold baby carriage from Dresden that carries a brightly-coloured child, a gaudy rooster, a shoe which turns out to be a candy box, and a stag are among the treasures.

A very specialized branch of Christmas collecting is represented by ornaments of cotton and crêpe paper. These engaging toys are surprisingly durable. They are often sprinkled with glass shavings, which glisten like newly fallen snow. Nestled in the Forbes tree are skiers, boys and girls on sleds, angels, a stork whose wing lifts to reveal a candy container, a little girl in a crêpe paper dress poised to throw a cotton snowball, and a lone ox which seems to have strayed from a Nativity set.

Party crackers offer a particularly interesting challenge to the collector. By their very nature, they are here today and gone tomorrow. Intact boxes which survive to be collected tend to be untouched shop stock. Some of the elaborate and expensive trinkets contained in the highest quality crackers of the late Victorian and Edwardian eras can bring big money in the salerooms. However, the mass of present-day cracker contents, mostly originating in the Far East, will never make the collector lists unless as subject matter for record and curiosity.

Tom Smith, a firm of longevity that is said to have made more crackers than other, claims to be the pioneer of the whole idea of Christmas with a snap. According to tradition, Tom Smith, an impoverished pastry cook in the second part of Victoria's reign, thought he could improve his fortunes by introducing to Britain the popular Parisian motto comfit, a sweet or sugared almond wrapped in a screw of paper which carried a motto. Sales resistance was strong, however, and Smith was sitting disconsolately by the fire wondering what to do next to save himself from ruin, when a log suddenly exploded into flame. That was Smith's inspiration. He was the first man to put a bang, or snap, into the bon-bons. Crackers, in fact, were often sold as 'bon-bons', and became a firmly rooted British tradition at Christmas. One large and expensive box of Smith creations of the 1880s was called 'Tom Smith's Snap Shots' and contained 'magic photography' devices.

Collectors of Christmas artefacts in the United States have much more opportunity to pursue their hobby than those in Europe. Specialist dealers are now dotted across the country from coast to coast. A typical holiday antique show in 1986, organized by enthusiast Jim Bohenstengel of Oak Park, Illinois,

attracted more than 2,000 collectors from 30 states, scrambling for the stock of 53 dealers. In addition to Christmas, homage was paid to Easter, the Fourth of July and Thanksgiving. Prices for small collectables ranged from a few dollars to £1,000/$1,500 for a rare Heubach candy container of George Washington on a horse. Dresden ornaments were seen in a vast variety. One enchanted visitor reported: 'Feather Christmas trees (swathed in turkey or goose feathers) as large as 8 feet (2.5m) tall were dripping with unusual ornaments. Black cats and orange jack-o-lanterns stared from every corner. Easter animals darted from table to table. Santa waved his lantern and held bags full of toys. What a dream!'

Christmas and greetings: Collector rating

Scope and variety	9
Investment potential	B
Prices range	A few pounds or dollars to £3,330/$5,000

CIGARETTE CARDS

Above. Pin-ups of another age, each one with a price on its head, this series of Actresses and Flowers was issued in 1899 by Myrtle Grove cigarettes. The series, 24 out of 25 shown here, was a popular collecting line in its day and is now soaring above an average £50/$75 per card, in sets.

Far right. The Big Top in cigarette cards. Taddy's legendary Clowns series represented by 19 out of the full set of 20. The auction catalogue observed: 'Lacks three dogs on see-saw.' At £4,600 – nearly $7,000 – the dogs' absence didn't seem to matter to the collector who bought them in 1985, but since then a full set has left this price far behind. The firm of Taddy's suffered a sudden and dramatic demise owing to industrial trouble.

The clowns are laughing all the way to the bank. Some twenty of them entered the ring in the last years of Queen Victoria's reign and now, the best part of a century later, their antics are still drawing an eager audience. It is a very serious audience, for these clowns are no joke. One of the world's rarest sets of cigarette cards, Taddy's Clowns are a highly expensive act.

Their cash performance reflects the fact that only about twenty complete sets are known. In 1970 a full team was sold at an English auction for £105/$160. By 1973, the price was up to £1,000. In mid-1985, Phillips in London established a world record for a group of cigarette cards when a collector paid £4,600 – more than $6,000 – for nineteen out of the twenty Taddy's Clowns. Cartophilists cheerfully predicted that in the next decade the clowns would be taking home £10,000/$15,000, or an average of £500/$750 per 2 inch card. Collectors call them the Penny Blacks of cigarette cards.

James Taddy and Company was a small London tobacco firm renowned for its beautifully produced cards. They have a particular rarity value due in part to the company's dramatic and sudden demise during an industrial dispute. Taddy's had been founded about 1740 as 'purveyors of tobacco, tea and snuff'. After more than a century and a half in business, the firm was successful and prosperous when its Clowns came on the scene; its cigarettes, such as Myrtle Grove and Premier, were popular: a bright future seemed to lie ahead. Taddy's owner, Gilliat

H.I.M. Emperor of Germany

Ogden's *Guinea Gold Cigarettes.*

Baron von Ketteler.
German Ambassador at Pekin. Murdered June 1900

Ogden's *Guinea Gold Cigarettes.*

H.M. EDWARD VII.
KING OF GREAT BRITAIN & IRELAND,
EMPEROR OF INDIA.

Ogden's *Guinea Gold Cigarettes.*

King—Manager of Chinese Telegraphs.

Ogden's *Guinea Gold Cigarettes.*

One of our "Handy Men" of
H.M.S. "Powerful."

Ogden's *Guinea Gold Cigarettes.*

120   EDISON
Famous Electrician.
Inventor of the Phonograph & Cinematograph

Ogden's *Guinea Gold Cigarettes.*

The Empress of China

Ogden's *Guinea Gold Cigarettes.*

532   MADGE LESSING.

Ogden's *Guinea Gold Cigarettes.*

Hatfield, was an enlightened employer who gave his workers fair wages and conditions, thus, in his eyes, dispensing with the need for a trade union in his factory.

In 1920 the cigarette industry was hit by a wages strike. Although Taddy's non-union workers were already paid more than the union was claiming, they came out on strike. Hatfield felt betrayed. He issued an ultimatum: 'Return to work or I will close the factory.' He was as good as his word. When there was no sign of a return to work, Hatfield sacked everybody and closed Taddy's for good. Furthermore, in his anger, he destroyed the firm's books, correspondence and records and refused to sell the goodwill of the business to anyone. As the firm was one of the earliest in Britain to introduce packed tobacco, which led to cigarette cards being used as stiffeners, in the last quarter of the nineteenth century, the destruction of Taddy's archives has robbed historically minded collectors of irreplaceable material.

This is a great pity because cartophilists are far from united when it comes to charting the origins of cigarette cards. There are, however, two facts on which they agree; the cards began as stiffeners for cigarette packets; and they made their first appearance in the United States, probably in the steps of general traders who had since the 1860s given away little picture cards to encourage sales of wares. The oldest cigarette card known to exist is in the Metropolitan Museum, New York, an American issue by Marquis of Lorne cigarettes, showing the nobleman's portrait and dating from 1878.

The first pictorial cards had plain backs. The story goes that in the late 1870s, Edward Bok, a successful American journalist, picked up a cigarette card in the street. It depicted an actress on the front; the back was black. It struck him that this was a waste of word space – and he launched the fashion for putting text on the reverse side of a cigarette card. Those earliest text-backed cards merely carried advertising messages for the cigarette maker. Factual material relating to the picture was to come a few years later.

American cards from the 1880s to the end of the century, in good condition, are very scarce, largely because it was the custom of American collectors to glue them into scrapbooks, thus damaging the backs. The international collecting spotlight switches to Britain in this era, therefore, where the tobacco industry was in the throes of trade warfare thanks to transatlantic rivalries. At the heart of the battle was the ruthless James B. Duke, who formed the American Tobacco Company in 1890. From humble beginnings selling tobacco from a cart, he had seized control of about 250 firms by 1901 and was looking to Britain for further conquests.

In true entrepreneurial style, Duke is said to have disembarked at Liverpool docks, walked into the factory of Ogden's and bought it out, lock, stock and cigarette cards. He went to work issuing huge amounts of cards for Tabs and Guinea Gold cigarettes, two names enshrined in collector lore. Tabs cards, of a multitude of subjects, were so popular that many decades later the word 'tab' was synonymous with 'cigarette' in the north-west of England. Guinea Gold's series of photographic portraits of personalities – which had begun some years before Duke set foot in Liverpool – ran to many thousands of different 'sitters'; some enthusiasts claim that as many as 20,000 different Guinea Gold cards were issued, making them a massive catchment area for collecting and a specialized field in themselves.

Duke's depredations triggered what was to become known as the 'tobacco war', with American and British companies at each other's throats, and millions of cigarette cards being turned out as ammunition in this international commercial conflict. For Britain, Wills and a dozen other firms combined in the Imperial Tobacco Company. It was a bitter and expensive fight for a few

Left. Guinea Gold cigarette cards: this famous series of small size photographs of personalities ran to many thousands of 'sitters'; some authorities claim that as many as 20,000 different Guinea Golds were issued. *(The Atkinson Collection)*.

Below. A display of cigarette cards when collecting was in its heyday. Cigarette cards began in the United States, probably as the result of the lead given by traders who gave away little picture cards to stimulate sales of the wares from the 1860s onwards. *(The Atkinson Collection)*.

years, in the course of which Ogden's was wrested back from American control. The result was an armistice and a compromise in which the American Tobacco Company held sway in America and Cuba and a newly formed British-American Tobacco Company (BAT) handled other overseas interests.

National honour was upheld: British cigarette cards remained thoroughly British, with English roses of the London stage, county cricketers and royalty by the ton holding the allegiance of collectors then and now; American presidents from numerous sources and Allen and Genter's Celebrated Indian Chiefs had their day on the western side of the Atlantic.

The history of the 'tobacco war' helps to explain why the period covering the closing years of the nineteenth century and the early years of Edward VII's reign is regarded as the golden age of cigarette cards.

Errors in cigarette cards are revered like mistakes in postage stamps. One hallowed howler is in the Famous Escapes series of Carreras cigarettes. Napolean III's daring getaway from the Prussians is depicted on the front of a card, but the reverse side

gives an account of Winston Churchill's break-out from Boer captivity in 1899. In a Player's cigarettes series on Dandies, Benjamin Disraeli is shown as a fashionably dressed young man of twenty-two, with Big Ben in the background. But Disraeli was twenty-two in 1826 – and Big Ben's clock did not go up until 1858. Aberrations like these put a premium on cards.

Here is a newspaper item of early 1987: a new picture card series produced by the tea manufacturer Brooke Bond was described as 'garbage' by an international group of scientists. The 'educational' series, Unexplained Mysteries of the World, deals with subjects such as ghosts, levitation, UFOs, monsters and fairies. No sooner were the cards issued than the British secretary of the Committee for the Scientific Investigation of Claims of the Paranormal weighed in with the complaint that 'this series perpetuates some of the world's greatest fallacies and hoaxes under the guise of being educational'. This sort of controversy, documented and stored, is the stuff of tomorrow's collecting lore – especially if dissent leads to the premature cancellation of a series.

Above. Waterloo – rare British cigarette cards which Wills prepared in 1915, but the set was unissued. The year marked the centenary of the battle. By 1915, however, Britain and France were allies in another war, and perhaps it was considered diplomatically unsound to be seen to be celebrating a victory over the French, who had become comrades in arms against the Germans. A key card in the set of 50 was Napoleon.

On the whole, however, cigarette cards have been remarkably accurate. Historians collect them. Film companies have often resorted to them as basic research material. Schoolboys by the million have been inspired by them to seek further knowledge of subjects. The words on the back have been hailed as 'models of conciseness'. Surprisingly, little is known of the authors of these texts. One writer commissioned to compile nuggets of information about fifty butterflies in 1925 was paid little more than £2.

Brooke Bond, notwithstanding its brush with the paranormal boffins, has enjoyed a good reputation for the accuracy and quality of its textual matter, and has for many series publicized both the compilers and authors. The issue of cards by cigarette companies has almost died out, but trade cards, such as those issued by the tea companies, survive as a collecting ground for tomorrow. Some issues obtainable at filling stations might find themselves in collections in the future, too. Breakfast cereal is another potential hunting ground. In the United States, bubble gum cards of the Fifties and Sixties are already priced like antiques, with hundreds of dollars turning on an ultra-rare card – a sporting subject or, as often happens, a depiction of a wartime atrocity – that will complete a run of, say, 200.

Left. A good collection of military issues of the late nineteenth and early twentieth centuries, including cards by Liebig, Player, Taddy, Faulkner and the American Tobacco Company. Current wars were often chosen as themes – for example, the Russo-Japanese conflict in a Taddy's series.

As issues of cigarette cards dwindled progressively through the 1950s to the 1970s, collecting came on apace. It is now an extremely well documented area, with price guides listing the going rate for practically every card and set recorded in the Western world – and many others elsewhere. Chinese cards are not unknown; Thailand has a history of cards; Japan has been a disappointment. While American and British cards dominate the collecting scene, Continental Europe has produced some interesting issues and legends.

Germany was late in the game, producing some of its earliest cards after World War One. Much of German production has been lost because it was traditionally on thin paper to allow collectors to stick the cards into albums. However, some of the cards reached a strikingly high standard of design and pictorial reproduction, not least during the Third Reich. Hitler feared cigarette cards might distract young people from more serious studies. His attitude is said to have changed when Goebbels pointed out their propaganda value. Certainly some of the Nazi-slanted cards of the Thirties are among the world's best for technical detail and reproduction.

Considering the fortunes of cigarette cards – the destruction of them in two world wars, the ravages caused by children's games in which a flicked card 'won' those it partially covered as it landed – it is remarkable what an enormous variety remains. Incomplete sets or single cards do not have the same pro rata value of full sets. Sets stuck down in albums do not make as much as similar sets of loose cards. (In the 1920s and 1930s some British firms followed the earlier American custom of issuing adhesive-backed cards to go into albums.) Condition is all important; collectors reject cards which have been creased or soiled by schoolboys' flicking games. Like many branches of collecting, cigarette cards are no longer child's play.

Cigarette cards: Collector rating

Scope and variety	8
Investment potential	D; B for rarities
Price range	Pennies to £10,000/$15,000

CINEMANIA

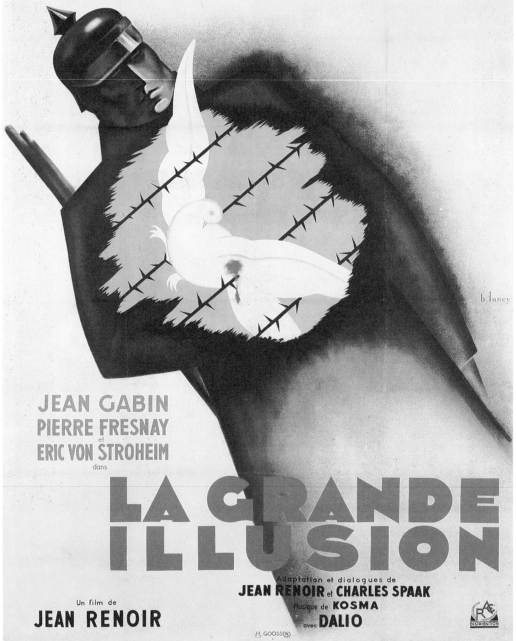

Above. Screen printed blue glass jug featuring child-star Shirley Temple.

Right. A powerful 1937 poster for Jean Renoir's anti-war film, *La Grande Illusion*. The movie was banned in Germany and Italy at that time. The poster (62 inches, 157cm high) is by Bernard Lucy who gave the subject strong allegorical treatment. A valuable item, heading towards five-figure value.

You can pay thousands for something unique such as the shoes in which Judy Garland danced along the Yellow Brick Road to Oz, or a few pounds or dollars for a Laurel and Hardy salt-and-pepper set manufactured in large quantities during the 1930s. Mrs Miniver's apron, worn by Greer Garson, and Pussy Galore's catsuit rank some way behind Marilyn Monroe's mock mink bikini – but that's showbiz for you.

The rules of collecting cinema memorabilia work a bit like the Hollywood star system. There is billing (bottom, middle and top), and fortunes sometimes depend on a fickle following and rapid changes in demand and popularity. Today's collectors are playing to a new scenario, one that has changed dramatically in the last twenty years. In 1974, movie enthusiasts from both sides

of the Atlantic flocked to Britain's Shepperton Studios when contents were auctioned, but much of the material was technical, and obsolete booms, gantries and camera dollies have a limited appeal even for the most enthusiastic collectors. An 11ft (4m) long replica which had sailed through studio clouds in the title role of the film *Airship* sold for £120/$180, a bargain at not much more than £10/$15 a foot. Collectors still marvel at this snip, as its price would be considerably higher in comparative terms today: there are now many more wealthy collectors in the market, happy to take on a cinematic memento of such large proportions and, coincidentally, airships generally are collectors' high-flyers (see Aviation on page 34).

A billion celluloid reels after the first moving pictures

flickered on to the world's screens, cinemania is big business. Hundreds of new titles on cinema subjects appear on publishers' lists every year. In the salerooms, record prices for modern ephemera are clocked up by buyers of film stills, cartoon drawings, set designs and posters. Superlatives abound in this collectors' world, dealing as it does with a dream industry which has peddled the spectacular throughout its existence.

Big as cinemania is today, it is a fairly new collector boom, as we have seen. At the start of the 1970s it was not unusual to see batches of stills change hands at international auctions for under £6/$10. The author recalls being the underbidder on just such a lot of twenty rare stills from Marlene Dietrich films. Within the space of about five years, however, things changed rapidly.

A milestone event for cinematic collectors came at an auction after Phillips in London was handed several large boxes of brown paper parcels which had been, almost literally, thrown out of a warehouse which was closing down. 'See what you can do with these,' said the vendor, a young woman. Paul Viney, who was handling sales of ephemera, recalls opening packet after packet of glossy film stills, many going back to the earliest years of the cinema.

'There were stills from more than 1,000 films, and pictures of hundreds, yes hundreds, of stars,' he says. 'In the time available the problem was how to classify them. To tackle it by subject matter – situation comedies, epics, gangster, war, etc – would have meant weeks and weeks of work.' He settled for alphabetical classification. So the first lot ran from *All Quiet on the Western Front* to *Duck Soup*, taking in *The Count of Monte Cristo* and *David Copperfield* on the way. And so on, down to *Ziegfeld Girl*, with rare gems from movies such as *Gone With the Wind* and *Hell's Angels* finding their places in the catalogue.

There were not only stills, but original studio press releases, glossy brochures with designs for productions such as the 1936 version of *The Lost Horizon*, treatises on camera work and film stunts, programes, magazines and newspaper clippings. 'There is,' said a cinema buff who came to view, 'enough fresh material to keep half a dozen publishers going for a year.' The subsequent sale proved a truism of collecting: a mass of material appearing for sale at one time, such as a definitive collection, does not necessarily depress the market, but often acts as a stimulus to the entire collecting field. In this case, cinemania was established as a dynamic area of collecting.

Stills, being the most accessible commodity for collectors, are none the less in far from unlimited supply. They were issued in hundreds of thousands but were usually destroyed after use, and those that remain today are often the only photographic records – apart from the reels themselves – of early films. At a premium are some of the early shots taken by the stills cameramen for Technicolor films and subsequently displayed in glass-fronted panels on the exterior of the cinema as a enticements for patrons. It is exceedingly difficult to price stills. Some can be picked up at rummage sales for next to nothing, or in inexpensive batches; specialist dealers in movie ephemera have a complicated scale of charges: a rare still from, say, a James Dean classic might have an inflated value within the circle of Dean fan clubs which it would not enjoy on the open market.

Cinema posters are a fascinating area of study and collection – 'a medium that was unique: loud, brash, vulgar, braggart, using the human form as a provocation and the letters of the alphabet

Top. Two of Britain's offerings among the flood of film annuals between the 1930s and the 1960s – packed with information and gossip about the lives of the stars, on and off camera. The *Daily Express* book dates from 1935. Annuals like these can often be picked up cheaply in street markets.

Above. Watercolour by Mike Margolis of Groucho Marx, captioned with characteristic Marxism: 'Sometime this Bitter ache will pass my love – Time wounds all heels!'

Above. Original watercolour conception for a cinema of the 1920s by John Alexander, a British designer who was responsible for the interiors of many picture houses throughout Britain. The Victoria and Albert Museum in London preserves some of his designs.

Below. *Father Noah's Ark* was a Walt Disney Silly Symphony produced by United Artists. This 1933 poster (41 inches, 104cm high) would grace any collection of cinema or Disney material. It changed hands in the early 1980s at more than £3,000/$4,500.

as a violence, declaring an irrepressible and irresistible vitality, making intoxicating use of form and composition and rhythm.' The description comes from David Robinson, a British film historian and film critic of The Times. Many cinema posters achieve four-figure prices in the collector market – and they can rise higher when executed by celebrated poster artists (see Posters on page 138).

Campaign books are regarded by some collectors as the most desirable area of collecting, representing the essence of Hollywood. These were sent out by the major film companies to exhibitors, advising how best to publicize titles and decorate cinema foyers. One idea offered on the release of *The Buccaneer* was to blow up a straddle-legged figure of Fredric March to giant size so that patrons could enter the cinema through his legs.

The old fan magazines, a branch of literature which is unique in style and content, have their own devotees. Early British film magazines seem sedate compared with the bumptious, keyhole-peeping, yet basically adulatory, flavour quickly adopted by the American pulp factories. *Photoplay* in 1911 was the United States' first fan magazine, to be followed by a host of 10-cent dream sheets, such as *Motion Picture* ('Will marriage ruin Loretta Young's film career?'), *Silver Screen*, *Modern Screen* and many others. The magazines had their heyday in the 1930s. If you followed them regularly you would learn that Garbo and Harold Lloyd paid £60,000/$100,000 a year income tax, all about 'Hollywood's unmarried husbands and wives', and 'What's the matter with Lombard' (actually, it appears, she was simply being inaccessible to the press). You would know how stardom came to, among others: Virginia McMath, Maureen FitzSimons, Ella Geisman, Frederic Austerlitz, Tula Finklea, Harlean Carpentier, Hedwig Kiesler, Joe Yule, Lucille LeSueur, Greta Gustafsson, Frances Ethel Gumm, and Spangler Arlington Brugh. Spangler Arlington who? Virginia McMath became *Ginger Rogers*; Maureen FitzSimons *Maureen O'Hara*; Ella Geisman *June Allyson*; Frederic Austerlitz *Fred Astaire*; Tula Finklea *Cyd Charisse*; Harlean Carpentier *Jean Harlow*; Hedwig Kiesler *Hedy Lamarr*; Joe Yule *Mickey Rooney*; Lucille LeSueur *Joan Crawford*; Greta Gustafsson *Greta Garbo*; Frances Ethel Gumm *Judy Garland*; and Spangler Arlington Brugh became *Robert Taylor*.

The magazines were a vital stream of the dream-industry's lifeblood. Today, expect to pay several thousand dollars for a definitive run through several years of one of these magazines. Bound copies of such a series are in the price class of fine antiquarian books.

Among Britain's contributions were *Picturegoer, Picture Show, Film Fun* and *Film Pictorial*. Collectors can dip into a past world of mind-boggling trivia: Gracie Fields was worth £2 a minute; it took 15,000 drawings for a 10-minute Mickey Mouse; Hedy Lamarr hated mustard. Special offers flooded fan clubs with autographed photographs, often bearing printed signatures (Jean Harlow, who is said to have been nearly illiterate, is now accused of having employed her mother to sign the photographs she sent out from the studio). If you had bought Britain's *Film Pictorial* of 30 September, 1933, you could have subscribed to six records at 1s 3d each of numbers from *Sally in Our Alley* and *Cuban Love Song*, and other films; surely collectors' items now.

And after the magazines came the film annuals, high on collectors' lists today. In a Sussex antiques arcade in the mid-1970s, the author came across a film book of 1935 produced by the *Daily Express*. How's this for a stirring contemporary film review in true blue Express style, by the critic Ernest Betts: '*Lives of a Bengal Lancer* is a tale of treachery and spying on the North West Frontier of India, and of how the British army keeps a stern hand on millions of its Indian subjects. It convinces you,

The lifeblood of cinema collecting – stills used for display outside the picture palaces of the world, including several from the heyday of Technicolor. In their working times, untold thousands of display stills were thrown away when they were no longer required. Routine stills are relatively inexpensive to collect and 'job lots' can often be found at minor auctions.

it thrills you, it moves you with extraordinary feelings of pride and patriotism.' At £2 it had to be bargain for that antique of a review alone.

One critic of the cinema's architectural development has noted that multi-screen picture houses have made the act of watching a film akin to 'sitting in a shoebox'. But it was not always so. The dream palace era of minarets, gothic arches and caryatids comes back into life in the designs of the great cinemas of the 1920s and 1930s, often the only remaining evidence of the cinemas' original appearance. These designs are keenly collected, both for their artistic value and as echoes of the past. One leading designer of the cinema interior in Britain during the 1920s and 1930s was the John Alexander studio. In the 1970s, a visitor to Alexander's home noted a number of huge drawings by the dustbin and alerted the Victoria and Albert Museum. Thus a unique record of a vanishing age was preserved. Only the previous week, Alexander had paid the dustman to take away another stack of drawings.

The wholesale demolition and drastic conversion of fine cinemas to make way for bingo halls and discos have meant the loss of part of our architectural heritage. Many of the picture palaces were neo-gothic temples or splendid examples of art deco design. Recently, groups of enthusiasts have combined to save some of the architectural furnishings, if they cannot save the buildings themselves. At least some fragments of the cinema's glorious past are being preserved.

The ultimate in cinema collecting, however, must be to possess one's own theatre organ. 'Wurlitzer, famed throughout the world for its perfect action and tonal beauty' was how the souvenir programme announced the introduction of the organ at the opening of the Gaumont cinema, Holloway in north London, on 5 September, 1938. On the first night, patrons not only got Dorothy Lamour in the film *The Hurricane* and a live stage performance which included Jessie Matthews, Will Hay, the Two Leslies and Will Fyfe; they also (boasted the programme, itself a collectors' item now worth three figures) enjoyed 'ten tons of music' from the Wurlitzer. Here and there, maybe in a garage, an old warehouse, or even a garden room, incurable victims of cinemania have preserved a musical dinosaur that once rose, glowing pastel green and pink, to herald the interval before the main feature.

Cinemania: Collector rating

Scope and variety	10
Investment potential	B
Price range	£10/$15 to many thousands

COMICS, MAGAZINES, ANNUALS

The world's most expensive comic is American. It is issue number one of *Action*, introducing Superman and dating from 1939. It would leave very little change out of £13,000/$20,000, and at that price it would have to be mint, untouched by schoolboy hand. The exact figure is problematic, as it is about as rare as any collectable item can be. 'When you are into rarities like that, it's simply a matter of how many megabucks two people would be willing to bid at an auction, whether public or private, just supposing the item were to come up at all,' says an American collector.

Danny Posner, a British collector of comics, magazine archivist and dealer, agrees. He feels the same way about the first issue of *Beano*, which is the most valuable British comic. *Beano* number one came out on 30 July, 1938, at twopence, with Big Eggo on the cover and a free gift inside of a Whoopee mask. 'It has a legendary value,' says Posner. 'One hasn't come on the market for many years, so nobody knows exactly what the price would be. Some say it could make £2,000 [or more than $3,000] for a single copy, but others say that's just a lot of inflated nonsense.' Indisputably, however, some pre-war issues of *Beano* fetch more than £20/$30 a copy, and possibly more than $40 in the United States where prices tend to be higher and collecting comic papers has become almost religious in its zeal.

Huge numbers of comics were consigned as so much waste paper for salvage during World War Two, preparing the way for rarity and modern-day collector demand. 'As a schoolboy I suppose I robbed the war effort of the equivalent of several Spitfires, as I was the one who was always raiding the big salvage dumps instead of adding to them,' says Danny Posner, admitting to an incorrigible bent for collecting even in his wartime childhood at St Ives, Huntingdon, in the east of England.

Later he used to head a busy public relations firm and would escape from the rat race into a panelled den where he stored his comics collection of some 30,000 items. His idea was 'to get together a specimen copy of every kids' periodical ever produced'. Then in 1975 there came an opportunity of sharing a little shop in the West End of London, from which he had been in the habit of buying his old comics. It was business and pleasure combined, but it was to be fateful for his *personal* collection. The commerce of comics grew and Posner branched out, eventually owning the thriving Vintage Magazine Shop in Soho, with a separate office that supplies archive material and illustrations to researchers and publishing concerns. In the process of becoming a dealer, he could not resist the blandishments of customers who had designs on the stock of his long-established collection. Desperate Dan, Korky the Cat, Lord Marmaduke, the Wolf of Kabul and a treasure of penny dreadfuls were at stake. What the customers *didn't* get, went into a sacrosanct archive that is the basis of much of the firm's business. None of the archive is for sale, but Posner no longer regards it as his private collection.

A writer once referred to collectors of early boys' papers as 'gentle suburban men with long memories'. In this connection, Danny Posner has deep reservations about buying comics as an investment: 'I think they reach an optimum value, then decline. Many people buy them to remember the good old days of their childhood. As those people fade away, so do the values of the comics that meant something to them.' He sees it in terms of a generational demand. In the early 1970s the 50 and 60-year-old

collectors were heavily buying their childhood memories in *The Gem* and *The Magnet*, and these boys' papers of an early era were the current cream of the market. (The most coveted *Magnets* are the red ones; there are also blue and whites, so called because of the colour of the front cover.) Fifteen years later, a middle-aged generation brought up on *Wizard, Hotspur, Rover* and *Adventure*, and caring little about *The Magnet* and *The Gem*, was dictating a new direction of trade in the comics market. And so the wheel moves on.

Americans emerged as the world's most avid collectors of comic papers in the 1950s. Their sights were set not only on their own heritage – *Marvel, Action* and their fellows of the Forties – but on British comic and story papers such as *Boy's Own*, the incomparable *Comic Cuts* (Alfred Harmsworth's 'one hundred laughs for a halfpenny' which dominated the early market), and *Chums*. Aware that the comics were social documents, learned institutions joined the scramble. *The Young Gentleman's Magazine*, a brief flicker on the scene as early as 1877, survives today only in the university libraries of Yale and Illinois. *Superman* and *Batman* too have gone into storage in the temples of scholarship.

Dez Skinn, who has edited or published many comics, collects them and sells American examples by the ton at a comics shop in south London, believes they have built-in investment attractions that makes them irresistible collector material.

'Of all the different forms of printed work, comics are without doubt the best investment for the financially-minded collector,'

Above. A poster by the American Edward Penfield advertises *Harper's* magazine for June, 1897. The magazine is such good summertime reading that our young lady can't wait to get to her seat in order to begin devouring it. A Penfield set of the months of the year is a collector's dream.

Left. Intrigue and romance in Paris. Steinlen (see Cats & Dogs) designed this 1899 poster for a magazine, *Le Journal*, to announce a torrid new serial on white-slavery. The villainous trafficker stands impervious to the women's despair.

he wrote in the magazine *Collectors World*. 'Popular stories are often reprinted, with the best-selling books remaining constantly in print. Comics, on the other hand, are rarely reprinted and have a limited shelf life of a week or a month. With their audience of between 10,000 and 100,000 per issue and national distribution, they have a very strong and loyal following. It is this high print run and short shelf life which can quickly convert the reader into a collector.'

He observes that American titles dominate the collecting market. With only *Eagle*, *Beano*, *Dandy* and a few more as exceptions, British weeklies do not have the same collector demand as the American monthlies. The Americans have the advantage of featuring one central character in a complete story, and are printed throughout in colour on good quality paper. 'Somehow the British black and white publications, with eternal cliffhanger endings to single-page stories, and as many as 20 characters per issue, often confuse rather than inspire the imagination.'

Quirks of distribution and demand can cause some strange anomalies in the prices of American comics, which often appreciate in value the minute they are published. Collectors talk about the case of *The Mighty Thor*. In 1983 this modern US comic had a change of artist, commonly a landmark event that can cause a beneficial blip in the comic's market fortunes. The November cover issue took the usual two months to reach the British news-stands; by the time it went on sale to the general public in the United Kingdom at 25p, or about 40c, it was already retailing in the United States as a collectors' back issue at nearly *thirty* times that amount.

Christopher Forbes, of the American business-magazine publishing family, has a large collection of *The Flash* from its first issue in January 1940. The comic story paper and the character accelerated to fame in the golden age of comics, 1940-50. Number one, introducing The Flash, 'the fastest man alive', The Hawkman, Johnny Thunder, The Whip and Cliff Cornwall, now has a value well into four figures. Christopher Forbes's copy bears the pencilled name and address of the original recipient, a Mr. Hollender in West Virginia, who paid 10c for it in 1940. *The Flash* has a habit of going through career crises: it 'retired' for a short time and then was reintroduced in 1956. Its most recent reincarnation after apparent demise came in 1987.

In the golden age, many of the comics on both sides of the Atlantic published bumper issues in hardback form at Christmas time; these annuals provide a major theme of collecting. They come in many forms; some with collections of comic strips interspersed with short stories, others bearing stories at greater length, and some excellently informative publications that are mini-encyclopedias. On the author's nostalgia bookshelf is *Film Fun All Star Annual* of 1940, picked up in an antique market for a couple of pounds. It mixes the American flavour of Buck Jones, Ken Maynard and William Boyd with the quintessentially English appeal of Max Miller ('In his latest scream') and George Formby. 'Eddie, the happy editor', urges readers to buy *Film Fun* weekly at twopence. In the same serendipitous purchase came *Tiger Tim's Annual* of 1955, issued by *Rainbow* comic and packed with the adventures of Tim, Porky, Jumbo, the Bruin Boys *et al*.

Some collectors concentrate on a branch of boys' reading matter known as 'libraries', medium-length series stories which were usually bound in covers more substantial than the comics, but not as durable as the annuals. Western and gangster stories were popular American topics; in Britain, Robin Hood, the highwayman Dick Turpin and the detective Sexton Blake were leaders. Inevitably, the influence of Hollywood made its mark

Top left. Copies of the British comic *Eagle* from the 1950s have found a place in collectors' hearts. But the experts warn that fashions in collecting – and values – can change from generation to generation.

Left. A *Film Fun* annual of 1940: 'Hundreds of funny pictures and thrilling stories of the films inside', with the cover framing a central star picture of George Formby, Britain's homespun, ukelele-playing, comic hero.

Right. The first issue of *Flash* comic of America, January, 1940, a treasured gem in Christopher Forbes's *Flash* collection … introducing the fastest man alive, with support cast of The Hawkman, Johnny Thunder and The Whip.

on the libraries in the Thirties.

Significantly, Danny Posner's business has branched out beyond comics into the supply of old magazines or the information and artwork from them. Certain artists' talents appearing in copies of, say, the *Illustrated London News* in the first two decades of this century can put a premium on the price of the magazine. The *ILN* and in America magazines like *Harper's*, when found in long, bound runs, are the stuff of antiquarian book sales. The Studio magazine is often expensive at top auctions of art nouveau and deco in New York and London. Some collectors will pay high prices for old magazines containing text and illustrations on military, scientific or fashion topics. Posner has a word of warning about this: 'I once bought some story papers from a lady in Bayswater Road, London, who also sold Victorian dolls. When I looked through afterwards, she'd snipped out all the bits about clothing.' Issues of the American magazine *Esquire* from the war years can reach nearly £65/$100 a copy at swap-meets when they contain representative and extensive examples of the art of Alberto Vargas.

The reputation of the artist is commonly a factor in the collector appeal of comics. Alan Clarke, a British computer consultant, 'comic sage and communicator', and his wife Laurel have spent many years amassing a large comic collection which includes original art work. Their regular bulletin called *Golden Fun* has produced specialized studies on artist Leonard Matthews and Teddy Tail of the *Daily Mail*, Alfred Bestall and Rupert bear, and Hugh McNeill's achievements in drawing the eventful life of Our Ernie in *Knockout*. One of their more recent works is a book celebrating the 60-year contribution to comic art made by Reg Parlett, trailblazer of the British adventure comic strip. When the book was about to be published, the Clarkes announced that they intended sending copies to Mrs. Margaret Thatcher and other political leaders. Now, that sounds an eminently sensible idea.

Comics, magazines and annuals: Collector rating

Scope and variety	8
Investment potential	B
Price range	From current new-issue prices to thousands

COMMEMORATIVES

Above. No subject has created more commemorative ware than British royalty, going back to the eighteenth century and progressing up to contemporary times with the current happenings in the royal family. Birthdays, deaths, weddings, coronations, abdication, jubilees, visits, investitures, even illnesses have been remembered in fine porcelain, cheap pottery, gold, silver, pewter and enamel. This group of royal china commemoratives stretches from Queen Victoria's time to the present-day celebration of Charles and Diana, the Prince and Princess of Wales (mug, lower right).

For 30,000 schoolchildren trooping into Hyde Park, London, on a June day, being British must have seemed the greatest thing that ever happened to them. The sun was shining (the same sun that touched rose-pink the largest empire the world had ever seen), six military bands were playing marches and music hall tunes, and their queen had been half a century on the throne. The children were drawn from the board and other elementary schools of London, equipped with Union Jacks and marshalled into columns to receive a royal handout. Each child was given the Jubilee Memorial Mug, a slightly tapering earthenware beaker bearing portraits of Queen Victoria, both when she was a new incumbent of the throne and as she looked then, in 1887, after 50 years of reign. Doulton of Burslem in Staffordshire made the mugs – 45,000 in total, most of which were destined for schoolchildren.

The scene was duplicated the length of the land that June, and ten years later it was repeated at the Diamond Jubilee. At Derby in 1897, for example, the children received a tin enamel beaker decorated with colour prints and the motto 'The Queen's Earliest Resolve – I Will Be Good'. The mayor of Derby, Sir Thomas Roe, added his name to the beaker's inscriptions, contained in a framework of designs exuding national and civic pride. Only when the beakers were upended would a patriot have experienced a slight pang of disappointment. On the bottom were to be found the words, 'Made in Austria'.

Queen Victoria's Golden and Diamond Jubilees, in 1887 and 1897, were remarkable for the amount of commemorative china

they inspired. The dates provide a useful bench mark in that anything that came later can be said to fall into the category of antiques of tomorrow.

Charles II appears to have been the first monarch to have his coronation – in 1660 – commemorated in china (the original picture, it seems, was meant to be of Oliver Cromwell, and only the face was hastily changed). It was during the Victorian era, however, that commemorative items reached their peak of popularity on a rising tide of spending power brought about by the industrial revolution and advancing education.

Sadly, the flood of jubilee commemoratives was accompanied by a drop in quality and design standards. There are two schools of thought about the general question of quality: one says that collecting commemoratives is a rewarding area because only the better quality material tends to survive the ravages of time; the other argues that even the poorer quality items are worth collecting as examples of social history and the 'pop art' of times past.

At the time of Queen Elizabeth II's Silver Jubilee in 1977 the Commemorative Collectors' Society estimated that £12.5/$19 million worth of jubilee souvenirs would be sold that year, and its chairman, Sir Lincoln Hallinan, was quoted as saying that most of those souvenirs were 'dull, unimaginative and pedestrian'. Four years later, during the celebrations of the wedding of Charles and Diana, the Prince and Princess of Wales, the debate took place again in the pages of collector and general magazines, reviewing the huge choice of contemporary royal souvenirs.

'Choice is determined by emotive impulse,' said Steven Jackson, secretary of the society. 'Commemoratives by their very nature are mass-produced items and very few have artistic merit.' But what, asked Rosemary Prior, of the Sussex Commemorative Ware Centre, is artistic merit? 'There are many different opinions on what is collectable or not, which is just as well since all tastes must be catered for.' John May, a leading antique dealer who specializes in documentary items, advised: 'Get something that pleases you within the price range you can afford and you won't go far wrong. The pleasure that you buy yourself because you enjoy collecting is what counts.' Ian and Rita Smythe, who rule over a splendid display of royal commemoratives at Britannia in Gray's Antique Market in the centre of London, had cheer for investor-collectors: 'Even so, no commemorative has stood still.' They cited some of the cheapest mugs having appreciated eightfold in four years.

The post-war era of royal commemoratives opened with the wedding of Princess Elizabeth to Philip, newly created Duke of Edinburgh, in November 1947. Restrictions were widespread and the potteries were recovering from the effects of the war. The souvenir field was limited to brooches, lapel badges, handbag mirrors and small compacts, a glass tumbler and a rather crude pottery mug issued by the Euwenny Pottery in Wales. Elizabeth's coronation in 1953 saw a quickening of interest: a Royal Crown Derby loving cup in limited edition, then a little over £12 or about $20, had appreciated tenfold by the early 1980s, and has since made similar progress.

The investiture of Prince Charles as the Prince of Wales in 1969 was a stimulus to collecting. Four years later, when Britain celebrated the marriage of Princess Anne, the souvenir china industry was in full swing. Wedgwood, Coalport and Aynsley were among the leaders at this beginning of the great commemorative boom, which reached massive proportions during the Queen's Jubilee celebrations of 1977.

On the occasion of the Charles-Diana wedding in 1981, the editor of *Art & Antiques Weekly* opened: 'What is it about royal events that apparently causes such a drying-up of the creative juices? The symbols of royalty never change – but is it really

Below. Will they become the antiques of tomorrow? The answer may lie in how few of these inexpensive modern Charles and Diana souvenirs last through the ravages of time. The Charles 'Big-ears' mug stands a chance on oddity value, but very little else.

Right. A Minton porcelain vase created for the 1947 wedding of Princess Elizabeth and Prince Philip. This attractive souvenir was made in a limited edition of 500. In the late 1980s its value was over £700, or more than $1000.

Bottom. Tastefully produced commemorative ware of the 1890s, made in large numbers for popular sale – the sort of material that forms the basis of any collection of royal souvenirs.

Top. An attractive plate, obviously aimed at the Irish market since it is nicely decorated with shamrock. It was issued to celebrate the golden jubilee of Queen Victoria. She reached the landmark of half a century on the throne in 1887, and this plate appears to anticipate the event by one year.

Above. Decorative glass plates, like this Victorian example, were popularized all over the world by firms using the medium to commemorate a huge range of events including the doings of US presidents and European royalty, the opening of railways and the success of international trade fairs. They were especially popular in America. This plate celebrates the silver wedding of the Prince of Wales, later Edward VII.

necessary to incorporate them into every design? Heraldic devices, coronets and Prince of Wales' feathers are all very well – but when exploited in such profusion they quickly become very boring … Disappointingly, when a company does manage to dream up something out of the ordinary, more often than not it's just plain vulgar.'

But what's wrong with a little healthy vulgarity, now and again? The people flocked to buy Prince Charles 'big-ears' mugs, in which the handle is formed by a gigantic ear. 'Big-ears' have begun to appear in the salerooms, but they are not yet making the price charts, as they tend to be grouped in multiple lots among other cheap souvenirs. Nevertheless, their value is believed to have narrowly beaten the inflation rate.

And what will collectors of the future make of a £5/$8 package produced by Woody Enterprises in the midlands of England at the time of the royal wedding? It consisted of a lifesize colour photograph of Prince Charles, with Princess Diana peeping out demurely by his side, and in front of them two lifesize hands. The adhesive-fronted photograph was meant to be applied to a rear side window of a car, affording a likeness of the royal couple so believable that onlookers might believe that the driver was chauffeuring the newly-weds, verisimilitude being added by the royal hands which juddered in impersonation of a wave as the car moved. The royal 'passengers' somehow slipped through the rather loose controls which tried to apply an official seal of approval on the flood of souvenirs, as did tens of thousands of T-shirts which had been ineffectively discouraged.

In the end, did the back-seat royals have any less relevance than, say, an upmarket souvenir such as the Wilkinson Royal Wedding Sword, sold at £450/$675 – a wall decoration whose hilt was adorned with the couple's names within bows, and issued in an edition limited to 1,000? Harrods sold Dunhill lighters bearing the royal face (at £80/$120) and Garrard, the Crown jeweller, produced, of all things, a £575/$860 wedding barometer, limited to 200 examples. In ten or twenty years' time, it is a fair assumption that a packaged, mint version of the Woody Enterprises pop joke will have appreciated in collector value more than the posh souvenirs from Harrods and Garrard, if only because of the rarity of an essentially ephemeral product.

Comparison and confusion abound in commemorative ware. A classic combination of both is to be found in the relative fortunes of souvenirs produced for the coronation-that-never-was of King Edward VIII and the actual coronation of his brother, George VI. Edward, of course, abdicated for love of the American Wallis Simpson in December 1936, six months before he was due to be crowned. Phillips, which holds regular auctions of commemorative china, receives a procession of callers bearing Edward 'coronation' mugs. 'They must be rare because the coronation never took place,' is the refrain of the hopefuls. The truth is that industry was well prepared for Edward's coronation and the market was flooded with china. The records of the Commemorative Collectors' Society list no fewer than 137 designs for Edward mugs alone, as well as 295 designs for plates, jugs, vases, bowls, busts, plaques, tin boxes and trays, handkerchiefs, flags, books and special magazines. Multiply those figures by units of mass production, and you see why Edward VIII and rarity often fail to match.

Rita Smythe, of Britannia, explains: 'The fact that Edward was never crowned leads to delusions of rarity. At the time of the abdication the warehouses, shops and stores were stuffed with tens of thousands of cheap pottery mugs in a multitude of designs, waiting for Edward's coronation. Today they are worth just a bit more than the corresponding ones for George VI and Elizabeth. But that is not the whole story. A good many factories were working rather more slowly on better quality pieces, and

Left. A Minton porcelain two-handled goblet vase, produced for the wedding of Princess Elizabeth and Prince Phillip in 1947. It is printed in colour and decorated in enamels and gilt. It is one of a limited edition of 100.

Below. Souvenirs of the 1937 coronation of King George VI and Queen Elizabeth, later the Queen Mother. Britain had just experienced Edward's abdication and commemorative ware for George was rushed into production.

these are still around in smallish quantities. These are the ones that had their production runs halted, the lines that finished almost as soon as they started. In some cases they were smashed up as worthless – and perhaps a few got away.

At Minton, a superb beaker in a fitted wooden box was being made in a limited edition of 2,000. It is not known how far they got (three-figure numberings are not frequent) but all the finished pieces were given away to the staff. Today the *price* is well into three figures. These are the Edward items worth looking for, the bone china pieces, well enamelled and gilded – and there is a surprising variety, in small quantities.'

Some of the keenest collectors of British royal commemorative ware are Americans, who treat it with a regard equalling that for their own, home-produced souvenirs of US presidents and political campaigns. In Britain pressed glass tends to be neglected by commemorative collectors but it is much appreciated in the States, where it originated in the mid-nineteenth century. 'Sandwich glass' was first made by the Boston and Sandwich Glass Company on Cape Cod. The author has come across this type of glass retrospectively commemorating Henry Clay's campaign against Andrew Jackson in 1832, and celebrating the bicentennial of George Washington's birth in 1932.

The assassination of President James Garfield in 1881 provided some macabre commemoratives. Although it was realized from the first that he had been mortally wounded, it was 11 weeks before the president succumbed to his bullet wounds. This gave potters time to prepare their commemoratives and one of the most commonly found is an Anglo-American Garfield memorial mug made at Burslem in the British midlands. It has a black transfer portrait framed by a laurel wreath, an eagle, the Union Jack and Old Glory. On the reverse are principal biographical dates and a verse said to have been composed by Queen Victoria. The initial letters of the lines spell out the name *GARFIELD* and the eulogy links the grief of Mrs Garfield with that of Victoria for Prince Albert.

Commemoratives of Woodrow Wilson, Warren Harding and Calvin Coolidge are scarce, reports Roy Busby, a London collector of American material. However, he does have a Toby jug of Herbert Hoover, 'his grim expression foreshadowing the depression his four years of office would bring and contrasting with another of his Irish-American opponent, "Smiling" Al Smith from New York'. Both were made in the USA for Patriotic Products of Syracuse in 1928. Many American souvenirs were made in the British pottery industry. As a memorial to President Franklin Delano Roosevelt after his death in 1945, Jonroth of Staffordshire produced a rose-bordered plate in pink or blue, with a portrait on one side and an extract from FDR's 'Freedom from fear' speech on the other.

The rules for commemorative collectors are similar to those in any other branch of collecting: the collector should avoid damaged pieces, go for the best quality the pocket can afford, and choose a theme. The Smythes of Britannia say: 'The great joy about collecting is the chance of the unknown turning up. We've sold tens and tens of thousands of pieces over a score of years, but every two months or so we come across an item we never knew existed. There has never been such a demand for commemorative china as there is now. It starts like this: people buy current mugs – a royal wedding, Prince William or "Fergie" design. Then they happen to pass by a shop like ours and see the huge spread of commemoratives. "I didn't know all this existed," they say. They are hooked. They start collecting.'

The Smythes admit to a 'small, very eccentric' personal collection in their own home. It has an unusual theme – 'oddities with unflattering likenesses, and that sort of thing'. The ugly mugs, in fact.

Commemoratives: Collector rating

Scope and variety	8
Investment potential	C
Price range	£4/$6 to four figures

CRESTED CHINA

Crested china is a very British collecting field. The vast numbers and varieties of small china novelties applied with the coats of arms of towns and cities have been called 'a celebration of day-tripper art'. Above all, they are representative of English seaside resorts. Like many other fields of collecting, however, crested china has for some time attracted the keen attention of American collectors. The wares of the Goss factory are at the forefront of this collecting phenomenon; indeed, to many people Goss has become synonymous with crested china.

Collecting Goss was such a wildfire craze in Edwardian days that 90 per cent of British homes had some of this crested novelty ware. After the 1930s, in the words of Nicholas Pine, collector and author on Goss, 'the country spent 40 years throwing it away'. Perhaps only 5 per cent of the original massive output survives as Goss goes through a new boom.

Typical white Goss, often decorated with colourful touches and inscriptions, includes parian busts, cottages, fonts, crosses, figures, vessels, shoes, clocks and even tanks, guns, dug-outs and bombs of World War One. This eclectic genre of Victorian, Edwardian and later pop art encompasses Shakespeare, Sir Walter Scott and Peeping Tom, Isaac Walton's cottage, 'The Devil Looking over Lincoln', a 'Large Cornish Pasty', loving cups, travelling bags and trench mortars. In the view of auction house specialists, Goss is set to rise moderately in value during the forthcoming decade. Many areas are considered under-priced: it is still possible to start collecting in Britain at about £10/$15 per item.

Highly desirable items are Goss cottages, such as those of Anne Hathaway or Robert Burns, heading slowly towards the £1,000/$1,500 mark. Cottages, like most of Goss's output, remain small in dimensions, seldom larger than six inches (15cm) in length. Some were designed as night-lights, with candlelight glowing through porcelain windows, and smoke rising from the chimney.

William Henry Goss, who produced wares at Stoke on Trent, Staffordshire, broke into the big time by thinking small in the 1870s/80s when his son, Adolphus, persuaded him to make miniature crested china. Adolphus realized that there was a

Left. Crested with the arms of the City of London, a five-inch (13cm) figure by Carlton Ware of Stoke-on-Trent represents Old Bill, Bruce Bairnsfather's redoubtable World War One cartoon character. It is one of the very few three-dimensional Old Bill appearances, the vast majority being in cartoon form on china and paper ephemera.

Below. Goss, the factory that 'thought small' as a means to big success, demonstrates the versatility of the shape and subject matter of its output in this group of ornaments. Few Goss items exceeded six inches (15cm) in length. Cottages make up the mainline of Goss collecting, but some collectors concentrate on the busts and the somewhat whimsical figures.

Above left. A model listed in the Goss catalogues as The Feathers Hotel at Ledbury in the midlands of England. The owner of the hotel is reputed to have commissioned this model to give away to honeymooners staying in his hostelry.

Left. Goss and its imitators had no more fruitful selling ground than the English seaside. The Beach hut bears the coat of arms of Eastbourne, and the Blackpool Tower landmark was a best-seller in that northern resort.

growing market in providing for the day-tripper who had emerged on the British social scene thanks to the introduction by law of holidays for workers and the expanding network of railways. All this had heightened the popularity of the seaside. Adolphus Goss's idea was that visitors to resorts and other places would like to take home as a souvenir a miniature china ornament embellished with the town's coat of arms.

He did not have an easy time persuading his father about the new wares. At first he was turned down and told that the scheme was not viable. But he made a prototype glazed parian model with applied coat of arms in the form of transfers hand-painted with enamels, and managed to get William to agree to the venture. It was not long before this heraldic ware replaced the factory's previous output of figures, busts and everyday vessels.

Adolphus became the firm's traveling salesman, signing up agencies all over the country. He considered himself the commercial foundation of the family business and revelled in calling himself 'Goss boss', a term which did not endear him to his father, with whom relations were always strained. Nevertheless, William could not deny the success of his son's idea. He was forced to draw up a five-year building plan to treble the floor space of the factory in order to cope with the immediate and overwhelming demand.

The selected Goss agents were allowed to sell only their own town's coat of arms or transfer-printed view. If you wanted a Land's End crest, you had to go to Land's End to buy it. But after 1883, as Goss fever spread, the agents could order any shape instead of being restricted to their own local shapes. Crests remained a local monopoly. On the whole, Goss was cheap for the working-class trippers. Most items were threepence or sixpence; but rarities – such as some of the cottages – were as much as seven shillings, a large amount in late Victorian and Edwardian times. There are 2,500 known Goss shapes, and it is not uncommon for collections to comprise many hundreds of these types.

In the wake of Goss's success, 200 other makers churned out crested miniature china. Among the leading competing products were the following wares: Arcadian, Carlton, Foley, Fords China, Grafton China, Macintyre, Melba, Nautilus, Podmore, Savoy, Shelley, Tuscan and Victoria. There were many others – including foreign firms, who sometimes came unstuck on the complicated heraldry of British coats of arms. One English enthusiast wrote in indignation to a collecting magazine: 'I have a foreign item with 13 errors in the City of London arms!' Other collectors have reported finding forged Goss marks on novelty china from other countries.

A trade decline forced the Goss family to sell out to Cauldron Potteries in 1929, and the line ended in 1940 when production ceased entirely. The Goss ovens still stand at Stoke, protected by a preservation order. A Goss model of one of those ovens is an essential item in any true devotee's collection.

Crested china: Collector rating

Scope and variety	7
Investment potential	D
Price range	£10/$15 to £1,000/$1,500

CYCLING

Above. A tricycle incorporating a wooden hobby-horse, dating from the late-nineteenth century – the sort of oddity that turns up in auctions of cycling memorabilia.

Below. A silver trophy awarded by Muratti, a cigarette company, in a motorcycle competition in Ulster in 1905. It was auctioned for £12,000/$18,000 in 1987.

You have to pedal hard to keep up with the enthusiasm of a cycling collector when he starts talking about his hobby. Free-wheeling comparisons are commonplace. Examples: 'It was the two-wheeled Rolls Royce of those days', and 'A spendid investment, so rare, so fine, a Tissot among cycles.'

The 'Rolls' under discussion was a Dursley-Pedersen bicycle of approximately 1904 vintage belonging to Sydney Denton, a British collector with a simple credo: 'As an enthusiast I collect for pleasure. As a businessman I collect for investment.' His business is selling new bikes at Oxford, and hiring machines in vast quantities to the students: 'We keep the wheels of the university turning.' None that he hires out is more radical in design, *avant-garde* or fashionable than the Dursley-Pedersen was in its day.

The machine was hand-made, patented in 1893 from a design by Pedersen, a Dutch inventor working at Dursley in Gloucestershire. The revolutionary light frame had a daringly futuristic look based on a series of scientifically designed triangles. There were twin brakes, mudguards and a comfortable hammock saddle. Still made as late as 1914, it was one of the most luxurious bikes of the Edwardian age, and beyond. 'At something like £25/$40 new, it was a "Rolls Royce" price in 1904,' says Sydney Denton.

We talked shortly after he had brought home in triumph from a Phillips auction his 'Tissot', a Meteor rear-steering tricycle of 1882, by Starley and Sutton, an elegant contraption that has been used on many long-distance veteran tours. At £3,500, or more than $5,000, it was, he admitted, his most expensive purchase so far in 1987 (but February was not yet out). It would not be ridden on any more rallies, but treasured as a gem in his collection, a three-wheeled hedge against inflation.

The Denton collection – ranging from rare machines to a wonderful array of cycle lamps – is a cross-section of cycling collectables. It includes a French velocipede of the nineteenth century and three examples of the penny-farthing, or 'Ordinary' as it was known. Until the arrival of the competing Meteor tricycle, the pride and joy of the collection was a four-wheel 'Sociable' of 1886, on which two people may sit and pedal side by side. 'One of the trade reps came to my shop and said he had seen this strange machine in Wales. I bought it for £125/$187, a bargain, and spent £500/$750 on restoring it. It's a marvellous machine that converts to a tricycle if you wish.'

It was while out riding on a 'Sociable' of his own making that the engineer James Starley conceived the idea of differential gearing. This was a means of enabling a machine like a tricycle to turn and track smoothly, even though the outer wheel on a turn was travelling faster than the inner one. Until then, tricycles were notorious for their spectacular spills. A similar device is now fitted to almost every motor-driven vehicle in the world. Starley's development earned eminent recognition. Queen Victoria ordered two of his Salvo Quad tricycles in 1881, commanded him to give a demonstration, and presented him with a silver watch. The royal interest gave the cycle industry a welcome shot in the arm.

Out of the engineering excellence to be found among today's bicycles, what will future generations regard as a treasured collectable? Mr Denton has no doubts that present-day high-tech bikes are far superior to anything made in the past. They are lighter (as light as 16lb/8kg) faster (45mph/68kph) and

better made. 'The Moulton bicycle, of radical small-wheel design, built on an aeroplane principle, and costing £500-£700/ $759-$1000, is the aristocrat that will become *the* collector's item of tomorrow,' he says.

Cycling began with a crude 'hobby-horse', little more than a beam on wheels, in France in the late eighteenth century. Hobby-horses were cumbersome, wooden-framed machines and a menace to pedestrians. They could not be steered and worked on leg power. Their popularity spread across Europe and to America in the early nineteenth century, and dandies took to them with delight, propelling them through the streets with the abandon of early Hell's Angels. The velocipede in the early half of the nineteenth century brought with it the refinements of steering and pedal power. Kirkpatrick Macmillan, a Scottish engineer who did much for the development of the velocipede, went down in cycling history for another reason: he is the first man known to have been fined for a cycling offence – knocking down a child; he was fined five shillings by a Glasgow court. The development of lighter wheels with spokes in tension ushered in the penny-farthing, or Ordinary, around 1870. They are more robust than they look and make surprisingly frequent appearances at cycling sales, ranging in price today from the mid-hundreds of pounds or dollars to well into four figures.

Why did the penny-farthing have such a big front wheel, which can often be 5ft (1.5m) in diameter? It geared the machine up while the smaller wheel acted a stabiliser. The front wheel was made as large as possible in order to cover a good distance between each revolution of the pedals. Moreover, because the rider was placed high up, he escaped the mud. The penny-farthing had a run of about 25 years. Few reached anything like the speed of a horse-drawn carriage: the rider was more concerned with stopping than racing. Downhill riders were advised to hook their legs over the top of the handlebars so

Above. This 1911 original design for Rudge motorcycles by Guy Lipscombe was used by the company on postcards and posters to advertise its products. Its dramatic impact appealed to those who wanted speed and excitement.

Below. The most famous cycling 'oldie' of all: a late 19th century penny-farthing, termed by the cognoscenti an 'Ordinary'. Examples reach into four figures at auction, but collectors should be wary of conversions and replaced parts.

that if they came off they could perhaps roll out of the way to escape injury. Any hapless pedestrian in the way had no such chance.

The use of gears and chain drive eventually made cycling a less strenuous and much safer hobby. A breakthrough came in the mid-1880s when the Rover 'Safety' bicycle was produced, with a Dunlop pneumatic tyre following a few years later. From the 1890s the bicyle contained most of the present requirements for relatively safe and well controlled transport.

At about the time of the arrival of the Safety cycle, the idea of the motor-cycle was beginning to make itself heard. In early models the engine was mounted vertically between the wheels and the drive transmitted to the rear wheel by an adjustable leather belt. Several variations on this theme followed until the Werner family, of Russian origin but living in France, experimented with the notion of fitting an engine to the Safety bicycle type. By 1900 the Werners had devised the prototype of the modern motor-cycle. The motor-cycle today ranks alongside the unpowered cycle as a branch of collecting in its own right. Rare machines or combinations with sidecar can range up to £10,000/$15,000 at specialized auctions.

A typical sale presents a glorious kaleidoscope of wheeled history. Dominating the lots may be a giant five-wheel Centre Cycle, an unwieldy contraption festooned with wicker baskets, tried out (unsuccessfully) in the 1880s by the Post Office as a delivery vehicle. Its central large wheel and four satellites earned it the nickname 'Hen and chickens'. Potential bidders, apparently fearing nothing for life and limb, try out boneshakers

and extraordinarily perilous Ordinaries. There are trophies for cycling and motor-cycling events, badges, medals, and clothing designed for the pioneers of the road (a huge silver trophy, given by the Muratti cigarette company for motorcycling prowess in 1905, changed owners at £12,000/$18,000 in February 1987). Books, trade catalogues, posters, prints and old photographs are eagerly sought. Gleaming brass, chrome and steel cycling lamps come in a variety of forms, ranging from The Neverout, a kerosene lamp made by the Rose Manufacturing Company of Philadelphia, to a candle-powered ancient of velocipede days. King of the Road acetylene lamps abound, and there are others with names like Pathfinder, Sultan and Panther. The degree of devotion that collectors show for history's 'scrap iron of the road' is touching.

To ride a bicycle, H.G. Wells explained in *The Wheels of Chance* in 1896, is very like a love affair: 'Chiefly, it is a matter of faith. Believe you do it, and the thing is done; doubt, and for the life of you, you cannot'.

Cycling: Collector rating

Scope and variety	7
Investment potential	B
Price range	£20/$30 to many thousands

Far left. Vibrantly coloured, delightfully 'tinny' – a toy for a modern collector; this motorcyclist comes from the Soviet Union. The *sputnik* era produced some inventive models and put Soviet tinplate toys on the collecting map.

Below. A collector-restored example of a Clement Garrard single-cylinder motorized bicycle of 1903, in the £2,000-£3,000 class ($3,000-plus). The auction catalogue enthused: 'This rare and delightful veteran machine, with a certain amount of tidying up, could be made presentable for *concours d'elegance*.'

Bottom. Glamour and romance: how to sell bicycles at the turn of the century. This lithographic poster was produced by an unknown artist, a member of the 1890s school of Parisian poster art that led the world in terms of style and stunning impact. Bicyles never had it so good.

DISNEY

Each type of auction in the saleroom has its own distinctive coterie of followers. Jewellery views are peopled by Cyclopean gentry with magnifiers screwed into their faces. Furniture men bury their heads in commodes' innards, muttering in muffled Italian. Picture buyers are the best dressed. Art nouveau and deco attract the beautiful people. The suntan quotient rises significantly at sales of sporting memorabilia. It is at its lowest among bibliophiles, but they are the most polite. Disney collectors are very, very serious.

Mickey Mouse on the xylophone was giving his all when the author came across him in the course of a saleroom audition. Up and down pumped his arms, frenetically battering out a tuneful tinkle. Goofy tap-danced half a dozen encores as Donald rattled out enthusiastic accompaniment on a drum. And not a flicker of a smile showed on the face of a middle-aged collector who was watching the performances. He probed glumly into the clockwork mysteries of Goofy's inside, peered closely at the paint on Mickey's cheeks, rubbed the dust off Donald's tufted bottom, and committed other indignities which surely no other Hollywood stars are asked to suffer. With prices for Disney memorabilia sometimes reaching levels set by the more

traditional, blue-chip saleroom stock, Mickey and Co have become serious business indeed.

At his ripe age, Mickey Mouse must be feeling wanted in a way undreamed of in 1928 when he first came with Minnie into the flickering light of the day as star of *Steamboat* (although completed later, *Steamboat* beat another Mickey short, *Plane Crazy*, to the cinemas). There have been Disney collectors for many years, but the 1980s saw a tremendous upsurge of international interest in Disney as an investment and collecting area.

Collectors recognize two main streams of Disneyana. First, there is the highly specialized field of studio ephemera. This ranges from original watercolours and 'Cels' – the hand-painted celluloid sheets used in the animation process – to production memos. The artwork is in the £660-£1,000/$1,000-$15,000 class, and memos signed or notes written by Walt Disney are very expensive. An example of cheaper items is *Dispatch*, a magazine published for Disney personnel in war service, with Donald on the cover throwing a tomato at Hitler.

A wider collecting field, however, embraces the millions of artefacts bearing the Disney label and turned out worldwide.

Collectors versed in their lore know that a Dopey doll is more popular than a Bashful doll, therefore more expensive. Mickey wristwatches of the Thirties are like gold. But a pair of his plastic snap-on ears can change heads at much less than £6.50/$10. There are even 'combat insignia stamps' – wartime Disney stickers that American pilots pasted on their planes to signify 'kills' or identify squadrons.

Collectors know their datelines. Mickey was 'released' with Minnie on 18 November, 1928 (his 60th birthday year being 1988), but before him in 1927 there was Disney's Oswald the Rabbit; a six-inch (15cm) celluloid crib toy of Oswald has changed hands in America at £130/$200. Pluto barked into life in 1930, but he was not named until 1931. Goofy appeared in 1930. The irrepressible, irresistible Donald Duck made his debut on 9 June, 1934, as a bit-part player.

Clarence Dent, of Los Angeles, who was the voice of Donald through nearly half a century, claimed, with some justification, that the duck he helped bring to life was the most popular of all Disney's characters. But Donald, as everybody knows, has his ups and downs. A sample entry in a toy-price guide published by Richard O'Brien, of New Jersey, illustrates the changing

Far left. **Donald Duck Rail Car** by Lionel Corporation of New York, 1936. 'Quack, Quack, Quack' it says on the box: Donald and Pluto frenetically spin round a circular track. Their price, new, in 1936 was $1.25. Half a century later they rode to £1,300/$2,000.

Right. **Minnie Mouse in bronze** makes a striking car mascot for the Disney collector.

Below left. An animation celluloid of Mickey Mouse as the Sorcerer's Apprentice in *Fantasia*, 1940 (10 inches, 25cm wide). 'Cels', as collectors know them, are at the heart of Disney production memorabilia and often command prices in the thousands.

fortunes of collecting: 'The duck mania recorded in the last edition has abated, and although Donald Duck is still a big draw, Mickey and Minnie Mouse seem to have put more distance between themselves and the terrible-tempered Donald.'

O'Brien reckons that Mickey devotees concentrate on toys of the 1930s because 'collectors generally agree that he was aesthetically at his most interesting during that period'. With prices from a few pounds or dollars to several thousands, the range of Disney artefacts is immense. O'Brien estimates that more than 50,000 different types of Mickey Mouse items alone have been made. Toys in the Disney image include cars, carts, clockwork figures, dolls, games, jack-in-the-box novelties, toy-soldier type figures, masks, paint books and boxes, puppets, puzzles, tambourines, tool-chests, tops, trains, xylophones and all manner of other musical instruments.

Then the collector faces a plethora of general items: advertising ephemera, ashtrays, books, bottles, buttons, calendars, charms, Christmas cards, clocks and watches, clothes, combat insignia stamps, comics, dishes, drawings, egg-cups, figurines, films and projectors, glasses, gloves, hairbrushes, jewellery, lamps, letter openers, money banks, musical boxes,

Above. Wind him up and he plays, enthusiastically if not tunefully. Mickey on the xylophone (6 inches, 15cm high) probably dates from post-war years, has not yet become wildly expensive but would be a reasonable investment in the under-£60/$100 class.

comic weekly can be enjoyed only by those with hundreds to spend. A couple of 1937 production paste-ups of the magazine's front cover have clocked up more than £100/$150 at auction in London. Comic strips from the magazine, by identified artists, have sold for several hundred dollars in New York and Los Angeles.

The magazine, in definitive runs, is highly valued because of its ephemeral quality. Equally ephemeral is a now scarce offshoot which the weekly supplied by mail order in the 1930s, a cardboard cut-out called 'Disneydrome'. It was a complete cinema of typical Thirties style which could be assembled by a child old enough to handle scissors and paste. In addition to the cinema auditorium there were the organ, foyer and box-office. Children were encouraged to 'manage' their cinema by changing the programme each week, the 'movies' being the comic strips clipped out of the *Mickey Mouse Weekly* every Friday. There were even little posters to announce the attractions. Collectors, while mourning the unavoidable mutilation of magazine copies to provide movie strips, revere this delightful Disney promotional item as one of the very rare pieces of memorabilia.

No round-up of Disney collectables would be complete without an examination of the impact made by Disney's first

pillows, playing cards, pocket knives, popcorn cans, porringers, posters and lobby cards, pottery, pyjama cases, rocking chairs, rugs, salt and pepper cellars, slides and projectors, soap, suspenders, tiles, toothbrush-holders, wall plaques.

Every one of these categories has appeared at auction since the Disneymania boom got under way. Within each group there are sub-divisions of type: a child of 1938 might sleep on a Seven Dwarfs pillow, then currently ousting a Mickey and Minnie pillow in popularity; children's cotton rugs might feature a solo appearance of Pinocchio or Bambi, or be peopled with a host of characters in a bedtime Silly Symphony.

The skills of Disney illustrators have lifted the prices of some of their original studio work to levels that equal those for minor old masters. Highly valued from the Disney stable are the works of artists such as Gustave Tenggren, Al Taliaferro, Floyd Gottfredson and the incomparable Carl Barks who took a leading part in the visual development of Donald Duck and his daffy 'family'.

On the way, Disneyana achieved a British Arts Council accolade when it appeared in 'The Thirties' exhibition at the Hayward Gallery in London in 1980. The catalogue recalled a British issue of *Mickey Mouse Weekly* dated 4 April, 1936. It was a University Boat Race edition revealing Donald Duck rowing – and angrily sinking – for Cambridge. Twopence every Friday – 'Fun for the whole family': today, however, pre-war runs of the

Top left. Donald on skis, demonstrating his splenetic determination to overtake his arch rival Mickey Mouse in the collector popularity stakes. Some collectors would not think of buying anything but images of the ill-tempered duck, who was born on 9 June 1934. A figure similar in dimensions, pedigree and value to xylophonist Mickey on the previous page.

Left. 'Snow White slightly soiled and the Seven Dwarfs in mint condition, with original labels,' said the lot description in the auction catalogue. Snow White stands at 1 foot (30cm), the dwarfs half her height. They were made by the British doll and toy company of Chad Valley in 1938 for the premiere of the block-busting Disney full-length movie. In popularity, Dopey quickly emerged as the way-ahead leader.

Bottom left. From the great American dream factory of Marx comes this Donald Duck Duet. Goofy hoofs it to the beat of Donald's drum. The toy dates from about 1946 and would stand muster in its own right as a highly desirable item in a tinplate collection.

full-length, full-colour cartoon feature, *Snow White*, which premiered in the USA in December 1937 and burst on a delighted Britain, and a further dozen countries, the following year. Even before the London premiere – at the Regent Street New Gallery cinema on 24 February, 1938 – many department stores mounted Snow White promotions or used the story as a Santa Claus grotto theme. After the United Kingdom release, store displays were assisted by Kamen of Wardour Street in London who sold display props consisting of 2ft (0.6m) plywood-backed paper cut-outs of the principal characters, collector items in their own right now. There were also 2ft (0.6m), three-dimensional figures in composition available for 16s 6d/$1.20 each; a collector might pay thousands today to have a full set of these lifelike figures in his den.

But who, indeed, were the main characters? When the movie's razzmatazz was sweeping the USA and Europe, toy firms put their money on what they considered were going to be the most popular central figures, Snow White and the prince. They were largely unprepared for the emergence of the seven dwarfs as the public's idols. Snow White got by, of course, and no set of dolls that included the dwarfs could possibly omit her, but the fairy prince was another matter. The British company of Wade Heath was one of those caught out. Many china figurines of the prince, which it manufactured in high hopes and proudly showed at the 1938 British Industries Fair, ended up as scrap. Perversely but understandably, collectors now seek them as unusual souvenirs of the time. Not for the first time, a marketing disaster of yesterday has become a desired object of today.

In the United States there was an avalanche of material related to the sensationally popular cinematic blockbuster. Precise dating of American-made toys is often difficult as Snow White merchandise was made throughout the 1940s, despite the war, with some lines in almost continuous production from the time of the US premiere in 1938. Silverplate cutlery was a best-seller from Roger Brothers, with a baby spoon a $1 and a spoon-and-fork set for $1.75. The advertising prominently featured the dwarfs, with Dopey accorded a pre-eminent position. Millions of paper and rubber party masks of the dwarfs were sold from coast to coast. Grumpy was a fairly popular line, but again it was Dopey who outsold all his colleagues. Hi-ho, hi-ho ... off to work went Dopey and his brethren in one of the biggest, most successful merchandising enterprises ever associated with a Hollywood motion picture.

Disney: Collector rating

Scope and variety	10
Investment potential	A
Price range	£7/$10 to £10,000/$15,000

DOLLS

In the saleroom they are aristocrats with prices on their heads, cool, elegantly gowned beauties, demure country charmers, doe, sloe and almond eyed, lips open in amazement or pouting petulantly, pale faced or pink cheeked, golden haired or dark. They belong to the large family Jumeau, and they are stunners all. What other ladies would win a beauty competition at the age of 100? Wherever doll collectors collect, Jumeaux are the show-stoppers. They command the attention – and the highest prices, frequently running into several thousands.

The doll antiques of tomorrow will come from the twentieth century, but whatever appeal they have – realism, fantasy, quality of manufacture, durability, fashion-consciousness or just fun – their development owes a great deal to their nineteenth-century ancestors. From a long roll of honour of dollmakers' names, perhaps Jumeau, a 'royal' dynasty of dolls, might be allowed homage here as an example of excellence.

Pierre François Jumeau founded this remarkable doll family in the 1840s and his pretty *bébés* and fashionable *Parisiennes* conquered little girls' hearts throughout the latter half of the century. *Bébés*, as the cognoscenti call them, were children's dolls meant to be played with, dressed and undressed. *Parisiennes* were, in effect, gorgeously gowned fashion models, dressed in the latest mode, and as much a toy for mother as for daughter. It mattered little that some had bodies of leather stuffed with sawdust: they came kitted out with wardrobes of dazzling clothes. When popular magazines published patterns of Jumeau clothes, women readers copied them to wear themselves. The firm even made Jumeaux with shawls – anathema to the fashionable French, an indication that they were meant for the American and British markets.

In 1881 85,000 Jumeau dolls were made. By 1897 the figure was up to 300,000. In the meantime the family firm had extended so much that there was a special factory for making the dolls' captivating eyes. They were produced by techniques similar to those for expensive paperweights and women workers had to serve a five-year apprenticeship. In the Gay Nineties came the ultimate Jumeau – a talking, singing, laughing beauty called *Bébé Phonographe*. The firm ran a competition in the magazine Mon Journal in which children were invited to devise a monologue. The automaton had a cylinder mechanism in the torso: when a lever was pressed the doll trilled her delight at a forthcoming visit to the theatre with mother: *'Je suis bien contente. Maman m'a promis d'aller au théatre … tra, la, la …'* there was laughter, a jolly song, and the recording ended: *'Merci, ma petite maman.'* Dolls had proved that they were not just pretty faces.

By the early years of this century dolls were also proving that they were attractive investment prospects. The Americans should be recognized for their perspicacity in rescuing dolls from international and deplorable neglect in the view of a foremost British doll expert, Constance Eileen King, a writer who has collected a large and well-loved 'family' ranging from rare aristocrats to funny rag characters: It was the Americans who really fostered doll-collecting among ordinary people in the first few years of the twentieth century, some of the most important pieces even then being acquired by general antique dealers. At first Europe was a great source of supply, and we have to be grateful to the Americans for saving so many pieces that would otherwise have perished for lack of interest. There were two national doll-collectors' associations in America by

Far left. A jaunty sailor from HMS
Active, as portrayed in the first
decade of this century by the German
firm of Kämmer and Reinhardt. He
stands about 13 inches (33cm) in
height, has a bisque head, and steps
easily into four-figure value.

Top left. The incomparable
French-doll-genius Jumeau
produced this high-fashion beauty,
with a bisque head. She is wearing her
original dress.

Below. Britain and America were
flooded with German imports in the
1920s, such as this attractive
glove-puppet of a monkey.
Nevertheless, they are now desirable
collectors' items.

1948, as well as a large number of small local clubs where
enthusiasts met to discuss their common interests, arrange
exhibitions and pool knowledge. Eleanor St George, the first
well-known writer on dolls, estimated that in 1950 there were
about 10,000 collectors in the States and commented that dolls
were becoming desirable items in Europe as well. Interest
boomed in America during the 1960s, and a whole range of
collectors' suppliers for wigs, eyes, body-parts and costumes
made the hobby into big business. Many of the finest pieces at
this time were purchased in Europe for American collections, as
prices were so much lower.

One result of the strong US interest was the mushroom
growth of doll conventions where displays, free gifts, kits,
accessories and advice are on offer. Some of them stage
workshops where techniques of making and restoring dolls can
be learned. Many American dealers now concentrate entirely on
the conventions and fairs and no longer maintain shops.

Interest in antique dolls, Miss King observes, had grown
steadily in Britain during the 1960s, but the really large price
increases occurred when the Germans, Dutch and Japanese
entered the market, often indiscriminately, and the British
dealers were forced into paying bloated prices. Coupled with
this factor, there was the desire of British collectors during a
period of high inflation to put their money into antique dolls.
For several years euphoria reigned as dealers believed their
customers would be prepared to pay ever-increasing prices. The
doll market, however, is prone, like the stock market, to
irrational peaks and troughs.

Nevertheless, the appreciation rate of good Continental dolls
from the late nineteenth century is impressive. An investment of
£4,000, or $6,000, in 1980 on a French Bru *Jeune* with her
original clothes, a Jumeau bisque example with original clothes,
and a German Simon & Halbig Oriental bisque doll, would
show a profit, in real terms after allowing for inflation, of more
than £5,000/$7,500 some five years later. There is no reason to
think that the rate of appreciation has not been maintained since

Above. A fashion parade of largely nineteenth-century German and French dolls is fronted by a rare Kestner bisque-headed, googlie-eyed charmer worth several thousand pounds. Doll-collecting fever is at its highest in the United States where collectors' conventions and exchange-markets abound and the prices exceed those paid for dolls in Europe. The American collectors and dealers have long been aware of the investment potential of dolls, especially of the superb products of the leading French and German factories. American museums, too, have taken dolls seriously and house some of the world's finest collections.

Far right. The Gay Nineties are personified in this French Jumeau doll of the era. *La mode* was an obsession of the Jumeau makers, and real fashion often aped that presented by the latest models to come off the doll production line. A fine and expensive Jumeau doll would arrive fully equipped with a dazzling assortment of clothes and fashion accessories.

Buying is recommended in two areas considered 'neglected and underpriced': cloth dolls of the twentieth century, and nineteenth-century Japanese dolls. Prices start at about £100/$150 and peak at about £500/$750. American firms traditionally led the way in rag dolls. British firms, such as Dean's Rag Book Company, Chad Valley, Merrythought and Norah Wellings, made a multitude of cloth dolls, covered in velvet, stockinette, stiffened net or felt. These dolls do not break, but they are susceptible to moths, so they must be kept in the open rather than in a drawer. The Japanese dolls are appealing little characters with faces made of a paste from crushed shells called *Gofum*. The bodies are part cloth, part *Gofum*, with a built-in squeak. If a *Gofum* doll has big toes separated from the other toes, and jointed ankles and wrists, it is likely to be from the nineteenth century. If not, it is probably one of a legion of modern copies.

The twentieth century means character dolls for many collectors, although such dolls, with expressive faces, were not unknown to nineteenth-century dollmakers. Miss King sums up the current collecting fascination: 'To me, dolls made after 1930 are items of curiosity rather than collectors' objects, but the price of old dolls is now sufficiently high to have forced many people into the collecting of dolls in general rather than those with any antique interest.'

Character dolls smile, pout, sulk and flirt with their eyes. The firms of Kämmer & Reinhardt and Gebrüder Heubach led the way in Germany. American influence helped make the googlie-eyed doll popular on both sides of the Atlantic. From US factories came composition-headed dolls with the marketing promise that young owners 'can't break 'em'. From Germany came 'The Jointed Boo-Boo Doll' and others carrying the slogan, 'Realism united with Beauty'.

In Britain dolls found themselves a subject for the election hustings – through the intervention of the most unlikely of protagonists, Beatrix Potter of children's book fame. In the early part of this century she desperately wanted to make Peter Rabbit dolls commercially but found the London doll industry (and particularly that based in Camberwell) depressed by cheap German imports under Free Trade. German Peter Rabbits and Squirrel Nutkins from pirated designs infuriated her. 'My father just bought a squirrel in Burlington Arcade. It was sold as a Nutkin,' she wrote. So strongly did she feel that she campaigned in the 1910 election for tariff reform; one of her hand-drawn posters (collectors please note) showed a limp doll with the slogan, 'Poor Camberwell is Dying. Killed by Free Trade.'

But new blood was on the way. The rag doll trade was given fresh life by the launch in 1903 by Samuel Dean of Dean's Rag Book Company; there was to be born a whole new generation of dolls, collector material for the present day. There were some lovely characters from many makers. In World War One Dean's made cut-out rag dolls of a British Tommy wearing a red bedroom slipper over his wounded foot; he was made specially for and sold at Boots the Chemists.

Royalty was, of course, a highly popular doll subject in Britain. In 1930 Chad Valley produced 17-inch (42cm) dolls of Princess Elizabeth; she was chubby with curly blonde hair, pearl necklace and a frock of tiered frills from waist to hem. Later in the Thirties as the two little princesses commanded world attention you could buy Elizabeth and Margaret Rose (it was always *Rose* then) in blue or pink colour schemes, with double-breasted coats over flowered dresses or party frocks. There were many other personalities from which to choose. After Hollywood released *Hurricane* in 1937, there was a demand for Polynesian-style beauty in the Dorothy Lamour mould and the Ideal company in the USA brought out a brown doll to capitalize on the film's success. Louis Amberg and Son of Ohio had a Charlie Chaplin in 1915, France had its *Charlots*, and in Britain Dean's made a foot-high (30cm) Charlie with a 'Tru-to-Life' face. Joe E. Brown, Gene Autry, Deanna Durbin, Margaret O'Brien, Sonja Henie – they are all there, lying forgotten in trunks or closets. A longtime favourite was an American doll of heavyweight champion Joe Louis, with latex head, heavily padded cloth body and huge boxing gloves.

Advertising dolls were churned out in thousands. Sunny Jim, 17 inches (42cm) of printed fabric, strode along with a packet of Force Wheat Flakes in his hand. Jimmy Whiteshine promoted a popular polish. Little Betty Oxo could be obtained in return for coupons saved from the meat-extract packets. Some time later the Bisto Kids, with composition heads and rag bodies, sniffed the gravy ecstatically, their jackets fastened with two huge safety pins like a couple of premature punk rockers.

Paper dolls, like all others, are descended from earlier centuries. In Britain, Raphael Tuck was king, with offices in London, New York, Paris and Berlin. The wares of Dennison, a premier American name in paper dolls, are widely collected on both sides of the Atlantic. Paper dolls have been made in endless variety. The best have jointed limbs and an extensive wardrobe of fabric or fancy paper clothes. An American catalogue of 1907 listed activated Indians, black babies and 'prima donna' actresses. No collection is complete without Shirley Temple, whose Hollywood success inspired a spate of dolls in the 1930s; in paper, she is found as big as three feet (1m) tall.

Shirley Temple is most expensive today when found in a fine quality version of wax over composition, with blue glass eyes. A re-issue of the golden-haired moppet in recent times failed to win the approval of the former superstar, by then a distinguished

ambassador of the State Department, and it had to be withdrawn. Collectors place a premium on the value of a top-quality Shirley when she comes complete with original hair net and badge. She was made in vast numbers, and in many different materials. Surviving Shirley Temple dolls are often faded, flaked and cracked. In the marketing charts, she has been superseded by the Barbies and the Sindies, and by *their* successors, but she endures today as the best loved doll of all time.

Dolls: Collector rating

Scope and variety	9
Investment potential	B
Price range	£12/$20 to many thousands

DOLLS HOUSES & CONTENTS

Thomas Batty, of Drighlington, near Bradford, Yorkshire, spent 22 years building, embellishing and furnishing a large dolls' house that gave pleasure to thousands of people all over Britain and raised considerable sums for charities. It consisted principally of four good-sized rooms positively crammed with furnishings harking back to various periods. In its public lifetime of many years it came under much scrutiny through its role as a display piece. The purists criticized the ensemble for including mixtures of good craftsmanship and 'amateur fumbling', for out-of-scale accoutrements, for such aberrations as a chandelier which patently revealed its plebeian origin as a glass salt cellar. One critic (who, admittedly, had some warm things to say about the *oeuvre*) even referred to it as the 'perhaps aptly named "Batty Doll's House".' Nevertheless, when it stood on display for several pre-Christmas weeks in the front hall of Phillips salerooms in London during 1984, the dolls' house illustrated here drew nothing but admiration from the hundreds of people who stopped to look at it. A collector from New Jersey eventually paid out more than £7,500/$11,000 for the house and shipped it over to the United States, where it still pleases today, warts and all.

Some dolls' houses are masterpieces of scaled-down artistry. Few can reach the exactness, the excellence and the lavishness of the palace built and furnished in 1920 by leading specialists of the day under the leadership of Sir Edwin Lutyens and presented to Queen Mary. It stands in Windsor Castle, a paragon among dolls' houses, scaled at 1 inch to 1 foot (2.5cm to 30cm) and holding such esoteric chattels as a set of toy soldiers in the nursery, miniaturized precisely by the premier lead soldier firm of William Britain.

It is a reasonable assumption that nobody has ever actually *played* with Queen Mary's dolls' house. On the other hand, the great majority of dolls' houses surviving from the eighteenth and nineteenth centuries and those which are the antiques of tomorrow, from the present century, have been the object of juvenile attention. As with teddy bears, to be well loved is to be well worn. Perfection is not everything. Much of the late Victorian and Edwardian dolls' house furniture was mass produced and was often crudely made. Even in some of the early cabinet houses – creations intended as much for domestic instruction as for play – the quality of furnishings was uneven.

It can be argued that some of the dolls' house furniture of the 1930s, particularly metal items produced with the assistance of relatively advanced technology, is of better quality than pieces of earlier days. Moreover, a huge amount of reasonably made reproduction furniture is now available. Miniature furniture, for display and collecting in its own right as well as for furnishing dolls' houses, is a booming industry. Miniatures have caught the public fancy. The wholesale turnover for miniature furniture in the United States, which was around £16/$24 million in 1979, was estimated to have reached about £230/$350 million by the early 1990s. More and more craftsmen are finding that they can make a living creating miniatures of all types for the growing market. Hong Kong, Taiwan and Korea have joined the trade,

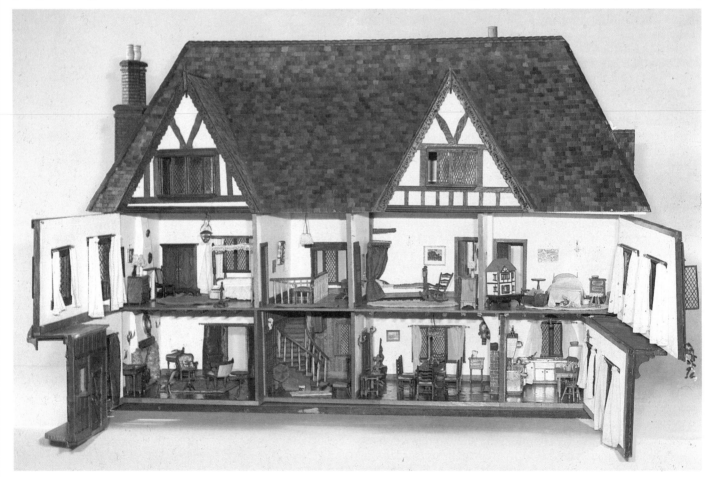

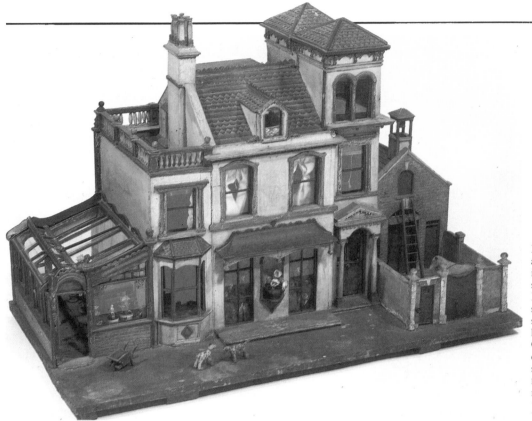

Left. The child of the late-Victorian age (in the 1890s) and her dolls lived in the make-believe world of this splendid residence called 'The Regency Villa'. In keeping with its station in the social scale, it boasts stables with enclosed yard, kennel, hayloft, bell tower and conservatory. On a more mundane level, an earth closet is housed at the foot of the stairwell. The house is just over three feet long (96cm). On the toy real-estate market it is in the £3,000-£5,000 ($4,500-$7,500) price bracket.

Left. The child of the early eighteenth century was presented with this house not to play with, but to store her clothes. It is a wardrobe, designed by Edmund Joy, an English craftsman, who signed his name and the date 1709 on the side. It is illustrated to show the lineage of dolls' house development. The architectural style is Anglo-Dutch. The interior has shelves and drawers. The house sold at Phillips in 1985 for £11,000/$16,500.

Far left. The child of the 1930s, living in the age of mock-Tudor, housed her dolls in this timber-framed symbol of suburbia. Delightful features are the parquet flooring and the dining suite's ladder-back chairs. The auction catalogue description had a whiff of Thirties' quaintness: 'Each room fitted with electrified light.' It is twice the length of 'The Regency Villa'; worth about half the price, but steadily appreciating.

Left. Superbly crafted mahogany bedroom suite, including a half-tester bed. It is not dolls' house furniture: it was made at the end of the nineteenth century for use with full-size dolls. Suites such as this come close to cabinet-makers' samples.

Below: Lithographed paper dolls from Germany, for cutting out. These dolls, which were very popular in Europe and the United States through the latter half of the nineteenth century and into the present century, came with many changes of clothing.

producing many ranges of dolls' house furniture that will stand the test of time. In the salerooms it is not unusual to find the finest quality dolls' house furniture making prices not disimilar to those achieved for its real Victorian counterparts.

Dolls' house dolls, models scaled down to be at harmony with the miniature rooms, are at a premium; a house without inhabitants is a museum, not a home. In the past, many a little girl raided the Christmas tree to people her dolls' house. Today a growing number of dealers specialize in the miniature, paying high prices to find dolls' house denizens, including models of humans, cats, dogs, ponies for the stables, and even mice. In the USA during the late nineteenth and early twentieth centuries many contents of dolls' houses were sold by mail order, and the catalogues are today a useful source of research into the subject. A Schwartz Bros catalogue for 1913 advertised dolls' house dolls thus: 'We have a large variety of small dressed dolls, such as gentlemen and ladies in different costumes. Maids, nurses, waiters, butlers, cooks, etc. The dolls measure from five to seven inches and range in price from 50c to $1.50.'

A number of dolls' houses are nearly always included in any specialized doll sale at the major auction houses of Britain and the USA, and in occasional toy sales held in Germany and France. The star performers in the miniature property market are, of course, the 'listed' and 'landmark' buildings of the eighteenth century. Increasingly, however, mock Tudor of the Thirties, Bauhaus modernism, the British archetypal detached house of suburbia, the town house, the holiday chalet, and even the duplex apartment of metropolitan America are appearing. Realism is a desirable factor. It is no longer sufficient to provide four compartmentalized boxes of rooms for the house-owner. There must be a staircase – and it must connect with the rooms. But these houses are not for play. Values have forced the young out of the market. After one particularly volatile auction at which doll property prices soared through the roof, one disgruntled middle-aged collector was heard to mutter: 'At this rate, we'll all be into time-sharing.'

Dolls' houses and contents: Collector rating	
Scope and variety	8
Investment potential	B
Price range	Houses, from low hundreds to many thousands
	Contents, from £5/$8 to £500/$800 plus, per item

The matching suite of dolls' house furniture above, demonstrates how finely made these toys can be. The furnishings of the Batty Dolls' House, created by an English craftsman over a period of twenty-two years to 1930 and illustrated on this page in exterior and interior views, are not up to the same standard of excellence, but make up for this in their cheerful profusion. The dining room bookcase is stacked with miniature books. Thomas Batty originally started the model for his future grandchildren but his only son was killed in war and he concentrated on making an exhibition piece. The house has raised large sums for charity. In 1984 it was auctioned, partly for charity, and went to a new Jersey collector for more than £7,500/$11,000.

FAIRGROUND

Stuart Cropper, a London collector and dealer known to the author as a man with a shrewd and affectionate eye for old tinplate, came across a small toy called 'Sea on Land', in which tin sailing boats revolved by clockwork around a central canopied spindle. A delightful but improbable piece, he thought; surely no fairground would have a ride with sailing ships on it? Then he came across a 1902 catalogue of Savage Brothers, fairground-ride makers of King's Lynn on the Norfolk coast, showing the full-size prototype with its description: 'The roundabout ... has delighted many thousands of visitors to our English fairs. The motion resembles the rocking of a boat at sea ... six boats with patent rocking motion, awnings to same.'

There was still some mystery about the toy, since it bore no maker's mark. It was not until Stuart Cropper found a photograph in a reprint of a catalogue issued by the German firm of Distler. There, on a shelf in the workshop, was a line of the 'Sea on Land' rides. Savage Brothers had specialized in making fairground rides, and exporting them, and it was probable that a copy of the firm's catalogue had reached the enterprising toy maker.

We have to look for the clues to old fairground memorabilia. In this case, the tin toy itself, the 1902 Savage catalogue, and the Distler catalogue reprint (in the absence of an original) are all collectors' pieces. Sometimes the pictorial evidence of old fairground equipment exists in old postcards. By these means, another collector identified a tin toy called the 'Flip-Flap', consisting of two crane-like arms with a passenger car at the top of each. The contraption seemed to offer such a 'tame' ride that it appeared that it would have had little appeal to a paying public. But there, in the evidence of two postcards, one for the Franco-British Exhibition of 1908, and another for the Latin-British Exhibition of 1912, was the 'Flip-Flap', by which customers were raised through an arc of 90 degrees until the crane-arm was vertical – surely the tamest ride on earth.

Nothing could be tame about American carousel art, however. Look at the prancing hooves of the horses. Thrill to the snarl of the menagerie tiger. Roll up! Roll up! Join the fun of the fair! A landmark auction in this field of collecting took place at Phillips New York on 3 May 1986, when half a million dollars' worth of carousel horses and other animals, most of which began going round together in the Gay Nineties, came under the hammer. It was – in true fairground vernacular – the greatest, most magnificent sale of American carnival art, 48 beautifully carved carousel horses, a massive stalking tiger, two prancing goats, a realistic furry stag and assorted carousel accessories, all of which came from a museum formed by the circus king John Ringling and his wife Mable.

These carvings are examples of the mastery of Charles Looff, originator of the Coney Island style of carousel art. The carousel to which they belonged was made in Brooklyn, New York, in 1895-1900, and many of the figures demonstrate the influence of master carvers Charles Carmel and Marcus Illions, who were employed by Looff at that time. Both Carmel and Illions later formed their own companies and became the most celebrated of carousel carvers. When the carousel was returned to the factory for renovation and conversion around 1915-20, the works of other master carvers were added to the ensemble. Carousels often had a mixture of carvers represented, especially after reconditioning.

The flourishing of carousels in America was directly related to the invention of the trolley, or tramcar, as owners of this new form of transport stimulated weekend and evening business by building amusement parks at the end of the trolley lines. The first successful American carousel company was formed in Philadelphia in 1867 by Gustav Dentzel, a German cabinetmaker. In contrast to European figures, the more imaginatively

posed and ornately decorated American carousel animals can be identified by their elaborately carved right side, which, when the machine is in action, is the side facing the viewer: most European machines have a clockwise movement, and American carousels revolve counter-clockwise. The most intricate carvings and elaborate trappings decorated the animals on the outside row, and these are consequently the most expensive in the collector market.

Whirling in a kaleidoscope of flashing mirrors and coloured lights, with a mixture of chariots and animals which moved only horizontally for the timid and up-and-down jumpers for the brave, the carousel became the jewel of the amusement park. Its appeal is no less strong to the collector of today – but the stakes are high. In the Ringling sale, one collector paid a world record £15,000/$23,000 for a carousel horse, which he intended standing by his swimming pool. The tiger sold for more than £25,000/$38,000.

As often happens, the provenance of the collection exerted influence on the sale prices. John Ringling established his

Above. A large 'stander' (as distinct from 'jumper'), the handiwork of Charles Looff, originator of the Coney Island style of American carousel art. This splendid merry-go-round horse has a value in the USA of more than $20,000 (£13,000).

Top left. George Churcher, a British retired wedding cake decorator, spent two years constructing a multi-piece model of a fair, of which this is a fraction. Wired for sound, light and movement, it fills thirty trestle tables. Mont Blanc Airways, one of many rides, is the size of a bus wheel.

Right. Dame Laura Knight, an artist of the Modern British school renowned for her paintings of circus scenes among other characteristically 'Knightly' subjects, calls this jolly canvas 'Laugh, clown, laugh'. Her clowns achieved a price of £10,000/$15,000 at auction in 1985, but the value of her works – and of the Modern British school generally – has been steadily appreciating since that time.

Below. A Royal Doulton figure, 'Sentimental Pierrot', designed by C. J. Noke (5.5inches, 13.5cm high). The figure was introduced in 1914, withdrawn in 1938, and had reached a price tag of around £1,000/$1,500 by the mid-1980s.

museum at Sarasota, Florida, in 1929. It is based not only on his circus and fairground memorabilia, but on his enormous collection of baroque art which appealed to his showman instincts through its theatricality. The John and Mable Ringling Museum of Art has officially been the state museum of Florida since 1980. Proceeds from the sale of the carousel items were being put into a fund to revitalize the circus part of the collection.

Collectors of fairground memorabilia who do not have the sort of money demanded by the carousel market have long been attracted to fairings. These cheap china groups, usually with a jokey subject, were sold for a few pence or a shilling or two, or given away as prizes, on English fairgrounds from the 1860s to the 1914-18 war. Beginners should be wary of modern reproductions, which have proliferated since the rarest fairings – especially cycling subjects – went through the four-figure barrier. Nevertheless, it is still possible to buy genuine late nineteenth-century china jokes for around £35/$50 and there is a huge variety of the semi-rare groups in the £250-£400/$375-$600 bracket.

No fairground/circus denizen is more documented than Jumbo:

Jumbo said to Alice, 'I love you,'
Alice said to Jumbo, 'I don't believe you do;
For if you really love me, as you say you do,
You wouldn't go to Yankee-land and leave me at the Zoo.'

The ditty was sung lustily by Victorian England at the height of the furore over the most famous elephant that ever came out of the African jungle … 'the biggest brute walking the earth', as showman Phineas T. Barnum billed him. Immortalized in song (which sympathized with his abandoned sweetheart Alice), the subject of High Court litigation and of patriotic fervour, and finally the focus of national mourning, Jumbo inevitably went into posterity as two Staffordshire portrait figures, examples of the glazed pottery which reflected so much of late nineteenth-century social history.

Jumbo came to London Zoo in 1865 and quickly bocame a

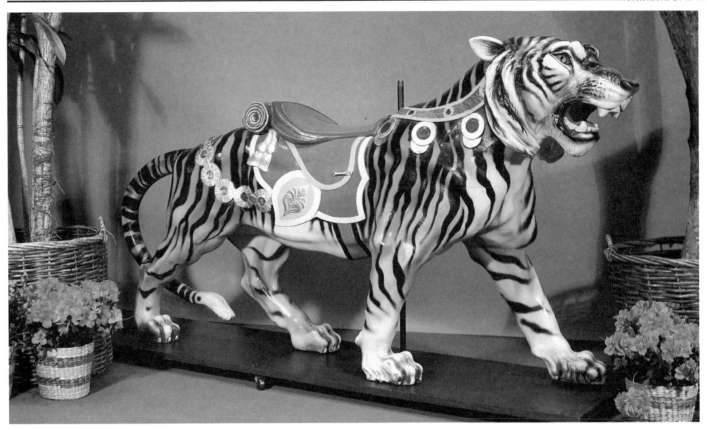

national hero. When the Zoological Society accepted a £6,500/$10,000 offer for him from Barnum in 1882 (he weighed six tons and had become somewhat dangerous by this time), Victorian wrath exploded. An attempt to seek a High Court injunction against his emigration failed, and Jumbo crossed the Atlantic to become the star of Barnum's circus. In 1885 he died when he charged and derailed a freight train in Ontario.

Pottery is not Jumbo's only memorial; he has been celebrated in prints, paintings and a mass of contemporary magazine ephemera, all of which are collector material today.

Barnum posters also record the great elephant, among a wealth of advertising ephemera which is one of the main lines of circus collecting. The price of American circus posters – the cream of the choice – varies enormously, depending on rarity, age, condition, subject matter and artist, but the following are likely to be in the £200-£800/$300-$1,200 range.

There is no question of modesty or subtlety in this vivid art. A Barnum & Bailey sheet of 1903 offers an oriental extravaganza as 'A grand transcendental spectacular pageant of imposing glory, royal pomp and imperial splendour.' Another (1916) promises: 'The most gorgeous oriental display ever seen in any land since the world began.' Forepaugh & Sells Brothers, a huge circus that travelled in a train of 47 cars, announces 14 fully grown polar bears in 1904 as 'more than the human eye at one time ever saw before'. Barnum & Bailey trumpets the chaotic attractions of '150 amazingly clever clowns presented at the same time', and lauds the prowess of James Teddy, 'The Human Aeroplane', who could jump over 80 chairs.

Above. This massive stalking tiger with eyes burning bright is a 'menagerie' animal from the same stable as the horse on an earlier page – the kaleidoscopic world of American carousel art. It was sold from the John and Mable Ringling Museum of Art (the state museum of Florida) to raise funds to revitalize the collection's circus complement. The tiger found a new American owner at $38,000/£25,000.

Fairground, carousel and circus: Collector rating

Scope and variety	7
Investment potential	C
Price range	£35/$50 to tens of thousands

GAMES

There is little evidence to show that the investor in games and jigsaws is going to hit the jackpot or put together a fortune. In comparison with other children's toys – such as tinplate and diecast vehicles, lead soldiers, dolls and teddy bears – board and box games and jigsaws are very cheap indeed. This applies not only to twentieth-century material, much of it a mirror of its time, but also to the parlour games that kept the Victorian child occupied.

Collectors have suggested several theories to explain this: the lack of books or other documentation on the subject; the fact that many of the games are large with many pieces, making it difficult to display a collection; the essentially ephemeral nature of many components and their packaging.

In the knowledge, however, that neglected areas of the collecting market have a habit of suddenly 'taking off', the shrewd speculator might equally well argue that now is the time to start putting money into the *Hands Up, Kaiser* shooting gallery, *How the West Was Won*, or even early sets of *Monopoly*. Having a flutter on games, in effect, might not be such a trivial pursuit, after all – and will certainly be fun.

The jigsaw has a venerable pedigree. Credited with its invention is a young London cartographer, John Spilsbury. In the early 1760s he mounted some hand-coloured maps on thin mahogany board, cut round their country or county borders, and sold them, boxed, as dissected maps to help teach geography. The idea caught on, and other mapmakers followed suit. It took some twenty years before other subjects, such as kings and queens of England, were treated as 'dissected puzzles'; the word *jigsaw* was yet to be born. Engraving and hand-colouring gave way to lithography; mahogany gave way to whitewood. But the great jigsaw revolution was waiting for the twentieth century, and for Raphael Tuck to use the ingenious invention of plywood.

There were many ready to scramble on to the bandwagon. They realized that with a fretsaw – or *jigsaw* as the Americans called it – dissected puzzles could be fashioned into as many intricate and small shapes as the skilled cutter wished. Subject matter was unlimited. By 1914 the Army and Navy Stores in London was advertising a multitude of jigsaws, including a 1,250-piece representation of Disraeli's last speech to the House of Lords. Parker Bros, more recently famed for *Monopoly*, flooded America, and sent vast export quantities of jigsaws to Europe. A trademark of firms such as Tuck and Parker was the inclusion of jigsaw pieces cut into the shape of a duck, a dog, a top hat, a boot.

The Twenties produced even more jigsaws. Cardboard was

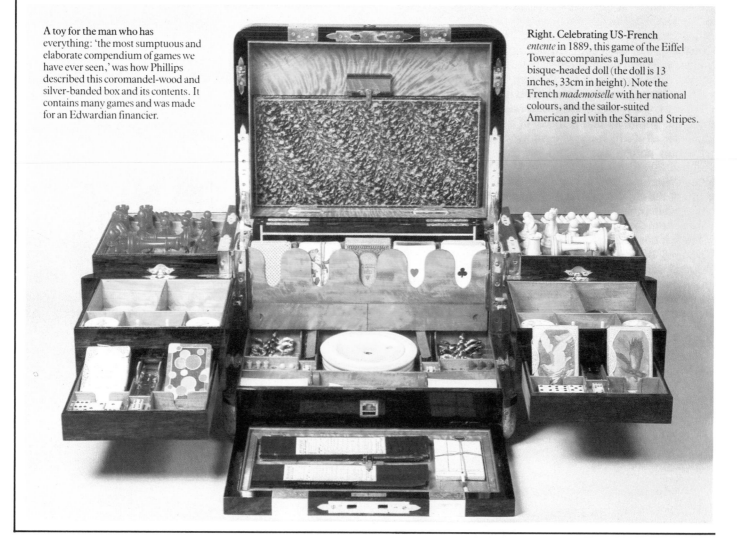

A toy for the man who has everything: 'the most sumptuous and elaborate compendium of games we have ever seen,' was how Phillips described this coromandel-wood and silver-banded box and its contents. It contains many games and was made for an Edwardian financier.

Right. Celebrating US-French *entente* in 1889, this game of the Eiffel Tower accompanies a Jumeau bisque-headed doll (the doll is 13 inches, 33cm in height). Note the French *mademoiselle* with her national colours, and the sailor-suited American girl with the Stars and Stripes.

Below. Gaming tokens and whist markers, mainly of the 19th century, are shown to demonstrate the enormous variety to be found in this field of collectables. The whist accessories come in ivory, tortoiseshell, mother-of-pearl, wood, silver and other metals, markers of an age of elegance. Although many of them are antiques in the true sense of the word, they belong here in a study of the lineage of more modern games and gaming paraphenalia.

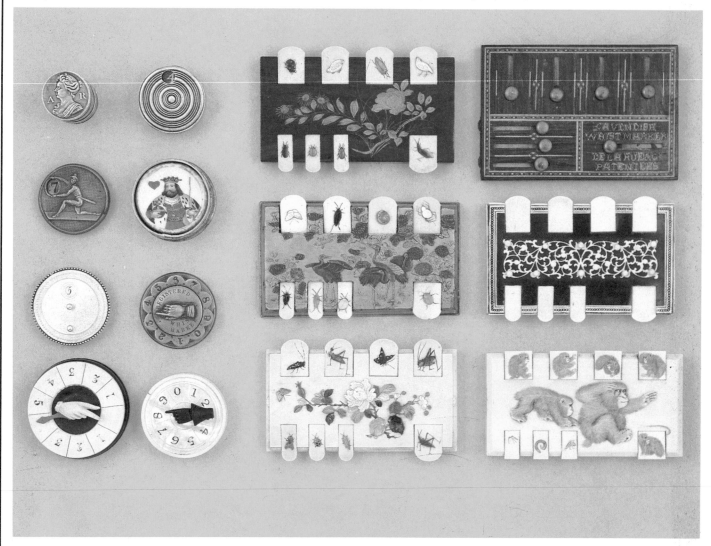

now to the fore. Raphael Tuck, dominant in the postcard market, had a new idea. Collectors' items today are the company's *Picture Postcard Puzzles*, which utilized the vast variety of current-issue postcard designs. These puzzles were made from light card, cut up into pieces and enclosed in a sealed folder with perforated edges; they could be addressed and posted like ordinary cards. So successful were they that Tuck introduced packets of six. These *Picture Postcards for Progressive Puzzle Parties* carried printed score sheets to record the time taken to complete a puzzle before moving on to the next. 'In passing through Pullman cars on a journey one is likely to find half the passengers working at the Puzzles, and at meal times there are notices, *Please do not touch*, on partly completed Puzzles all through the train', reported the *Daily Mail*.

Some few Victorian jigsaws earn the distinction of an auction lot to themselves at collectors' sales, but in the main jigsaws are grouped together in multiple lots. There can be some interesting finds. '*The Airship Puzzle Box*, a set of six printed paper on cardboard dissected jigsaws, depicting early airships, over Tower Bridge, London, and the Statue of Liberty, in original illustrated box, with printed guide on inside lid, by E.P. Dutton and Co, New York, circa 1903' – such a lot in a general collectors' sale may not attract the toy brigade, but at an estimate of less than £100/$150 it could be treasure for a collector of aeronautica.

It was not until the last quarter of the nineteenth century that commercially-made games became available for the parlour. Among the most popular were the miniaturized games based on outdoor pursuits, such as table croquet, carpet bowls, and parlour fishing in which magnets dangling on the end of small rods picked up metal fish. In the 1880s came *Histoire de France*, surely the forerunner of *Trivial Pursuit*, which incorporated a series of historical questions printed on a disk, with a pointer to be turned to the desired answer. By the beginning of World War One, boxed games had multiplied to enormous proportions. They cheerfully assimilated wartime propaganda, on both sides of the fence. British, French and American children threw dice for the *March to Berlin* and targeted spring-loaded sucker missiles at an Aunt Sally of the Kaiser's head. German children went on Zeppelin raids to London or tried to sink the British Grand Fleet. In World War Two, Hitler substituted for the

Left. A lawn golf set, dating from the turn of the century, has flagged hoop-like components to be used as the 'holes' and four 'golf clubs'. It speaks of leisurely, languorous days on the lawn in summers long ago.

Below. Lindstrom's 'Gold Star' Game, a Bagatelle-type of amusement, sold in vast quantities in the 1930s by the Lindstrom Tool and Toy Company of Bridgeport, Connecticut. Bagatelle can lay claim to being one of the world's most popular indoor games in the 1920s and 30s.

Kaiser, and the Luftwaffe's Heinkels took the place of the Zeppelin raiders.

Chess sets have a special place in collector esteem, and can hardly be said to share the 'neglected' label of games in general. There is an extensive price range. An amber set of the late seventeenth century can easily top £20,000, or $30,000, at auction, while £100/$150 might buy an ivory or bone travelling kit of the present century. Ivory predominates in chessmen, but there are also fine pieces in silver, silver gilt, pewter, bone, ceramics, boxwood, ebony, pearwood, bloodstone, agate, brass and amber. The permutations of material, intrinsic value, quality, age and craftsmanship are infinite in chess sets. These variations are to be found, if to a lesser extent, in other gaming collectables, such as dominoes, mah-jong, baccarat and solitaire items.

A games box fit for a millionaire, a supertoy, changed hands at £11,000/$17,000 in 1983; the years since then would have totted up several thousands more in value. It was a coromandel wood and silver-banded box – 'the most sumptuous and elaborate compendium of games we have ever seen', according to Phillips – and originally a present to the financier Sir Ernest Cassel some time near the end of the last century.

The box has to be seen to be fully appreciated. At a touch it opens on smooth spring action to reveal drawers, shelves and compartments packed with gaming riches: a horse racing game with 12 silver and silver-gilt horses and jockeys, plus fences and water jumps in silver; the board for the game, a collector's treasure in itself, in coromandel wood and ivory; a superb ivory chess set; ivory draughts; ivory roulette wheel and cover; a game of spillikins, which tests the steadiness of the hand; a collection of dice, dicebox, spinners, diabolos and counters in ivory and mother-of-pearl; whist-markers, scoring cards, pencils and several sets of playing cards. Its owner, Sir Ernest, became immensely rich through his wide business interests; he acted as financial adviser to King Edward VII; he was a prominent and popular figure on the social scene, and spent much time following his passion for the turf. History does not record whether he ever had any time to play with his toybox.

Games: Collector rating

Scope and variety   7
Investment potential   C
Price range   From £4/$6 upwards

GRAMOPHONES

'There is about the gramophone, particularly the horned variety, a certain elegance, a purposeful air of willingness to entertain, that makes it a natural candidate for a place among the frontrunners of that recently emerged group of bygones known as "collectables". It may be that the sharply cubic shape of the machine together with the flowing lines of the horn result in a whole that seems natural to the eye. Whatever the reason, there is no doubt that gramophones, both in their earlier varieties with horns, and in their later forms when they are pretty or interesting, are desirable.' The words are those of Graham Webb, collector, dealer, writer and enthusiast, who, through many years, built up a unique reputation in Britain for knowing most things about boxed music.

The gramophone owes its origins to the first talking-machine, or phonograph, which Thomas Edison introduced to a spellbound American public in 1876. Cylinder music reigned until Emile Berliner, a 37-year-old German-American, who had realized the advantage of discs over cylinders, patented his gramophone in 1887. The invention was dogged by teething troubles, not least the jerkiness caused by hand-cranked powering. By 1896, however, a satisfactory clockwork mechanism had been found and shellac discs, giving improved reproduction, took the place of zinc-coated vulcanized rubber discs.

Improvements came in quick succession during the early twentieth century. The period from about 1919 onwards is the threshold for tomorrow's antiques. The names of the models which modern-day collectors seek reflect the status then given to those occupants of the parlour: Aeolian, Vocalion, Duncan Phyfe (in walnut with reeded legs, a somewhat cavalier representation of the work of America's long-famed and fashionable cabinetmaker), Deccalion and Oranoca (in the form of a side table). Horns grew to enormous size after 1924, with the advent of electrical recording it was not uncommon to find a six-foot horn being given house room among the 'smart set'. Then, as the wheel of fashion revolved, the horn began to grow smaller, its function eventually being housed inside the set.

Today's collectors seek bargains among early French, German and Italian models of the first quarter of the century. Somewhat higher priced are the machines of the 1920s, with highly efficient mechanical parts and housed in craftsman-made cabinets. Portable wind-ups for picnics on the river are in demand, and some collectors concentrate on German toy-like machines, miniature hand-wound gramophones which once flooded the market in Britain and the USA. Old gramophones usually carry a metal plate giving details of their patent and date. It is not uncommon to find 'cannibalized' gramophones, in which desirable features are sparsely represented in a largely modern ensemble. Horns, being such prominent appendages, are vulnerable to wear and tear. The collector must be wary of modern replacements and forgeries – fibreglass has become a common weapon of the horn-faker.

A trawl through a recent collectors' auction (1987) revealed in two random lots how gramophones and their accessories are selling. Likely to hover around the £1,000/$1,500 mark for a few years is an 'Expert' horn gramophone of 1940 by E.M. Ginn, a stylish English maker. It has a cubistic oak cabinet and a large and elegant, yellow-painted horn of *papier-mâché*. Such a gramophone, it should be stressed, is a collectors' item and its value, owing much to its maker and the craftsmanship of its

Below. Musically minded collectors go not only for the boxes that make the sound but for all the accessories of phonograph and gramophone, including a wide range of decorated needle tins, and items such as this HMV 87 record cleaner. Needles, of course, are at a premium for the use of collectors of old gramophones.

Left. Close-up of an American-label 78rpm record by Decca of Louis Armstrong and the Mills Brothers in the 1940s period. Vocal and trumpet solo of *In the Shade of the Old Apple Tree* are by Armstrong. Such records usually go at auction for less than £10/$15 apiece.

Below. This gramophone dates from 1920 and is made by EMG Handmade Gramophones Ltd. The enormous horn is made of papier mâché.

Left. This British-made
gramophone was manufactured in
1912 and, according to a name plate
on the machine, is called the Apollo
Junior Sound Box.

Below. A selection of labels featuring
popular artists and big bands.

cabinet, is higher than most machines of the period up to 1940. The second lot is a group of gramophone accessories including eight boxes of 'Top Hat' fibre needles, an HMV cleaning pad, four 'Point Master' needle sharpeners, an EMG Davey needle cutter and a collection of needle tins; the value of this uninspiring collection of knick-knacks, not far off £200/$300, proves that enjoyment of collecting in a mechanical field relies heavily on the availability of spares and accessories.

The most essential accessory of the gramophone, and happily the most common, is the record. It remains, on the whole, a very inexpensive commodity. In the summer of 1986 when a London auction house dispersed between 30,000 and 40,000 78rpm records, it was computed that they changed owners at not more than £1,000/$1,500 a ton, or roughly 20p each on average. They covered the spectrum of musical sound from pop to classical instrumental, from jazz to opera. A sample lot, consisting of 130 records of Gracie Fields, carried an estimate of under £60/$90. Marilyn Monroe telling us that 'Diamonds Are a Girl's Best Friend' managed to seduce £50/$75 out of a collector, but a rare recording of Sarah Bernhardt reciting various theatrical classics made only £20/$30. A dealer in old records, Peter Machin of Chelsea Antique Market, London, explained to *The Times* after the sale:

'As with books, many old records have no real value. Equally, there are many which, although fairly common, represent the best examples of musical, theatrical and other entertainment of the first part of the twentieth century and are highly collectable, selling at between £2 and £5/$3-$7. They are generally collected for playing. With proper equipment, there is very little danger of damaging them. After this staple diet, most collections contain a few "prized items". Almost without exception, these records are rare either because they are old and few examples exist – many collections disappeared during the war – or else because, being unappreciated at the time, they sold in very low numbers.

'It is difficult to recommend records as an investment area unless the investor is prepared to spend a great deal of time becoming acquainted with the intricacies of condition, rarity and collectability which distinguish the junk shop piles from the magnificent collections owned by several well known actors, millionaires and musicians. Far better to enjoy the simple pleasure of collecting and listening to outstanding musical performances, comedy turns etc, which are unavailable in any other form, and build up in time a collection which will increase in value well ahead of inflation.'

One factor which discourages investment is that old records do not enjoy the benefits of a catalogue of values, as stamps do. Certain facts of record life are, nevertheless, well known to the collectors. On the international market there is a price difference of, say, £7/$10 for a popular Caruso recording of 1910 and £550/$800 for certain of the very rare recordings by lesser artists of the same period. On the other hand, a set of seven Caruso Zonophone records made in Italy in 1903 and put on sale in Europe for only a very short time is known to have changed hands at nearly £5,500/$8,000. It is thought that only three sets exist. However, were the other two sets to come on the market, the law of rarity, supply and demand would dictate a considerable drop from that value.

There are similar anomalies in jazz. Rare original American recordings by King Oliver, Louis Armstrong and their contemporaries are valued at thousands of dollars, while excellent later pressings of the same recordings in British Parlophone Rhythm Style series generally go for a few pounds or dollars. Peter Machin's summing-up is encouraging, however: 'Record collecting is a growth area and is by no means restricted to 78s. There is a very large interest in post-war LPs, EPs and singles, and the demand for some of these is higher because of genuine nostalgia for the sounds on them.'

Gramophones and records: Collector rating

Scope and variety	6
Investment potential	C
Price range	Gramaphones, from £60/$90 to four figures
	Records, from a few pence to thousands

ILLUSTRATORS

One of the literary delights of a wartime childhood in a north of England industrial town was the arrival, at infrequent intervals, of consignments of American magazines and comics at the shop that pursued a sideline specialization in these magical, exotic goodies within the huge indoor market. How those artists could draw! Alex Raymond's Flash Gordon, Milt Caniff's Terry and the Pirates, Chester Could's Dick Tracy ... with giants like these as one's allies across the Atlantic how could Hitler and Tojo last another day? As bewitching as the comic-strip wizards were, however, and in tune with this author's slowly improving literary tastes, it was the rare appearance of a *Saturday Evening Post* that swallowed up the weekend pocket money.

Stirring stories with stirring illustrations. The *Saturday Evening Post* illustrators, the best that astronomic commissions could buy, would take an incident in a story and translate it into a picture that made mere words superfluous. And the king of all, of course, was Norman Rockwell who painted more than 300 *Post* covers and whose pictures were stories in themselves.

Norman Rockwell had the common touch. He projected the old-fashioned virtues and the homespun characters of his native America with immense painting skill that transcended a literal photographic rendition of his subjects. From the vantage point of war-rationed, Utility-fashioned Britain, it seemed a romantic if folksy land of barber-shop choirs, drive-in cinemas, co-ed existence, soda fountains, leggy cheer-leaders, freckled and diminutive baseball-catchers, and homecoming heroes from Guadalcanal and the Coral Sea. Rockwell's images somehow filled gaps in the Great American Picture projected by Hollywood's glossy visions at the local Majestic and Roxy.

Rockwell's works – even the very copies of the magazines that published them – are collected not only as examples of most highly skilled fine art but as unerring reportage of the twentieth century. He died in 1978 at the age of 84 after a career in illustrating that spanned five decades. Within a year of his death one of his paintings, *The Bookworm*, sold at auction for £43,000/$65,000. Illustrators were beginning to achieve rightful recognition as practitioners of a main stream of art. By the time Rockwell had begun drawing and painting for a living – and he was a moderately successful commercial artist by the age of 18 – the tradition of American illustration was well established. Its golden age had occurred from the 1880s onward. Artists' works were used to illustrate popular books and magazines, with the aim of creating intriguing paintings that would entice the public to buy the publication and read the stories.

In the late nineteenth century a study group of artist-illustrators was established in the Brandywine Valley on the borders of Pennsylvania and Delaware. It became known as the Brandywine School, notable among its members being Howard Pyle, N.C. Wyeth, Frank Schoonover, Harvey Dunn, Dean Cornwell and W.H.D. Koerner. They were the forerunners of a tradition which later gave us Joseph C. Leyendecker, a prolific *Post* contributor and mentor of Rockwell, and Rockwell himself.

Leyendecker (1874-1951) was considered by his colleagues to be the greatest draughtsman of his day. Not only did he make a name for illustrations (like Rockwell, he contributed 300 *Post* covers), but he was in great demand as an advertising artist. He originated the dapper image of the man-about-town who wore Arrow shirts. His was the baby in diapers which symbolized the new year for millions of Americans on covers of the *Post* every

Above. Norman Rockwell, the prince of illustrators, shows his talents for recording The Great American scene in *The Homecoming Marine*, painted as a *Saturday Evening Post* cover of 1945. As usual in his pictures, Rockwell made use of the ordinary people around him in Vermont.

At last Johnny managed to nail all the pieces of wood together and there was a splendid case for his clock.

It had a door in front fitted with hinges and a round hole for the face.

But, of course, all this took a long time, because whenever his parents heard the sound of hammering they said, 'Oh dear! JOHNNY IS UP TO HIS NONSENSE AGAIN,' and made him help with the housework.

Only Susannah was excited about it and thought that he was a very clever boy.

Left. The delightful work of Edward Ardizzone, both war artist and children's illustrator, for a children's book of 1960, *Johnny the Clockmaker*.

Below. Joseph Christian Leyendecker (1874-1951) contributed 300 covers to the American *Saturday Evening Post*. This is a brilliantly decorative example which he created for the December 26 issue of 1931. He was considered by his colleagues to be the greatest draughtsman of his day.

year. Many of the American illustrators, of this century as much as of the last, were inspired by the evergreen subject of the West; their activities are dealt with in a later chapter, Wild West (on page 208). While the plains and mountains of wild America were the artistic domain of such illustrators, Norman Rockwell found his inspiration in his home town of Arlington, Vermont. Time and again his neighbours and his family appeared in his *Saturday Evening Post* covers.

His painting of *The Homecoming Marine* made a staggering £150,000/$230,000, a world record for one of his works, when it sold to a dealer at Phillips in New York in April 1981 (previously, the most expensive Rockwell had been his £43,000/$65,000 *Bookworm* in 1979). *Homecoming* was painted on a canvas measuring 45 by 41 inches (110cm by100cm) for a wartime *Post* cover of 13 October, 1945. The magazine's contemporary description is significant: 'Norman Rockwell's painting of the returned marine features Duane Peters, who was a marine ... This is Bob Benedict's garage in Arlington, Vermont. The proprietor is the man with the pipe. The fact that Peters is from Dorset, Vermont, rather than Arlington, is unusual in a Rockwell painting, for Rockwell almost invariably paints his Arlington neighbours. When he can't find a neighbour of precisely the right size, he has a couple of pretty good models even closer to home. That is Rockwell's son Peter, sitting beside the marine, and the other boy is Rockwell's son Jerry.' That was it: *real* people. Rockwell once explained that in World War One he had depicted Doughboys in France, 'but it had been fakery'; later, in World War Two, 'I didn't attempt to do battle scenes in Italy or Saipan. I painted people and scenes I knew something about.'

When Rockwell's output was at its highest in the 1940s and 50s, his paintings could be bought for as little as £65/$100 apiece. He had little respect for the cash values of his work. The story is told of his visiting the house of some hometown people to whom he was introduced by a friend. On the living-room wall was a framed cover cut from a *Saturday Evening Post*. It was a Rockwell illustration of two young girls at a dressing table. Shortly after the visit, the artist knocked on the family's door and presented them with the original of the picture. It had been in store 'doing nothing', he explained, and he thought they might like to have it.

The 1980s have seen a tremendous boost in the fortunes of

twentieth-century illustrator art. From being a backwater of demand, the genre has become a main stream. The major auction houses devote specialized departments and sales to the subject and galleries dealing in the illustrators have been set up in New York, Los Angeles, San Francisco and London. The art has become highly prized in Continental Europe where, notably, the Italians, French and Germans have a distinguished tradition of dramatic magazine illustration.

Many American illustrators are moderately priced. Among them is Charles Dana Gibson (1867-1944) whose finely detailed ink drawings of sentimental subjects or glamorous 'Gibson Girls' are evocations of the years that span the junction of the nineteenth and twentieth centuries. Howard Chandler Christy continued the Gibson tradition of portraying beautiful aristocratic-looking women, and in the 1920s Coles Phillips was known for his 'All American Girl'. Haddon Sundblom put a new zest into advertising with his early Coca Cola efforts, and other desirable illustrators who pass through the New York salerooms are John Falter, Stevan Dohanos (a touch of the Rockwell), Rose O'Neill, John La Gatta, Bradshaw Crandall, A.W. Brown and Harry Beckhoff.

The date of 14 May 1842, was an important one for illustration and pictorial journalism. That was the day of the first issue of *The Illustrated London News*, a sixpenny newspaper founded by Herbert Ingram who was able to base his venture into publishing on the fortune generated by a fast-selling laxative pill in the east midlands of England. The new weekly contained 16 pages and 32 woodcut illustrations. The latter found immediate success with the public and were to revolutionize news publishing. A new era opened for the home-based illustrator and the pictorial journalist in the field.

The arrival of the *ILN* had an almost immediate effect in France, where *L'Illustration* was founded, and in Germany, with the launch of *Illustrierte Zeitung*. The Crimean War of 1854-6, between Britain, France and Turkey on the one side and Russia on the other, consolidated the hold of pictorial journalism on the imagination of the general public. By 1868 the Tsar's subjects were buying *Vsemirnaya Illyustratziya*, a picture paper published in St Petersburg. From 1869 the *ILN* had strong national competition from *The Graphic*, and there was a bundle of lesser emulators. In the United States, *Frank Leslie's Illustrated Newspaper* was launched in 1855, and *Harper's Weekly* in 1857; within a few years they were to assign platoons of special artists to cover the most illustrated conflict of the nineteenth century, the American Civil War.

No event of news interest was left uncovered by the special artists and illustrators. On Saturday, 8 March 1890, the *ILN* published news pictures of the opening of Scotland's splendid new Forth Bridge by the Princess of Wales, an event which had taken place only four days earlier, on the Tuesday. How it was achieved was explained by the artist William Simpson in his memoirs.

He travelled to Edinburgh with an engraver, Forrestier, who carried a block. They reconnoitred the site, studied the details of the ceremony in advance and interviewed officials. Simpson then drew the basic scene and the engraver completed the block as far as possible. On the opening day, Simpson went to the ceremony and returned in a cab to the hotel where he added and corrected a few details. The two then caught the night train to London – which took ten hours – and arrived on Wednesday morning in time to put the block to press for publication on the Saturday. Pictures of events such as this were frequently published as slip-in supplements which could be printed after the main section of the issue.

The science of illustrating the news by drawings and paintings became largely obsolete with the development of mass printing techniques which enabled photographs to be brought speedily to the breakfast table. The special artists left a legacy of excellence

Right. Full-blooded, colourful American illustration from Dean Cornwell (1892-1960), *The Presentation*, for an historical adventure story. Detail is shown from an oil painting on board. Cornwell's work, once the nuts and bolts of story-telling, is now traded in the world's leading galleries.

Left. Strong, uncompromising, Soviet illustrator art of World War Two. The artist is Nyeprintsev who, in the painting *After the Battle*, portrays cheerful, victorious heroes of the Red Army enjoying themselves during a pause in the bloody fighting with Hitler's invading troops.

to be handed on to their twentieth-century successors: men such as William Simpson, Frank Vizetelly, Melton Prior, Frederic Villiers and Charles Fripp of Britain; Constantin Guys of France; Alfred and William Waud, Edwin Forbes, Winslow Homer and Frederic Remington of the USA. These were men of action: they went out to the news, in peace or war. In addition, there was a legion of home-based illustrators who often worked up the sketches, hastily scribbled by the 'specials' on the field of battle, into full-page or double-page spreads; the original work of one such 'office artist', Richard Caton Woodville of the *ILN*, finds itself today in a highly priced bracket of late Victorian painting.

The main purpose of twentieth-century illustration has been to complement fictional writing. Some of the finest work, the most eagerly collected, has been in the field of children's books. In 1978 the American trade journal *AB Bookman's Weekly* asked seven specialist booksellers to state what in their opinion were the best modern illustrated books. Among those mentioned most frequently for their illustrators' talents were the following: Arthur Rackham, *Peter Pan in Kensington Gardens*, 1906; Edmund Dulac, *Lyrics Pathetic and Humorous from A to Z*, 1908; E.J. Detmold, *The Fables of Aesop*, 1909; Kay Nielsen, *East of the Sun, West of the Moon*, 1914; W. Heath Robinson, *Bill the Minder*, 1915; Harry Clarke, *Andersen's Fairy Tales*, 1916; William Timlin, *The Ship that Sailed to Mars*, 1923; Maxfield Parrish, *The Knave of Hearts*, 1925; I.R. Outhwaite, *Fairyland*, 1926.

The quality of some present-day illustration for the juvenile market is among the highest to be found in modern publishing,

and it is to this area that the investment-minded collector should be looking. Children's illustration has taken enormous strides during the past three decades: the advent of the space age, with its mind-stretching technology and possibilities, has fired the imagination of some of the brightest and best to come out of the art schools of Europe and America.

From our own times, however, there are still nuggets of nostalgia to be mined gratefully. The author was looking at a 1950s issue of the magazine *Punch*, and there was a drawing by E.H. Shepard (who died in 1976 at the age of 96), probably the best loved children's illustrator since Sir John Tenniel. Then and there, Shepard's little boys were still being drawn in three-quarter-length knickerbockers – even in the Fifties, at the dawn of the permissive age and pupil power.

Illustrators: Collector rating

Scope and variety	9
Investment potential	A
Price range	Two to six figures

MODEL TRAINS

As the steam railway age struggled into existence it was inevitable that the modelmakers would have as much difficulty in developing workable systems as did the engineers building the full-size prototypes. It took many years before the model steam locomotive was safe enough to trundle around the nursery.

That the famous locomotive *Rocket* posed many mechanical problems for its creator in 1829 is understandable. Yet, more than three-quarters of a century later, in 1906, modelmakers of the veteran engine were still not having a smooth technical run. It was then that the go-ahead German toy firm of Märklin trumpeted the arrival of a model of the *Rocket* as 'a delectable difference from the advanced trains of today'. Not so delectable was Märklin's scaling (the chimney was too long, the driving wheels too small) and mechanics. Gustav Reder, a Spanish model railway enthusiast and historian, says that the exhaust steam condensed in the model's chimney and poured down into the hot part of the flue, producing a noise like the quacking of a duck. He once watched a demonstration of the *Rocket* model at a Madrid exhibition when people rushed from all directions to see 'the running duck'.

Model railway development was, in fact, such a slow affair that its main strides took place in the present century, eminently qualifying the results as a subject for this book. The first steam locomotive toys were not commercially made in number until the 1860s. British, French and German factories turned out simple steam models which were nicknamed 'Dribblers' in England from their habit of leaking water through the cylinders

when at a standstill. The infant Dribblers nevertheless provided the parentage for a long line of model steam engines which extends to the custom-built model engineering wonders of today.

Trains run on tracks. But it was not always so in the history of modelling. It was not until the end of the nineteenth century that rails became a universal part of the modeller's package. Collectors classify the early types of engines as floor-runners. Dating and identifying are complicated by the fact that models of a primitive sort were still being turned out by leading German commercial factories at the start of the twentieth century, and these were not far removed in quality and style from some of the pioneers of the 1830s. At the same time, these factories had expensive ranges of more sophisticated locomotives. Primitive or sophisticated, these model engines are highly regarded by collectors today. The names of the great makers are household words in the collecting world, and the history of a firm is often a story of family endeavour.

Märklin of Germany is a notable case. Märklin has produced a mouth-watering range of model railways and the firm is to be praised for its important role in standardizing wheel gauges, thus paving the way for sophisticated rail layouts with all their appendages of stations, signals, points and trackside reality. In 1859 Theodore Märklin, a tinsmith, was turning out dolls' cooking vessels and his wife Karoline ranged over south Germany and Switzerland making sales at toyshops. When he died in 1866 his indefatigable widow carried on the business and it became a thriving family concern with the help of her sons.

Model trains of steam – and the sensational new clockwork – attracted Märklin's attention, and in 1891 the company exhibited at the Leipzig Trade Fair a full railway which could be extended by the addition of stock components. The firm's fortunes carried it through two world wars and into a modern, highly competitive post-war model railway era. Some of the company's pre-war electric sets are the price of a minor old master.

Mention model railways, and the name Bing springs to mind. Entire auctions are sometimes devoted to the works of this company. Founded in Nuremberg in 1863 by the brothers Adolf and Ignaz Bing, the firm ensured that its products were made of the best materials by setting up its own workshops. In 1908 the *Nürnberger Spielwarenfabrik Gebrüder Bing* employed 3,000 workers under the slogan, 'The greatest toy factory in the world.'

Bing engaged itself in keen competition with Märklin, thus releasing a flood of ideas from designers in both organizations, which resulted in marvels of toy engineering, a delight to collectors of today. In the 1930s commercial pressures forced a take-over of the various departments of the Bing toy empire by other firms.

The tremendous part played by Germany in the development of model railways is shown in the long catalogue of makers' names – Schoenner, Falk, Carette (one of the first makers of electric models), Bub, Lehmann, Kraus, Haffner, Trix and many others. But German railways did not always have it all their own way.

Far left top. A 5in-gauge live steam model of Britain's London and North Eastern Railway A4 Wild Swan locomotive, with its tender, a streamlined shape which became familiar on many rail routes before the death knell of steam. Such a model is worth several thousands to a collector.

Far left bottom. The magnificent, record-breaking veteran, The Great Western, which thundered down to Britain's west country, is remembered in this 5in-gauge live steam model which is the £5,000-£7,000/ $7,000-$10,000 class. Nostalgia for live steam is growing.

Above. The rolling stock and trackside accessories shown here are mainly of German manufacture. In the foreground there is a splendid example of the good quality locomotives and carriages made to special order from Britain's Bassett-Lowke by the firm of Bing. The turntable on which it stands is Bassett-Lowke. The station, decorated with advertising signs for Gamages, Bovril and Sunlight Soap, comes from Märklin, a factory which excelled in the production of intricately-fitted railroad buildings. The water tower, again labelled with posters in English, is by Carette.

Below. Generations of boys knew this O-Gauge rolling stock from Hornby – cheerful, brightly coloured wagons plastered with the advertising signs of well known products and companies. Now they represent money on wheels.

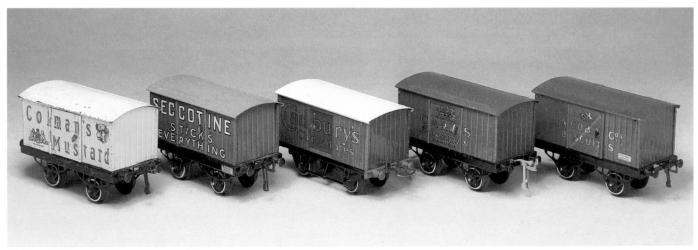

In an America fascinated by the technological revolution, model railways were steaming ahead. A traditional log-cabin success story is told about the great model-making firm of Ives ('Ives Toys Make Happy Boys'), a household name for half a century. Edward Ryley Ives lived on a farm in Connecticut where in his young years he experimented with small dancing figures which worked on a spiral turbine operated by the hot air rising from the family stove. His early crude experiments later led him into business and for several years Ives produced cast-iron, steam-driven floor-runners. In time, the firm moved in a big way into large railroad layouts on line systems.

Full-size German locomotives failed to find much of a market in the United States, but their modelmakers did. Thus cross-pollination of ideas between the model men of America and the Continent helped to stimulate the industry. Similar alliances were made between German makers and British counterparts such as Bassett-Lowke and Hornby.

It was World War One and the ending of the dominant German toy imports which stimulated the British model train industry. Hornby, famous for its Meccano constructional toys, introduced its first boxed clockwork Gauge 0 train set in 1920. It consisted of a small four-wheeled engine and tender, one open wagon, and a circle of rails. Hornby today is one of the fastest rising areas of the model and toy train market.

Aspects of model train collecting are similar to some in lead soldier collecting. Models made as recently as the 1950s or even 1960s can fetch as much as those of 80 years ago. Modern, custom-built rail models, correct in the finest detail, are frontrunners in the salerooms alongside primitive Dribblers and 'Stork Legs' (the name given to certain engines of tall, ungainly construction) made at the end of the nineteenth century.

The collector can decide to go for the scale-modelling aspect of steam or for the toy department, in steam, clockwork or electric. Many of the accessories of the bygone toy railways are a delight in themselves. For example, a prize collectors' piece is a Märklin station with its tin canopy, beautifully fashioned gas lamps, and cafe containing passengers enjoying coffee at parasol-shaded tables. There are exquisite ticket-vending machines of tinplate which issue half-size tickets to Magdeburg or Köln (each ticket being illogically as wide as a railway tie). And surely nobody could resist Bub's 'Whatsamatter Train': after a short run the train stops; the driver looks out through a trap-door in the top of his cab to investigate; after a pause he goes back and the train continues until the next 'obstruction'.

The quality of modern railway modelling is so high, the technology and layouts so sophisticated, that practically anything from a respected 'name' will qualify among the antiques of tomorrow. There will be more wonders to come in the microchip age. Modern models are cleaner, less noisy, more convenient to operate and certainly safer than the Dribblers and Stork Legs. But there's nothing like the thrill of watching a Black Prince of 1904 in the livery of the London and North Western Railway thundering down the straight, past the television set and into the sideboard tunnel under a good head of steam.

Below. A Gauge 1 clockwork tinplate locomotive made by Bing in Germany for Bassett-Lowke in Britain. The year was 1904. Bing material was well made and much of it has withstood the ravages of time.

Far left, top. A fine boxed electric set by Bing comprising a 4-4-0 locomotive and tender, three passenger coaches with interior lighting, a voltage reducer and track figures. Bing supplied a vast amount of material to the toy markets of Britain and the United States.

Far left, bottom. Märklin of Germany was renowned for its high-quality, sturdy, inventive and infinitely varied railway rolling stock and accessories. It took as eagerly to the age of electric as it had done to the age of steam. The models below are a pantograph locomotive, seen everywhere on the railways of Europe, and the streamlined Flying Hamburger.

Model railways: Collector rating

Scope and variety   9
Investment potential   A
Price range   £10/$15 to many thousands

PAPER MONEY

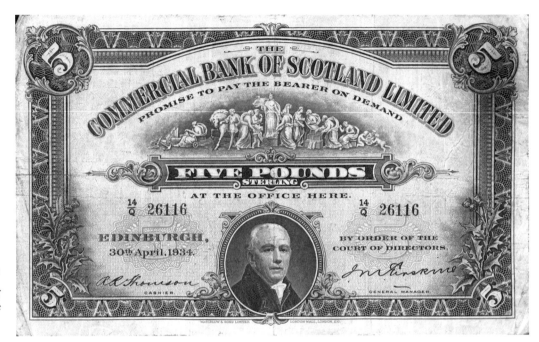

Right. British provincial banknotes have a strong following among collectors, thanks to their infinite variety. This £5 note of 1934 from the Commercial Bank of Scotland was known as a 'horse blanket' because of its large size, more than 8 inches wide (200cm). It is the sort of fairly rare collectors' item that can be found for less than £50/$75.

It's a wacky world where a dollar is worth $500, a busted bank pays out handsome dividends, and £1 million changes hands for £16,000. That's old paper money for you. But is it so crazy? The answer is, in fact, that paper money has some irresistibly sane attractions for enthusiasts and investors as a collecting area that has not felt the bitter winds of dramatic change in recent years. It has not suffered the result of unsettling rise and fall, like the coin market which saw speculators rushing in to seek a hedge against inflation during the late 1970s, and then fleeing in the early 1980s when inflation waned. Nor has it experienced the fluctuating hazards of some areas of the postage stamp market. Paper money has moved steadily forward and seems set fair to continue doing so.

The paper money collector can step into the past to dabble in the veering fortunes of British provincial banks of the eighteenth century, many notes of which are joined in the middle because the printers sent them by coach in halves to be joined up later by the banks as a precaution against the activities of highwaymen. Even further back in time is to be found the oldest surviving paper money, Chinese Ming dynasty banknotes of the late fourteenth century, each 12 inches (30cm) long and printed on mulberry bark paper: these are one-kwan value, a sum then so immense that you would have to be in the mandarin class to have one; now they can fetch about £500/$750 apiece.

In contrast, the collector may come right up to the present to concentrate on issues straight from the day's news; some early Sandinista notes from Nicaragua have already begun to make prices in the region of £130/$200. Certain issues of modern emergent states have great attractions because their leaders, conscious of their roles in posterity, pay for lavishly expensive engraving to produce colourful notes of distinction.

Auctions of paper money (which often include busted bonds) are now frequent affairs in many of the leading salerooms. Such sales bristle with superlatives. One might include the largest denomination note issued in Germany at the time of hyper-inflation, a 1923 Krefeld issue for 200 billion marks. At the time, it had a face value of about £3/$5. Such notes have been earning £300-£350/$450-$525 at auction. In world record terms the largest denominations were found in Hungary during World War Two. Banknotes have come in many different guises during wars; paper, mulberry bark, concentration camp currency printed on old letters or documents – one of the strangest materials for money is found in a 10-shilling currency note of 1902 during the Boer War. It is made from cloth of soldiers' uniforms and the note was issued by Britain's Uppington Border Scouts while fighting in a remote part of the veldt. One such scrap of Tommy Atkins' tunic has brought over £200/$300 at auction. Military issues are a common collector specialization: notes used by the British in the Western Desert in 1941, money planned by Mussolini to be the currency in Egypt after the conquest that never happened, American Doughboys' scrip from World War One, US issues in Japan in World War Two, and many others.

Mistakes in money make more money. There are Bank of England aberrations like the 1975 £10 note with most of Florence Nightingale missing, worth some five times its face value, and another tenner of the same period with the nursing heroine intact but part of her hospital missing. A certain British £1 note bearing a Dardanelles overprint for use in the World War One campaign against the Turks was selling at around £70/$105 in 1972; in 1987 it was being regarded as a very hot property worth £2,500/$3,750 in extremely fine condition, one of the highest grades of condition recognized by collectors.

The basic gradings, from the top, are as follows: UNC (uncirculated) clean and crisp as issued; EF (extremely fine) clean but with traces of folds, almost as issued; VF (very fine) minor folds and creases, a note with a little wear; F (fine) a note which is very creased or worn, but still perfectly clear; Fair, a note which is extremely creased or worn, one that has seen a great deal of use. Condition is one of the critical factors among

Left. Germany provided some of Europe's highest denomination notes. This sample is a modest 1000-Deutschmark note of 1910. Denominations reached some staggering levels during the Weimar Republic's sinking days of the 1920-30s era.

Left. The Hongkong and Shanghai Banking Corporation issued this $500-dollar note in the 1930s, an example of the vast amount of colourful and attractive paper currency which kept the wheels of commerce turning. This is a pre-issue specimen, therefore it has added collector interest.

Above. Of little or no value, but a decorative item to add to any collection is this Spanish 100-peseta note issued by El Banco de España in Madrid on 1 July 1925.

banknote collectors, and an otherwise valuable note of rarity can plummet in value if it is not up to scratch.

Enthusiasts often specialize in a closely defined field such as American Confederate money, French Revolution issues, Tsarist Russian or African banknotes. Wars produce much interesting material for collectors, particularly prison camp scrip. Paper money has also been much used as a weapon in wartime. Governments try to destabilize the enemy currency by flooding the opposing side's country with forged notes and showering from planes reproduction notes carrying propaganda messages. A crude forgery of an American $1 bill which was distributed by Germany in France during World War Two folds out to reveal heavily anti-Semitic propaganda which claims that America was using the power of the dollar to pay for the 'Jewish War'. As a collector's item, it is worth about £46/$70.

Bank crashes have underwritten the value of some notes for collectors. There is a rare 1869 £5 note of the City of Glasgow Bank which closed its doors in 1878 with £6/$9 million losses in the most disastrous bank crash of Scottish history. It caused a major scandal and resulted in prison sentences. Glaswegian misfortunes of the nineteenth century are good news to modern collectors: the £5 note is now worth in excess of £1,000/$1,500. In almost the same class is a much older note, a £1 issued in 1772 by Douglas Heron, a bank in Ayr that lasted only three years and went down in history as Scotland's earliest banking collapse.

Somewhere on the collector round is a rarity of rarities, a note which changed hands at £16,000/$24,000 in 1982, and has passed through various private collections since then. It is a £1

million pound note believed to be the last survivor of only 11 printed in 1948 and then ordered to be destroyed by the Bank of England which had second thoughts about their use for inter-bank transactions. One note, number D0000007, was held back, and cancelled, to give as a retirement souvenir to a senior Bank of England official. When he died, his family put the note into collectors' currency by selling it. If it were to come up for auction there would be no shortage of eager bidders to buy themselves into the ranks of the paper millionaires.

Paper money: Collector rating

Scope and variety	7
Investment potential	C
Prices range	Less than £1 to £20,000/$30,000

PHOTOGRAPHY

'You press the button, we do the rest.' With this motto and the Kodak box camera, George Eastman opened the door to popular photography in 1888. The company name was coined by Eastman as one which could be easily pronounced in any language; the word has neither meaning nor root. The snapshot age was born.

Anyone could now be a photographer as long as they could afford the £15/$25 for the camera. It came with a roll of film sufficient for 100 exposures (which yielded circular negatives). When the film was exposed the camera was returned to the factory where the film was processed and printed. The camera was returned to the owner with new film, the prints from the first load being sent on a couple of weeks later. Hitherto, the amateur had to master some basic chemistry before practicing photography; now, it could be left to the box and the system. Nothing could be simpler.

The first simple box, operated by a string, is an extremely rare item, so seldom seen that photographic specialists will quote only an imprecise value of 'thousands'. This is The Kodak Camera, produced from June 1888 to the following year. It is not to be confused with the Kodak Number One, which followed swiftly on its heels, in production from 1889 to 1895 and valued in the 'mid to upper hundreds' when in immaculate condition.

There were numbered variations on the Kodak model; some had to be loaded at the factory, some the owner could load, albeit in a darkroom. The Pocket Kodak of 1895 used a film based on celluloid with paper backing which allowed it to be loaded in daylight. It opened the way to a battery of daylight-loading cameras, the most famous among them being the Brownie range. The first Brownie was made of cardboard and wood, with a simple lens and an almost foolproof rotary shutter. It was amazingly cheap – one dollar in the USA and five shillings in Britain. Its success was instantaneous. In the first year more than 100,000 Brownies were sold, half of them in Europe.

The heyday of the box camera was in the 1920s and 1930s when these inexpensive models were bought by the million in their brown canvas carrying cases. Vast quantities have been thrown away. They were available on sale, although an endangered species, as recently as the end of the 1950s. The box was finally buried, unmourned by a gadget-minded society, in 1963 when Kodak, the box pioneer, introduced its sensational cartridge-loading Instamatic range with a new film size, 126. The new camera outstripped the original Brownie for revolutionary appeal. Practically every maker in the world chased after the Instamatic bandwagon. The box was finished.

In those heady days of the new photography of the Sixties it would have been possible to put together a collection of redundant twentieth-century box cameras – and the popular, pocket folding types – for little more than the price of a modern cartridge model. Nobody wanted the veterans. A quarter of a century later, boxes of the inter-war years and the period immediately after the war are respected as interesting relics of their time. Although they have increased in value, they are still inexpensive and a representative collection can be formed for an outlay of a few hundred dollars or pounds. The older rarities apart, it might be a decade or two, however, before such a collection would pay off as an investment.

While the American camera market in the twentieth century was dominated by Kodak, Britain produced a variety of makers of interest to collectors. From fine wooden cameras in the late

Below. In the final months before he gave up photography, Lewis Carroll (The Rev. Charles Lutwidge Dodgson), the nineteenth-century author of *Alice's Adventures in Wonderland*, took this photograph of young Leila, the daughter of a friend. It has historic meaning for collectors because Carroll's departure from photography was sudden, following adverse comment on his penchant for photographing little girls.

Left. George Eastman opened the door for popular photography with his marketing of the revolutionary Kodak box camera in 1888. 'Kodak' had no meaning or root: it could be easily pronounced in any language. The model shown here is a Number 4 Kodak panoramic camera of around 1900.

Below left. An early box type of the 20th century. It is a Rouch's Patent Excelsior magazine hand-camera, the body superbly crafted in mahogany and brass, a feature which never fails to attract the collector. Cameras such as this and the Number 4 Kodak panoramic can still be found in the lower hundreds.

although good-condition specimens are becoming more and more difficult to obtain. Leica (first model 1925 and subsequently more than a hundred different types) and its rival Zeiss Ikon have their own collector societies in Europe and the USA. America, Germany and Japan have far more collectors *pro rata* than Britain and prices tend to be correspondingly higher in those parts of the world. The slow development of national and international collectors' organizations helps further to explain the wide differences in price from area to area and from country to country.

The collecting of photographs shows similar market patterns. London was long the recognized centre of photographic auctions, but the 1980s have seen many fine sales being held in New York. The material spans two centuries.

The nineteenth century provides us with the highly priced works of such 'greats' as William Henry Fox Talbot, father of photography, Julia Margaret Cameron (who worked at the art for only 12 years), Roger Fenton (a barrister with a passion for photographing English landscapes and cathedrals, who is celebrated for a portfolio of Crimean War pictures), the renowned partnership of Robert Adamson and David Octavius Hill, Lewis Carroll (the Rev. Charles Lutwidge Dodgson), Matthew Brady (America's chronicler of the Civil War) and a host of others. Many of their works have climbed into the price bracket of middle-range old master paintings.

America has led the way in the study of photography; there, several universities offer degree courses in the history and practice of photography (a development now reflected in some European universities). Both Britain and the USA enjoy important museum collections of photographs and related material. Keen international competition between museums, universities, dealers and private collectors is the order of the day at the regular photographic auctions held on both sides of the Atlantic.

The question of whether photography is art has long been the subject of debate. In 1976 the British magazine *Art and Antiques* quoted Sam Wagstaff, formerly curator of twentieth-century art at the Detroit Museum, and an active photographic collector: 'I suspect that photography, which is surely one of the most common or garden pastimes of all, is one of the most difficult things to *see* (as an art form). It is quite easy to *see* paintings with a little bit of training but I find every day it is more difficult to *see* real quality in photography.' Philippe Garner, a Sotheby's specialist writing on the subject of photography, commented on this: 'It is easy to come to the conclusion that it is the very facility

Victorian era, many went on to produce high-quality miniature metal models. The Compass, designed by Pemberton Billing in 1937, was of such an intricate design that it could only be produced by Lecoultre, the distinguished Swiss watchmaker. Only 4,000 were made, masterpieces of miniature engineering, and those that survive are highly coveted by collectors. The cameras of Sinclair, Adams, Watson, Sanderson, Lancaster and Ensign are hotly chased. Collectors have come to realize that quarter-plate cameras, in infinite variety, with their gleaming wood bodies and brass-housed lenses fitted into attractive leather cases, are works of art as well as being functional machines. The north of England is a particularly good place to look for old wooden cameras, of all types and sizes, in view of the fact that many camera factories were established there.

Early twentieth-century cameras are relatively plentiful,

of photography that creates a prejudice against looking deeply into the genuine merits and delights of the images created by sensitive and imaginative photographers.'

Attitudes have arguably changed since 1976. The growth of the market in photographs, ancient and modern, has been been based as much on recognition of artistic merit as on rarity. It has been an exciting two decades for those engaged in the pursuit of the photographic image as a collectable. The works of Julia Margaret Cameron and her ilk command astronomical prices at international auctions. Just as interesting, however, are the discoveries of less exalted practitioners, brought about by the increasing interest in old photography.

More than a century after she travelled the English highways and byways in a horse-drawn darkroom, 'Great Aunt' Gertrude was one of these 'unknowns' who, in the mid-1980s, achieved retrospective fame as a stylish Victorian photographer. Gertrude Elizabeth Rogers's hidden talents produced a portfolio of photographs of rural life between 1861 and 1864. Locals, such as eel-pot fishermen, village children, old gaffers and field hands, posed for up to 20 seconds while she operated her cumbersome wet-plate camera. Gertrude would make her forays on sunny summer days from her family stately home, Riverhill House in Kent, using a box-like brougham which she equipped as a mobile darkroom: the collodian wet-plate process which she employed required swift developing of the negatives.

When Gertrude's photographic results came to auction at Phillips, the brougham was still at Riverhill, an eighteenth-century house then occupied by her great nephew, Major David Rogers. He and his wife discovered her bundle of photographs

Above right. Flashback to the great 'collector age' of photography, the 1860s. This was part of a portfolio of English village life captured on wet-plate glass negatives by Gertrude Elizabeth Rogers. She roved the highways and byways of Kent and neighbouring counties in a carriage which she had fitted out as a mobile darkroom: the collodion wet-plate process which she used necessitated instant development on the spot.

Right. Twentieth century progress and the customers' demand for more refinements swiftly developed the reflex camera. This is an Adams Tropical Minex reflex model – a work of art in substantial teak bound with brass. It has gone above the £2,000/$3,000 level in collector value.

Left. The results of early popular colour photography: a whole-plate Lumiere Autochrome portrait by Olive Edis, a Briton, taken in 1907. The process was one of the earliest popular colour services available. It was slow, tended to be expensive and was based on the use of a potato-starch emulsion. A collector will pay several hundred pounds or dollars for a print such as this.

Below. The children of Tsar Nicholas II were photographed in 1911 by Boissons and Eggler, a poignant memento which the Tsar's family signed on the mount. The pearwood frame bears the imperial crown and insignia. A collector's treasure at £4,400/$6,600 in 1986.

wrapped in old newspapers on the top of a wardrobe. Hugo Marsh, head of the photographic department at Phillips, explained: 'Gertrude roved in her horse-drawn darkroom through Kent, into Essex and Sussex and as far as Berkshire, but her hobby seems to have ended abruptly when she married in 1865. Her photographs were an important discovery, combining excellence of quality, composition and condition with historical value. She has left behind a delightful record of village life in distant summers: her photographs never appear forced or sentimental, but convey the feeling of hot days with a slight breeze blowing through the trees.' In a later summer, Great Aunt Gertrude's bundle of photographs changed hands at auction for £16,000/$24,000 and helped pay a very hefty repair bill at Riverhill.

In photography, however, age is not only necessarily a virtue. Many twentieth-century works by photographers such as Man Ray, Alfred Stieglitz, Edward Steichen, Walker Evans, Edward Weston and Ansel Adams are more sought after and more expensive than those by some of their Victorian forebears.

An auction of the works of modern photographers might include an eclectic selection of styles and sitters: Winston Churchill, photographed by Steichen, a co-founder of the American-influenced Photo-Secession of 1902, a group of practitioners dedicated to advancing recognition of pictorial photography as a fine art; or the same distinguished sitter captured by Yousuf Karsh, Canada's celebrated camera artist; a gleeful nun on a swing, recorded through the lens of Henri Cartier-Bresson, newsman-extraordinary; Jean Cocteau portrayed by Irving Penn; 'Grandma Moses' by Arnold Newman; or James Dean through the camera of Phil Stern.

The most popular and collected photographs of all have been the images of Hollywood. But these portraits of the stars, so common, so available, so much a part of the everyday scene, have been despised by many a serious collector. John Kobal, a collector of and writer on things cinematic, has done much to put this branch of photography in a more favourable light through advocacy and exhibition. George Hurrell's series of photographs of Joan Crawford, William Walling's moody Marlene Dietrich and many Hollywood works by Ernest Bachrach, among others, would be ranked with the desirable 'photographic antiques' of tomorrow.

Photography: Collector rating

Scope and variety:	9
Investment potential	Highest quality, A; others C-D
Price range	£40$60 to six figures

POP & ROCK

Above. Bright, solid colours in a New York radio station poster of 1966, at the time of the Beatles (35 inches, 89cm wide). It is by Milton Glaser, who has been for years one of the most successful and influential of graphic artists. Glaser posters change hand in the USA around the $100 mark.

A portrait of a typical Beatles collector, as deduced from some of the lots to be found in a sale of pop memorabilia, would be something like the following. Our subject is young, female, probably single, and shares a bedsit. Let's call her Lucy. The tights she wears (pantyhose if she is across the other side of the water from Liverpool) are adorned with the ubiquitous grins of John, Paul, George and Ringo. She makes up her face from a Beatles powder compact and uses Beatles talc. She dines off Beatles china and serves drinks in Beatles glasses on a Beatles tray. Her bedside table clutter includes a Corgi model of a Yellow Submarine, a signed photograph and a Beatles Fan Club card – and the walls sport the odd poster or two. After stepping out of the tub on to a Beatles bath mat and drying herself on a towel woven with portraits of the the Four, Lucy begins her day with cereal and coffee from a Beatles breakfast set; and she goes to bed with hot chocolate in a Lennon mug before snuggling down under a Beatles-decorated blanket.

In the Sixties, all those things could have been Lucy's for under £50 – or less than, say, $100 in the United States. In today's rarified collecting climate, the bill might be 30 or 40 times those levels.

Beatlemania is the most active and visible manifestation in the pop and rock collectors' market, and Lucy's treasures represent only a minute part of the vast amount of material available. The collecting field is defined roughly in three price segments: two figures, three figures, and above.

A typical pop sale includes a large choice in the lowest of the three ranges. China, tea towels, posters, dolls and toys (the nodding-head Beatles, 1964 composition figures, are popular), programmes, a plastic Lennon to jig about on a car rear window, belt buckles, a composition apple core (Apple Corps, get it?), any number of Beatles photographs and pressings (unsigned) … all this, in large quantity and variety, is the basic accompaniment to the middle and high performers. Like most things appertaining to the Beatles, it all has to be put to the acid test: is it genuine Sixties material, or is it modern reproduction from Taiwan or Hong Kong? If in doubt, seek the advice of an auction room specialist.

Three-figure items might include: a 1960s American bubble gum machine, all scarlet and chrome and bearing pictures of the Four in their early days; a mint Yellow Submarine or a celluloid from the cartoon film; a purple satin jacket with gaudy yellow lettering proclaiming a Beatles American tour of 1965; one of Paul McCartney's old sweat shirts; a psychedelic *Magical Mystery Tour* jigsaw; and autographs.

Autographs present a problem. A John Lennon signature on its own, for example, can have a value on the international market of more than £150/$250, but much depends on the circumstances in which it was written and what it was written on. If it is accompanied by an inscription, a jokey Lennonism, the price rises dramatically (see the chapter on Autographs on page 26, for the vital difference between 'autograph' and ' signature'). Substantial Beatle writings match the prices for antiquarian manuscripts. The Beatles were generous in signing and sending photographs, postcards, posters and programmes. However, no fewer than ten people were employed to sign fan club cards, and there is a theory that the writing machine, which reproduces signatures from a matrix, *must* have been deployed as well. And, of course, there are downright fakes. One specialist claims that only two or three out of a hundred signatures are genuine: again, expert advice is essential.

Gold discs, too, have attracted the fakers, not surprisingly when one considers that some genuine examples can make several thousands each at auction, while there are many priced in the hundreds.

Beatle-related clothing often fits the four-figure profile. A cotton mini dress was one of only eight made for the cinema usherettes at the royal premiere in London of *Help!* in 1965. It was hand-signed in ink by the group (Ringo signed twice), by Cynthia Lennon and by Brian Epstein. In 1985 it sold at Phillips for £1,000/$1,500. A Paul McCartney 1965 stage suit of grey worsted jacket and black trousers has doubled this amount, and is probably, ere now, fast gathering value, if not moths, in some collector's wardrobe.

Perhaps only a Lucy in the sky with diamonds could afford the most exotic Beatles memento. The ritziest car in show business became the costliest car in the world in New York in July 1985 when it changed hands at over $2 million. It was John Lennon's flower-painted Rolls Royce Phantom V, a dazzling confection of yellow, pink, blue and green. He decorated the Rolls as Flower Power arrived in Britain – flowing scrolls and gorgeous blooms. He kept the whole thing secret until one day in

Above. A satin jacket produced for a Beatles American tour of 1965. Such an item of clothing might sell in a pop auction for around £300/$450 or more; proof that a garment had been worn by one of the Fab Four, can multiply the value by 10.

Below. A Beatles breakfast mug of 1964, which is accompanied by a plate and a cereal bowl. Such souvenirs were sold in their thousands during the Sixties. Many have been lost or destroyed. The surviving sets are assured of a ready sale when they appear.

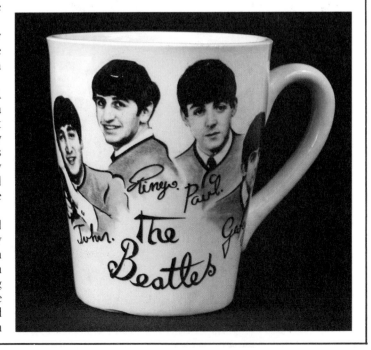

Right. A mini dress plastered with the faces of the Fab Four (and signed by the group) was made in an extremely limited number of 8 for the cinema usherettes at the London premiere of *Help!* in 1965. Cynthia Lennon and Beatle 'godfather' Brian Epstein also signed the dress. In 1985 it sold for £1,100/$1,650 at auction in London.

Below. They are somewhat crudely modelled, they are fragile, they are by no means exclusive, but the Bobb'n Head Beatles in plaster (8 inches, 20cm) find eager buyers whenever they put in an appearance. Collectors are warned to be wary of modern pop artefacts from Hong Kong and Taiwan, being manufactured to take advantage of the current Beatles bandwagon.

1967 when he drove home in his freshly painted car. As he turned into the drive of his mansion on the exclusive St George's Hill estate at Weybridge in Surrey, neighbours behind their curtains were astonished, and not a few were outraged, by the apparition.

Collectors love Beatle mementoes because they recall the evergreen stories of the Fab Four's great days. Don Short, a London journalist guarded over the years a few scraps of paper bearing closely-written handwriting that represented Lennon's first draft of *A Spaniard in the Works*. Short travelled with the Beatles all over the world between 1963 and 1970. He recounts: 'Beatlemania was almost in full cry. We were hurtling through 1964 on a nationwide British tour. Already John, Paul, George and Ringo were making headlines and I came to know them well as a newspaper columnist. In the process we were becoming close friends. We checked into a country hotel between Birmingham and Leeds. After dinner John disappeared into the loo and emerged nearly an hour later clutching a torn white envelope and two brown paper bags. He had scribbled notes all over them, and at first I thought he intended showing me the lyrics of a new song he had written.

'Instead, he explained that it was the start of "a great new book". John thrust the pages into my hand – after copying the text into an exercise book – and said, "Here, Don, they're yours. Flog 'em if you ever go broke." It transpired that John, while in the loo, had composed the first and title story of his book of short stories, *A Spaniard in the Works*, published a year later by Simon and Schuster in New York.'

Lennon's handwriting fills the opened-out envelopes and the paper bags with the 800-900 words of his opening story. In some places, the draft differs from the published text. But Lennon liked his introduction sufficiently to keep it as written: 'Jesus El Pifco was a foreigner and he knew it. He had imigrateful from his little white slum in Barcelover a good thirsty year ago having first secured the handy job as coachman in Scotland...'.

Who collects pop and rock? Auctions attract young and not-so-young alike: today's youthful followers of the modern bands, and yesterday's Beatle groupies, now approaching the threshold of middle age; musicians active and retired, and steely-eyed characters with their sights on investment potential. The Hard Rock Cafes of New York, Los Angeles and London have valuable collections of memorabilia. Establishments such as the London store *Elvisly Yours* and Jeffrey Walker's Beatles Museum of Vancouver, Canada, pursue their respective specialities. There are Rolling Stones fan clubs, Sex Pistols nostalgics, Liberace worshippers.

The Stones are a coming market. They featured in a rare 'single' at a 1987 auction, a 30-second tape of a Rice Krispies commercial for radio, performed by them in their early days : 'Wake up in the morning with a snap around the place...' Somebody thought its novelty value was sufficient to invest in it a bid of £200/$300. Bill Hayley and the Comets are well placed in the collector charts. So, too, are Genesis, Marc Bolan and Pink Floyd. Mementoes of Buddy Holly are scarce and expensive. Elvis has been assiduously bought by Michael Jackson, one of an international legion of his collectors. What, one wonders, is the eventual destination of Lot 549, the finale of a recent pop sale at Phillips? For a mere £200/$300, the buyer obtained 'Forty-eight plastic musical-box Elvis Presley statuettes revolving to the tune of *Love Me Tender*, all in original boxes and packed in trade boxes of twelve, by the Le Fare Company.'

Tony Fox, who turned his collecting hobby into a career by founding *Elvisly Yours*, talked about the lure of collecting in an interview for the *Glasgow Herald*: 'Prestige, having something which others don't have ... a strange fascination with having a

Below. The memory of Elvis Presley has a vast following of worshippers throughout the world, with a highly specialized dealer-industry geared to meet the demands of collectors and fans. His records, such as this RCA 78, are the staple diet of the industry. Anything with a personal Presley connection fetches big money.

"complete" collection of something you know you'll never be able to finish acquiring ... the difference between being a fan and a fanatic. There's an element of getting closer to the star you admire, but the whole thing's useless in many ways. I never actually play any of the rare Elvis singles and LPs I've got, once I've taped them ... PLAY a genuine 1958 Presley!!'.

The interviewer, David Belcher, admitted to some degree of bafflement about pop-collecting: 'This is perhaps not the most urgent or obvious of questions arising from a look through the catalogues of two forthcoming auctions of rock 'n' roll memorabilia – but just who took a needle and thread to Jimi Hendrix's trousers ("striped wool-mix worsted in khaki, scarlet, blue and emerald, some repairs")? Would the original wild man of rock ("even our cymbals are phallic") have darned them himself in quiet backstage moments before going out to trash guitars in the service of his muse? Did his mum sew them up for him?'

Jimi Hendrix's trousers, Paul McCartney's sweat shirt, Ringo Starr's waistcoat, an usherette's mini-dress ... hand-me-downs never had it so good.

Pop and Rock: Collector rating

Scope and variety	9
Investment potential	B
Price range	£20/$30, to the highest notes

POSTCARDS

FROM THE CLOUDS
29 August 1903.

"LIFE-BOAT SATURDAY"

Balloon Post

LOVE'S TOKEN.
Never sigh,
You and I
Will meet again
By and by.

Jeannie Bowden's balloon postcard, shown here, fluttered from the clouds in the north of England in 1903, and about eighty years later it was hailed as one of the few postcards that have broken through the 'sound barrier' of four figures. Jeannie and hundreds of others paid threepence each for their cards which were to be taken up by balloon and showered over the city of Manchester in a stunt to raise funds for lifeboats. Delivery depended on the finder's goodwill in popping the pre-stamped card into a mailbox. There was a hitch at the beginning of the enterprise when bad weather postponed the advertised and printed date of ascent, and the balloon went up some days late. Most of the cards went astray or have vanished over the years. Jeannie's has made it into history, franked, and carefully preserved, in collectors' terms one of the most desirable and valuable picture postcards out of the incalculable billions that were produced.

The postcard's golden era spanned the first twenty years of this century. Thereafter, there was a lull in collecting, brought about by various factors (in Britain, for example, an increase in postal charges in 1918 led to a significant drop in mailings and a parallel decrease in card manufacture).

It took nearly fifty years for postcard-collecting to climb back to anything like its former popularity. Today, those who collect postcards claim that they are second in number only to stamp enthusiasts. There is one outstanding difference, however, between today's collecting and that which was all the rage in the 1900-1920 period. Present day devotees seek *old* postcards, whereas the collectors of the earlier time eagerly bought new issues as they came from the printer. The old habits have helped the new: there was such a tremendous sale of albums that many postcard collections from the golden days have remained beautifully preserved in pristine condition, a wealth of excellent material for the modern collector.

Many postcards, however, cross the frontier into philatelic collectables. The attraction of a used postcard is that it was written and signed and franked at a given time: it is unique, a very personal piece of history, a message from the past. It is doubtful whether much of today's output of postcards will qualify for the term 'tomorrows antiques', owing to the proliferation of mass printing techniques. Most modern production is of the topographical type – or 'scenic', as it is known in America. The immense variety of subject matter which postcard collectors once enjoyed is now missing. Therefore the main collecting ground remains confined to the half century or more stretching back from the 1950s.

An understanding of the postcard in collector terms requires a grasp of its historical and social context. The earliest postcards were plain. The idea of a card with a picture on one side had spread from Continental Europe by the 1880s. Before then, in 1869, Austria is credited with the first officially recognized postcards – plain, prepaid, with the message on one side and the address on the other. Within a month, 1½ million had been sold. Other countries soon copied the idea.

As picture postcards began to appear in the next 10-20 years one side still had to be kept free for the address. Continental 'multiple-view' cards seemed to meet the need to provide message space. German makers excelled in cards which illustrated various scenes in vignettes, leaving a small space for a brief message. Finely printed and coloured, these cards have

Left. Jeannie Bowden's balloon card of 1903 which went into history many years after it was dropped from the skies over the north of England. It is a very rare item.

Lower left. 'Never sigh/ You and I/ Will meet again/ By and by.' Typical postcard with wartime sentimentality of 1914-18. Such postcards cards sold by the million.

become known as *Grüss aus* (greetings from), the phrase which universally appeared on them.

In Britain, the great postcard breakthrough came after 1902 when postal regulations allowed the address side of the card to be divided into two parts to provide space for a message without encroaching on the picture. 'In 10 years Europe will be buried in postcards,' intoned a London newspaper in 1903. Within six years, 860 million cards were being mailed annually in the United Kingdom. They appear to have caused a social upheaval. The 'antis' cited the views of Queen Victoria who had departed on the eve of the new-fangled development and seems to have remained stolidly unamused by the idea of sending messages by the postcard of her day. On the other hand, the 'pro' lobby quoted her former prime minister, William Ewart Gladstone, a prolific writer of postcards who reckoned he was indebted to their invention for prolonging his life. As early as 1890 a manual on behaviour had warned: 'Do not conduct correspondence on postal cards. It is questionable whether a note on a postal card is entitled to the courtesy of a response.' Joseph Pennell, an American artist friend of Whistler and self-appointed custodian of culture, pompously opined that postcards were not artistic because they were produced commercially; people took to them because they 'were too busy to use their brains to write letters'.

The symptoms of the new social disease were widespread. A correspondent of *The Referee* magazine reported on a tourist expedition to the Rigi mountain in Switzerland during the summer of 1900: 'Directly we arrived at the summit, everybody made a rush for the hotel and fought for post cards. Five minutes afterwards, everybody was writing for dear life. I believe the entire party had come up, not for the sake of the experience or the scenery, but to write post cards and post them at the summit.'

The London *Evening News* declared in 1906: 'The art of letter-writing may speedily become extinct.' But the postcard was winning. It was, said the Daily Express, 'no longer considered vulgar'. A stockist in the heart of London had 27,000 cards seized by the police and was summoned because his French ladies in moderately revealing *négligées* and silk stockings were considered too saucy for the Edwardian public. When newspapers reported similar arrests of two shopkeepers for selling postcards which transgressed the bounds of propriety *The Picture Post Card Magazine* announced: 'We cannot conceal our satisfaction that the persons guilty were not English tradesmen.' Within a short time the same magazine was able to exult that picture postcards were 'now used by the lowest and the highest in the land ... Today postcards are collected by the King and the coster and every class and condition between'.

And collected they were. There was a booming trade in albums for storing picture postcards, whose subject range was immense – views, politics, history, glamour, great events, jokes, transport, royalty, the US presidency, theatre, advertising, folklore, animals, flowers ... these contemporary hoards provide riches for today's collectors of the past.

There were some serious cases of postcard lunacy. An official decree of 1900 tried to forbid French postmen, under pain of dismissal, from reading messages on postcards. In Russia a fine of 10 roubles was imposed whenever any declaration of love was found written on a card. Miss Rita Kittredge of Belfast, Missouri, was in the habit of sending postcards to American presidents every few years, but it was hardly a case of 'just a few

"I just love mountaineering it's so embracing"

Above. 'I just love mountaineering. It's so embracing.' A jokey card of 1908, which is a tinted photographic type manufactured by Bamforth, one of the most prolific British makers.

Below. Delightful Art Nouveau postcard of 1920-30, designed by Elizabeth Sourel. Similar works of postcard art have changed hands at more than £100/$150 each at auction.

Above. Typical work of Donald McGill, recorder of the British seaside scene, who was known as the 'Leonardo of the saucy postcard' and the 'pastmaster of the posterior'. At his peak he was producing more than 150 illustrated jokes a year.

lines'. At the age of 77 she crammed 15,000 words on one side of a card, the text of President Cleveland's Message to Congress. A few years later she completed a 23,305-word postcard to President Garfield, who sent her a letter of acknowledgement. The annals of postcard verbosity also reveal an 85-year-old Norwegian who transcribed a 46,000-word novel; and a Dusseldorfer who found he had room to spare after copying down the first three books of the *Odyssey*, so he filled up his postcard with a record of a debate in the German parliament.

Postcards had a role to play in news reporting. When King George V and Queen Mary visited Dublin on 8 June 1911, a photograph of the event was taken at 10.30 a.m. It was processed, a half-tone block was made and a postcard was printed the same day. Disasters were given similar rapid treatment. Train and air crashes and natural catastrophes are a special branch of collecting, in which individual cards can fetch high prices. Probably no event was as well covered in postcards as the San Francisco earthquake of 1906. The results varied from the brashly coloured postcards of the Hearst newspaper company to the superior works produced by Adolph Selige and Britton & Rey. All were runaway sellers. They showed the devastation as well as relief work in progress, refugee camps and people in breadlines in the ruined streets. Furthermore, there was subsequently a heavy demand for pictures of the city as it had been before the earthquake.

American collectors, who like to call themselves deltiologists (from the Greek *deltion*, small card), have been going through a nostalgic revival which has inflated postcard prices on their side of the Atlantic. Similarly, American material which surfaces in European postcard auctions has a premium on its price: American buyers now closely monitor and buy at sales in Britain and the business of collecting is on an international basis. Postcards reproducing the works of the American artist Charles Dana Gibson are eagerly sought on both sides of the Atlantic; his cool and statuesquely beautiful Gibson Girls, while not yet emulating the eminence reached by the art nouveau beauties of Alphonse Mucha and Raphael Kirchner, have a glamorous price on their heads.

Many American 'scenics' increased ten-fold in the 1980s. An East Coast collector can remember in 1975 pricing his swap-meet stock of city views at two for 25c, a risible price when viewed now. Price-listing is made difficult by the fact that values differ across the States. It is easier and less expensive to buy a view in New England than in the mid-West, where postcards are in scarcer supply. Street scenes are in big demand – and even inside this theme there are crucial variations of price relating to subject matter: a postcard of a railroad station with a vintage locomotive standing on the tracks is double the price of one showing an empty station; fire stations are at a premium, but one with contemporary fire equipment drawn up outside has a significant edge in value to a collector.

The postcard is now widely acknowledged as a source of historical information. As a result, many classic photographic series have been skillfully reproduced and the sets are ready sellers in main bookstores. The assembly of the Statue of Liberty, the progress of railways and the building of such landmarks as the Golden Gate and Brooklyn bridges are typical and rewarding subjects. Given the increasing rarity of the original postcards, some of these definitive sets may well qualify as collectables of the future.

Social history, too, is encompassed in the postcard, often through the medium of humour. Nothing catches the essence of the British seaside ethic so much as the comic postcards of Tom Browne (1872-1910) and Donald McGill (1875-1962). Brownes still have the edge on McGills in value, but the latter are

Left. A magnificent collection of the cream of early twentieth century postcards: examples produced in Austria by the Wiener Werkstätte in Secezionist, or Art Nouveau, styles.

Below. A modern postcard taking a nostalgic look at Broadway, New York City, in the early 1900s.

increasing fast, especially his watercolour originals (usually double a postcard's size) which can top £500/$750.

McGill's gloriously irreverent jokes about fat bottoms and large busts in red bathing suits dominated the British comic card scene for most of six decades. His jolly, rotund women, henpecked husbands, red-nosed drunks, hopeful swains, ineffectual clerics and ambiguously innocent bathing belles are instantly recognizable from faked 'McGills'. The statistics of his output are as impressive as the waistlines he drew. Assessments of the number of his postcard designs vary from 3,500 to 12,000. At his peak he was producing more than 150 illustrated jokes a year, but he was sharp enough to sell variations of the same joke to several publishers. His top-selling postcard is said to have run to 6 million copies – 25 tons of postcards. It shows a little girl at bedtime prayers being harassed by a puppy: 'Please, Lord, excuse me a minute while I kick Fido.' The card went into several languages. Some of McGill's jokes defied translation into a foreign language: 'Do you like Kipling?' 'I don't know, I've never Kippled!'

In an essay on Donald McGill's art in 1941, George Orwell described his jokes as 'a chorus of raspberries'. The author found in the postcards 'something as traditional as Greek Tragedy, a sort of sub-world of smacked bottoms and scrawny mothers-in-law which is part of Western European consciousness'. The McGill archetypes were a skit on real life, and, as Orwell said, 'The slightest hint of higher influences would ruin them utterly.' Other writers dubbed McGill 'the pastmaster of the posterior' and 'the Leonardo of the saucy postcard'. Untold millions of holidaymakers simply had a laugh and wrote: 'Wish you were here.'

Postcards: Collector rating

Scope and variety	8
Investment potential	C
Price range	Pennies to four figures

POSTERS

Adolphe Mouron Cassandre (1901-68) was a Ukrainian-born artist who worked in France and whose dramatic graphic messages include the Triplex poster illustrated in this chapter – as well as his incomparable salesmanship for the liner *Normandie*, seen in Shipping on page 146. 'The poster artist,' he observed, 'is an operator: he does not *issue* a message, he merely passes it on. No one asks for his opinion; he is only expected to establish a connection: clear, powerful, accurate.' Painting, he believed, was a self-sufficient proposition; not so the poster. It was 'a means, a short cut between trade and the prospective buyer – a kind of telegraph'. With Cassandre's definition in mind, we present a few 'telegraphic' facts about the vast subject of posters and poster-collection.

Choose a theme; there are many: tourism, transport (ships, railways, aviation, motoring, cycles ...), theatre and cabaret, circus, pop, magazine and book advertising, political, fashion, food, drink, cosmetics, art nouveau, war, particular artists or periods. Esoteric ultra-specializations veer from Buffalo Bill's Wild West shows to Sarah Bernhardt's stage appearances.

Posters were meant to go on walls: so beware highly priced, so-called 'hand-signed' versions – few artists would bother to put a personal signature on something that was going on a hoarding at the mercy of rain and wind. Also, beware modern reproductions backed by old linen to make them look 'antique'.

If you have a good example of a genuine poster of, say, the Gay Nineties, treat it as a work of art. Strong sun and electric light will fade both the colours and the value.

What price a poster? Take your choice. Henri Toulouse-Lautrec's *Moulin Rouge*, featuring the dancer La Goulue (The Glutton), topped £33,000/$50,000 at auction, and that was in the early 1980s. Cassandre's *Normandie* is well into four figures. A British railway company's 'Come to sunny Bognor' message of the 1930s can make several hundreds of pounds. A browse around the print booths of a market might produce a collectors' item for a few pounds or dollars. Some reproductions of currently successful advertising campaigns are available gratis from the agencies.

Lautrec (1864-1901), the greatest poster artist of all, produced only 31 known posters. His approach was very personal. He once fell in love from afar with a woman passenger he spotted on a Le Havre-Bordeaux ship, and pursued her to Portugal where he gave up the chase. He immortalized her in an 1896 poster for an exhibition centre called 'Salon des Cent'.

Old posters are sometimes rarer than the artist's original paintings. Pierre Fix-Masseau (b. 1905) was constantly asked by admirers for copies of *Exactitude*, a celebrated poster which he executed for the French State Railways. He had kept none, and found it easier to dash off a quick painting of his impressive locomotive. More of these paintings are known to exist than examples of his 1932 poster.

Far left. Henri Toulouse-Lautrec's poster for an exhibition centre (15inches, 39cm wide) depicts a woman with whom he fell in love from afar on a voyage. Lautrec's poster art is at the top of the collecting scale, and is valued in many thousands.

Left. Lautrec again in his most famous poster, an advertisement for the dancer La Goulue, appearing at the Moulin Rouge in 1891. One of his original posters, measuring some sixty six inches (168cm) in height, fetches tens of thousands of dollars in New York.

Below. One of the most arrestingly beautiful of all Art Nouveau posters, a masterpiece created in 1900 by the designer Manuel Orazzi to advertise *La Maison Moderne*, an emporium and showcase of artistic artefacts in Paris (46 inches, 116cm wide).

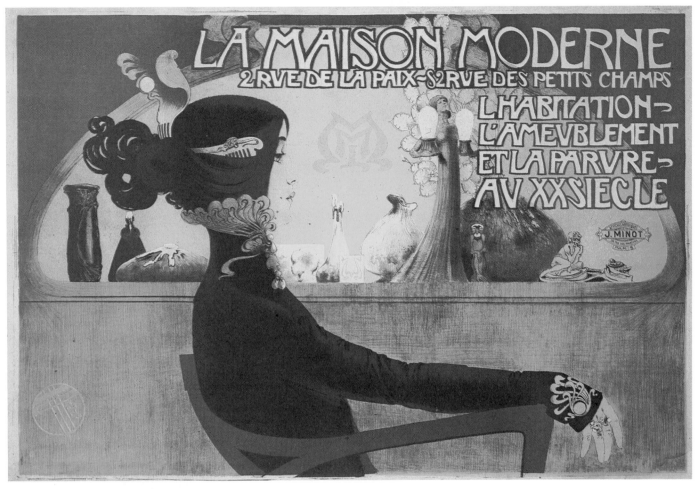

Bernhardt appreciated the hard financial facts about poster collecting. When the Czech-born artist Alphonse Mucha (1860-1939) produced a ravishing poster to advertise her appearance in *Gismonda*, she ordered 4,000 copies and sold them off over the years at a profit. Collectors wince today when they learn that copies of this poster, now worth more than £6,500/$10,000, 'quickly went to pieces in the London atmosphere' when it was on hoardings for a British tour.

Jules Chéret (1836-1932), known as 'the father of the poster', was so famed for his ethereally beautiful women of *La Belle Epoque*, that a song about his *Chérettes* became the rage of Paris. He used his beauties to advertise theatre shows and cabarets and such mundane subjects as coughdrops, soap, lamp oil and bicycles.

Chéret's role, wrote a devoted, if pompous, admirer, was 'to wrest the streets from the grey and bleak monotony of buildings strung out in long rows; to cast upon them the fireworks of colour, the glow of joy; to convert the walls into "decorable" surfaces and let this open-air museum reveal the character of a people...', Chéret was little impressed by such high-flown flattery and continued to produce, by the score, the prettiest girls that ever graced a poster.

Andy Warhol (1930-87) went the whole hog when he made a poster in 1968 for the RCA Color Scanner, a machine which electronically separates colour art for printing. No easy way for

him. He painted a real, live pig as a piggy bank at the J. Walter Thompson advertising agency, then had it photographed. The poster caption reads: 'Bank by Andy Warhol. Gaudy savings by RCA Color Scanner. Pretty as a pigture, huh?' Having reached £300/$450 at auction by the late 1970s, the poster has steadily appreciated in value. Inevitably, Warhol's death has put a premium on the values of his posters, along with other examples of his art.

The business of poster collecting – and big business it is – has been immensely stimulated in the past decade and a half by a series of auctions in New York, which became the undisputed centre of the poster trade. Now, even the illustrated catalogues for these auctions are changing hands at inflated prices. The contents of the sales have reached as far back as the 1880s, with some exciting travelling-circus material, spanned the the gaiety of *La Belle Epoque*, roared through the mechanically-minded and transport-conscious eras of the Twenties and Thirties, and come close to our times with psychedelic rock posters of the Avalon Ballroom, San Francisco, dating from the late Sixties, and the even later 'Smoking Camel' sensation of France, featured in the chapter on Advertising (on page 16).

Many factors contribute to the high price of certain posters. The artist's standing, the rarity of the poster, the circumstances in which it was designed or lithographed, its condition ... all these can affect values today. Lautrec, Mucha, Chéret,

Bank by Andy Warhol. Gaudy savings by RCA Color Scanner. Pretty as a pigture, huh?

Théophile Alexandre Steinlen (an example of the work of this Paris-based Swiss is to be found in Cats and Dogs on page 60), Cassandre and Fix-Masseau head an array of artists whose masterpieces have entered the multi-thousand-dollar class of collector art. Their works are rare and valuable partly because the ravages of street exposure have left few survivors.

Posters show a clearly defined line of descent from the famous names of *La Belle Epoque*, from the flowering of art nouveau, through this century's art deco movement, into the direct hard-sell of modern times. Surely it is not outrageous to assume that Chéret and Lautrec, Mucha and Steinlen would appreciate and respect what modern poster artists are attempting today.

A newcomer to poster collecting must be clear on the distinctions between authentic advertising posters and the reproduction or modern prints that go for smallish sums in a museum gift shop. Jack Rennert, a highly regarded and authoritative specialist in posters in the United States, says: 'A beginner's first question is always, "How many copies of this poster exist?" The answer is that no one knows. Posters aren't done as art. They get slapped on walls in the rain. A printer might keep a folded copy for his records, but the rest tend to vanish.' As in so many other fields of collecting, the lure of rarity, the thrill of the chase and the ever-present hope of finding a vanished one are the stimuli that keep the poster collector going.

Posters: Collector rating

Scope and variety	9
Investment potential	B
Price range	From nothing to many thousands

Above left. To make this 1968 poster for the RCA Color Scanner, Andy Warhol painted the pig at a New York advertising agency and then had the animal photographed by Irwin Horowitz (45 inches, 115cm wide). The method was dramatic and effective for a product which essentially meant colour. The entire event was filmed by Warhol's motion picture crew. Examples of Warhol art have inevitably increased in value since his death.

Below left. A powerful image for motoring safety glass – by Adolphe Mouron Cassandre. This poster of 1931 (47 inches, 120cm in height) is typical of Cassandre's symbolic, yet direct approach. It is not an easy product to convey, but here the image is clear and the message immediate.

Below. In this political poster of 1948 for America's Progressive Party, the artist Ben Shahn pokes fun at rival candidates Truman (at the keys) and Dewey, engaged in a rendition of the song *A Good Man is Hard to Find*. The teeth of both men are satirically frozen in bright evenness. A prize item for a politically-minded collector.

RAILWAY

Right. Looking back to the genesis of railwayana: a hand-coloured lithograph from John Cooke Bourne's book of 1846, History and Description of the Great Western Railway, which contained fifty of his magnificent illustrative plates. This one shows the locomotive Acheron steaming into history.

Far right, top. Pierre Fix-Masseau's irresistible poster of the late Twenties was created for the French State (Etat) Railways. Its dramatic *Exactitude* told the fare-paying customer what he wanted to know about the service.

Far right, bottom. In 1937 Muneji Satomi produced this striking advertisement for Japan's railroad system. The Japanese countryside, seen from a passenger car of a train, is a blur of colour rushing past.

Around the end of World War Two the British artist William Russell Flint was discussing with his lawyer, Arthur Underwood, the question of art and investment. In this case, however, the roles of counsellor and client were reversed and it was the artist who was advising the solicitor. Flint's advice to Underwood, who was seeking guidance on extending his art collection, was to explore areas of untapped potential, areas which – while providing pleasure and aesthetic rewards for the collector – would prove to be a good investment. In effect, Flint was proposing an incursion into 'unfashionable' art.

He could have pointed generally to Victorian pictures, for the artist must have been aware that this branch of art was notably neglected and underpriced, and the post-war boom in nineteenth-century paintings and watercolour was yet to take shape. But Flint, ever a practical man, was much more specific. In a nutshell, his advice was: Put your money into nineteenth century railway prints. From the standpoint of the late 1940s, that was the same as saying: Buy tomorrow's antiques.

The fact that Underwood heeded Flint's counsel resulted in

the formation of one of the most remarkable collections of this branch of art. The huge interest aroused by the collection's dispersal at a Phillips London auction in 1977 served to underline the growth of collectors' regard for railwayana in general. America and continental Europe have their rail enthusiasts, and in large numbers. But it is in Britain, the map of which was covered by a network of lines during and after the industrial revolution, that rail fever is at its most virulent among collectors. Their interests extend practically to the present day, thanks to re-equipping and reorganization of the railways, but they have their roots in the nineteenth century.

The Stockton and Darlington line opened in 1825, but it was the 30-odd years after the opening of the Liverpool and Manchester railway in 1830 that gave hand-coloured railway prints – and other commemorative rail material – their greatest stimulus. America underwent similar experience after the imported *Stourbridge Lion* made the first successful rail trip in 1829. The period from the 1830s to the 1860s formed the basis for Underwood's magnificent collection of 200 prints. He bought diligently and wisely, choosing lithographs and engravings only of the best quality and in immaculate condition. His buying grounds were some of the leading Bond Street galleries in London, the odd one of which found itself repurchasing prints it had sold to Underwood when the collection came on the market 30 years later. Being a careful and methodical man (and a model collector), Underwood kept a ledger of his purchases, and his neat entries made fascinating reading in the aftermath of the sale. The collection had been exhibited at the Victoria and Albert Museum in London in 1974, and on that occasion the catalogue hailed the prints as imparting 'both the excitement the artists felt at the unprecedented scale of the engineering works called forth by the Railway Age and their sense of social revolution which this technological advance was about to bring about'.

It is worth examining sale prices of some items and comparing them with the amounts paid for their acquisition by Underwood. They illustrate the remarkable rise in post-war years of rail ephemera. One print stands out above many of the others as a work with all the attributes of 'collectability'. It is a hand-coloured lithograph by F. Jones and W. Spreat of Exeter and is entitled, *South Devon Railway: Landslip near the Parson and Clerk Rock between Dawlish and Teignmouth December 29th, 1852*. It happened to be the highest priced single-print lot in the sale, selling for £800/$1,200, compared with the £12.12s (about $18) which Underwood paid for it in 1958. Today, the print's value would probably be quadrupled.

There were important factors that contributed to the print's value. Firstly, it was in excellent condition and a fine piece of art: Spreat is considered to have been Devon's finest lithographer. Secondly, it depicted an interesting incident. Landslips were common on this pioneering line and the print showed passengers being shepherded from one train held up by a rock fall, around the obstruction to board a waiting train on the other side. Mishaps were, and are, news on the railways, a point underlined by the premium attached to rail postcards showing disasters on the track and produced in large numbers during the early years of this century.

Probably the best-loved British rail system of all time has been the old Great Western Railway, which carried through into the present century the tradition of fine express trains thundering from London to Bristol and points west at record-breaking speeds, and with an efficiency of service unsurpassed by any rail company in the world. Here, the outstanding nineteenth-century artist was J.C. Bourne. A fine coloured lithograph of the magnificent GWR locomotive *Acheron* steaming out of Number 1 tunnel near Bristol formed the frontispiece to Bourne's GWR portfolio, and this print commanded £230/$350 in the 1977 sale. Underwood had paid £3.3s for it in 1958.

But railwayana – or railroadiana, as some Americans call it – is not all prints. The branch lines of railway collecting hold some strange treasures. Locomotive name plates can fetch four figures at auction. Station names signs are also ready sellers. Rail notices are sought for their historical worth and sometimes for their quaintness: 'None but the Company's horses allowed to drink at this trough.' The class system and old values are in evidence. The toilet facilities on the Cheshire Lines: 'These closets are intended for the convenience of passengers only. Workmen, cabmen, fishporters and idlers are not permitted to use them. BY ORDER.' A notice to cabdrivers outside stations of .the South Eastern and Chatham Railway: 'Any Cabman skylarking or otherwise mis-conducting himself on the Managing Committee's premises or Smoking whilst his Cab is standing alongside the Platform will be required to leave the Station immediately.'

Railwayana embraces books, guides, pamphlets, tickets

(some of which sell for outrageously high sums at auction), posters, brochures, crested china and cutlery of the operating companies, uniforms, buttons, insignia, and trackside equipment such as lamps and signalling paraphernalia. And there are postcards by the ton.

America has a richly varied choice of operating equipment for collectors. High on the list is the particularly American locomotive whistle. Early whistles are very popular; they are single-throat affairs which emitted a high, piercing shriek. They were later replaced by the 'chime whistle', with a more musical note. Engine bells, which were used not only to announce departure, but in signal combination with the whistles, are expensive items. History recounts that on the first run of the 'DeWitt Clinton', the conductor blew on a little tin horn to warn of the train's departure. Where is that precious collectors' piece today? Locomotive headlights, too, are typically American. The earliest electric, and, going back in time, kerosene and whale-oil, lamps are eagerly sought. Pioneering train runs were prudently undertaken in the daylight. In 1833, Horatio Allen, foreseeing the need for night-lighting, made an experiment. He arranged for the locomotive to push two flatcars ahead of it. The first was loaded with sand, surmounted by pitch-pine knots burning brightly to illuminate the way.

In fine art, American or European, the inclusion of a railway – however distant or minor in scale compared with the spread of the canvas – is enough to place a premium on a nineteenth-century painting.

Likewise, Victorian sheet music has a cachet if it deals with a railway theme. As early as 1836, Johann Strauss paid homage to the railway in his *Eisenbahn Last Waltz*, the sheet-music cover of which portrayed one of the first locomotives in Austria. Britain later had *Express Gallop* and the rousing number, *The Great Semaphore Song – There's Danger on the Line*, which celebrated the introduction of a safer signalling system following a train accident. On a more intimate level, an Alfred Concanen cover illustrated a ditty entitled *The Charming Young Widow I Met in*

Below. Railway tickets were one of the first categories of railwayana top be collected, partly because, like stamps, they require little space. This selection of tickets is mostly from the pre-grouping (1922) companies and includes a dog ticket.

Bottom. A Great Northern Railway Absolute Block Instrument, used to ensure that only one train occupied a 'block section' at a time. The design dates from the 1880s, and examples were still in use into the 1980s.

Top left. A rare Highland Railway lamp, believed to date from the 1870s and to have been a locomotive lamp. The brass plate 'Thurso' refers to the most northerly station and engine shed in Britain.

Below left. A collector's dream is this gouache painting by Bryan de Grineau, commissioned for the 1937-38 catalogue of Hornby's toy trains. It depicts the locomotive Princess Elizabeth travelling through a small station. The picture hung in Hornby's Liverpool boardroom until 1960. In 1985 it fetched £1,760/$2,640 at auction.

the Train. Collecting rail-oriented sheet music (from *Oh, Mister Porter* to *Chatanooga Choo Choo*) would suffice for some enthusiasts; others collect the lot.

Beside the front door of the Rectory at Cadeby in Leicestershire is a board saying, 'London, Midland and Scottish Railway', serving to introduce visitors to the remarkable collection of railwayana amassed by a man of the cloth, the late Reverend E.R. 'Teddy' Boston. 'The inside of the house is decorated with paintings of trains and engines, copies of *Railway World*, labels, tickets and models. Railway ephemera are to be found in all corners – above the beds, across the piano and in the crowded library, which is also well stocked with books on railway history,' write Susanna Johnston and Tim Beddow in their delightful book on acquisitive eccentricity, *Collecting. The Passionate Pastime.*

The Rectory garden is completely occupied by rolling-stock and engines. A notice, 'Passengers must not cross the line', warns people of the huffing and puffing presence of Pixie, a two-foot gauge 0-4-0 industrial locomotive which Teddy rescued from mouldering retirement in a local quarry. *Pixie* now steams happily again. When the Reverend's railroad came into being Teddy was a bachelor. According to the authors, when he was asked how his wife had taken to a train-filled Rectory and a steaming, flowerless garden, he replies: 'Well, she went into it with her eyes open.'

Railwayana: Collector rating

Scope and variety	6
Investment potential	C
Price range	£50/$80 to five figures. Much more for live steam.

SHIPPING

An explorer in shipping collectables – or nautica as some salerooms like to call them – will come across treasure unrivalled for variety in any other area of tomorrow's antiques. The 'modern' collectables, of the last hundred years, have a noble lineage as old as ships themselves.

Marine *antiques* range in value from the millions required for superb seascapes by Dutch old masters to the 'lower-deck' prices paid for the little tokens of love made or embellished by sailors for their sweethearts – embroidered pin cushions and pictures, decorated glass rolling pins, and the like. American whaling men have contributed scrimshaw in the form of carved whalebone, and helped make this enterprising craft industry an important branch of the decorative arts. The everyday tools of sea life are gathered into the collectors' trawl: compasses, steering wheels, binnacles, sextants, telescopes, charts, chronometers, lanterns, weapons, even anchors. Rich rewards are reaped in Bond Street and Madison Avenue for ship models in ivory, bone and wood, especially the exquisite labours of Napoleonic prisoners-of-war incarcerated in English hulks, or the works of captive seamen in the American Civil War. Sightings of figureheads are so rare that only the richest museums can afford these valuable relics.

Sail has given way to steam, motor and nuclear power, and the sea is still providing treasure for the collector.

The choice is richer than ever. The passing of the ocean liners has left a fabulous heritage of shipping memorabilia. Is there anyone, given a modicum of imagination and romanticism, who does not mourn these great ships? In a jetting generation few can resist the nostalgic attractions of the days of the Blue Riband Atlantic queens, the trans-Pacific leviathans and the giant flagships ferrying empire builders East of Suez. For those born in the liner age, the images were real, very real. Whether we experienced personally the luxuries of ocean travel is beside the point. A childhood nurtured on picture books, cigarette cards, glossy brochures and newsreels of royal launchings and star-studded maiden voyages introduced us to the vernacular of a magic age.

The trade in shipping memorabilia spans many specializations. Advertisements for the pride of shipping fleets (outstanding is the *Normandie*) take their place in poster sales. Tin battleships and liners appear in toy sales (see Tin Toys on page 172). Panels and other decorations from the interiors of liners, from the 1920s to the 1950s, sell with art deco collections; the visitor to the *Forbes* toy boat fleet on Fifth Avenue, New York, is greeted in an ante-chamber graced by eight magnificent ground-glass panels designed by Jean Dupas for the *Normandie's* grand saloon. Marine painting remains in the front rank of fine art. Ephemera of all types are to be found in sales of nautica – books, brochures, passage tickets and labels, programmes of shipboard events, seamen's manuals, shipyard plans, wartime ship-spotting books, and postcards by the ton. High prices are paid for furnishings and equipment such as officers' brass-bound chests, ships' crests and decanters, divers' helmets and boots, portholes and barometers. Nothing, however, finds sharper demand than ship models.

In the heyday of the big shipping fleets the making of

HOLLAND-AMERIKA LIJN

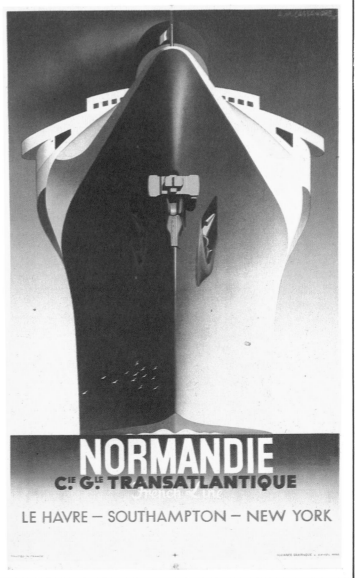

NORMANDIE
Cie G^{le} TRANSATLANTIQUE
LE HAVRE – SOUTHAMPTON – NEW YORK

Far left. Fine art on shipping themes is represented by a painting entitled *Young America* by the popular British marine artist Montague Dawson. His work has the very tang of the sea about it.

Left. A poster of 1937 for a Dutch transatlantic shipping company by Ten Broek (37 inches, 95cm in height). The artist uses the small yacht to give perspective and strength to the huge vessel. His work has important echoes of that of Cassandre, below.

Below. A towering triumph from the genius of Adolphe Mouron Cassandre in a 1935 poster created at the time of the inaugural transatlantic voyage of the French Liner *Normandie* (38 inches, 97cm in height). Nobody has ever bettered this image in trying to express the power, size and elegance of a great ship.

scale-model replicas of the famous and the lesser known vessels became a tradition. Many a big-city office of the shipping lines displayed them in their windows. Today, these magnificent models, correct in every detail and constructed of the finest materials, are all that remains of the giant liners, apart from film, photographs and drawings and the memories of an ageing generation. They have, of course, become collectors' pieces of exceptional value.

With the demise of the ocean liner, there came a lessening demand for publicity, sales, experimental and presentation models, and the craft industry was, naturally, reduced. Now, however, following the stimulation of collector interest by the appearance on the market of 'obsolete' models, a new lease of life has been given to the craft of restoring and re-creating model ships. There is a growing band of gifted amateurs, skilled in the building and restoration of both cased models (waterline and full hull) and working models run on steam or motor power for pond sailing. With developing collector interest, some people have found that their hobby is a healthy source of income and they have developed a virtual 'cottage industry', servicing a second segment of the model boat field – a small but highly specialized group of dealers catering for an international market in models old and new. Yet a third group consists of professional model-making firms undertaking construction and restoration to order.

The huge 10 to 20-footers built to grace the shipping lines' main showrooms are, generally speaking, excluded for most collectors because of their sheer size. Thus, per foot, they are relatively less expensive than more manageable cased models.

The problem of size arose in the 1970s when the P & O shipping line in London decided to sell one of its large stock of

models, a 15-footer of the *Orion*, to a private collector. There was a touch of the ship-in-a-bottle puzzle about the affair. The model, they found, was too big to be taken out of the company's building in Leadenhall Street. So how had it got in? The answer was that the model was taken to the ninth floor while the building was still being constructed. Finally, a carpenter found a method to cut the model in such a way that it could be rejoined later. When the sawing was finished a tattered piece of paper fell out bearing the names and addresses of three men who had made the model at the Vickers shipyard in Barrow-in-Furness 45 years earlier. One, 69-year-old Fred Wayles, was traced and he and his wife were given a free holiday by P & O.

Few models would exceed the *Orion* in size. As Laurence Langford, one of the world's leading model-ship collectors, puts it, 'The collector wants something he can place on his mantelpiece.' That, however, is hardly Mr Langford's own criterion. Talk to ship-model collectors anywhere in the globe and the name Langford crops up sooner or later. He is a leading London silver dealer and no one entering his silver galleries in Chancery Lane can be unaware of the proprietor's remarkable passion.

When the author went there a powerful looking Dreadnought occupied space enough in which to park a fair-sized family car. An assistant was putting the finishing touches to a display case housing a sleek destroyer of mantelpiece proportions. Masts and rigging soared above silver epergnes and coffee pots, and wooden half-models of tugboats and trawler hulls lined the walls like effigies in a mausoleum. But that was only the beginning.

Behind a steel door in the basement was the major part of the Langford fleet, case after case, piled ceiling high. He wasn't quite sure just how many models he has, but his collection can only be described as Titanic in size and comprehensiveness. He began collecting in the early 1960s. 'I was always interested in boats. My father once owned a fishing fleet and I suppose some of my interest stems from that.' His first model was a tug, which cost him less than £2. Collectors from all over the world flock to his door. However, in the nucleus of his collection there are boats he would never part with, although he constantly refines the fleet. It consists mainly of models of steamships of the twentieth

century, merchant and war.

Warships, incidentally, are more difficult to find than merchant ships, and therefore have a premium on their value. The most desirable of all, however, are models of steam yachts. There is a very simple explanation for this. By their *raison d'être* they embody luxury, therefore they offer most to the model-maker in the challenge of producing fittings of the best materials and following the details closely. Further, the model-maker indulges vicariously in the idiosyncracies of the owner or commissioner of any given yacht.

Quality of workmanship is the main factor to seek when collecting model boats. This is as true for the large builders' models, as it is for the smaller 'amateur-made' models. Such qualities demand care and protection. Models are best kept under glass because of dust. They should be maintained in an even temperature, not too dry, not too damp. Punishing central heating will burst seams and raise veneers, and strong sun or electric light will be detrimental to paintwork and fade sails.

Mr Langford said that over his collecting years he had built up a corps of gifted modellers – whom he calls his 'cottage industry' – and he uses their skills when he needs a model or fittings made to order or a particularly complicated job of restoration to be done. Restoration is a delight and a challenge to him. 'Look at that,' he said, pointing to an immaculate three-masted auxiliary sail vessel cruising on a glass-enclosed sea. 'You wouldn't believe the state in which it came to us. Masts broken, rigging in a tangle, bowsprit damaged. But 50 years ago it had been a fine model. We owed it to its original creator to make it shipshape again.'

There is one class of model, however, about which he holds very definite views when considering how far to take restoration. This is the block model – the half-boat and indeed sometimes simply a hull. They were originally made in the shipyards to act as a guide to the builders when a vessel was under construction. 'Invariably they are in poor condition,' says Mr Langford. 'After all, they received some hard wear and tear as tools of the trade. They make nice decoration, but there is not really a lot you can do with them. You can polish them up, but you should accept the nicks and bruises as part of the reason for their existence in

Far left. Scale models of vessels are rising rapidly in value, especially fine replics of warships. This is a 1:40 scale dockyard model of the British man-o'-war *Hogue* made by Vickers, the shipbuilder. The real thing was torpedoed at the beginning of World War I, her anti-torpedo nets proving to be markedly unsuccessful.

A magnificent toy boat in the *Forbes* collection – the *Tornado*, possibly by Bliss, and dating from about 1895. The vessel, made of wood, is a pull-along toy, and is remarkable for its delightful lithographed paper decoration (length 25 inches, 64cm).

the first place.' Half-boats are sometimes mounted by their owners in a mirror-backed case to give the optical illusion of a full-hulled or superstructured vessel. They are the darlings of restaurant owners and decorators. 'I am afraid,' says Mr Langford, 'that many of the mint-looking examples you see in pubs and restaurants these days are modern reproductions.'

A sophisticated extension of the half-model is the plating model, which shows the edges, butts and other details of the hull plates. Yet another type is the sectional model, with cutaway views of decks and cabins. Inevitably, however, it is to the whole scale models of ships in intricate detail that the collector pays most attention. These have an added value if the vessel represented had an interesting history or the model some special provenance.

One such model was an attractive 10-foot replica of the *Asama Maru*, a pre-war trans-Pacific liner of the Nippon Yusen Kabushiki Kaisha shipping line. Although it plied normally in peacetime between Tokyo and San Francisco, the outbreak of the war with Japan found the vessel in European waters. It was carrying Japanese nationals home from Europe when it was boarded off the coast of Ireland by sailors from an Irish navy vessel (among the crew of which was the writer and humourist Patrick Campbell). The liner was allowed to proceed, but later

in the war it was torpedoed and sunk by an American submarine while it was ferrying troops in the Pacific.

In the London offices of the Japanese shipping company there remained, however, the superb builder's model of the *Asama Maru*, and this was seized by the British government as enemy property after the outbreak of hostilities. It then had a somewhat chequered career, eventually being given to the First Carshalton Sea Scouts in Surrey. After the war, the scouts, anxious to raise funds for camping equipment, tried unsuccessfully to sell the model back to the reconstituted Japanese shipping company. Finally, many years later, they sent the ship for auction at Phillips in London. The Asama Maru joined the fleet of Laurence Langford.

Shipping: Collector rating

Scope and variety	10
Investment potential	B
Price range	£100/$200 to six figures

SMOKING

It looks like a dolls'-house-size garden temple and is made of porcelain resting on a wooden plinth. In the base is an electrical apparatus which provides the essential spark to enable the Temple of Vesta – for so this edifice is named – to perform its function. Through intricate machinery and piping sourced inside the building, the spark is united with a stream of hydrogen, and flames issue from the mouth of a brass lion which sits at the temple door. There, sir, you have a light for your cigar.

The Temple of Vesta came to the Science Museum, London, in 1937, as part of the Bryant and May collection of implements which preceded the production of the company's own safety matches. It dates from 1807 and is one of the world's first table lighters. But standing 20 inches (50cm) tall and filled with glass flasks of hydrochloric acid, to generate hydrogen, the temple had obvious mobility limitations as a smoker's companion. Indeed, this push-button wonder was meant to stand on a tobacconist's counter or in a gentlemen's club. Lighters, perforce, had to become more portable.

From the early pocket tinderbox to the slimline ignition of the microchip age, the lighter has had an evolutionary descent that fascinates collectors of smoking antiques. Our collecting field is the twentieth century, and it has endless variety.

In 1907 a small business was opened at Duke Street in fashionable St James's, London, by Alfred Dunhill, the entrepreneurial patriarch of a family dynasty whose shops now span the world. His store sold tobacco, cigars and pipes and a large range of smokers' requisites. On the subject of the manufactured artefact, Alfred's stated maxim to his suppliers, staff and customers, was: 'It must be useful. It must work dependably. It must be beautiful. It must last. It must be the best of its kind.' From that time onward, Dunhill lighters met these criteria, and they are among the most cherished smokers' antiques of tomorrow.

The oldest Dunhill lighter in existence is the prototype for the company's first model, called the Unique, which was mounted on a Colman's mustard tin. Watch lighters were among the early best-sellers and catalogues of the 1920s show several of this type. The selling power was epitomized in two undoubted attractions: one-hand operation and first-time lighting. For collectors' dating purposes, lighters of the Twenties have single-wheel action. Any lighter with double-wheel action would almost certainly be post-1930.

After a depressed beginning to the decade, the 1930s were to produce lighters in vast variety. Dunhill's last catalogue before the war shows a lighter in the guise of a stick of bamboo, another in the form of a leatherette-covered book entitled *The Light*, a tinder pistol and a Roman lamp. Earlier, in 1934, a table lighter appeared as a longcase clock, a museum piece today. Alongside these way-out novelties, however, the Dunhill legacy has given us a series of 1930s finely designed, functional lighters of convenient dimensions for pocket or purse. The Tallboy for ladies, and the Broadboy for gentlemen are two names that indicate marketing directions.

Ronson was busy, too, in the 1930s. Early on the scene were pencil format lighters, selling for just over £1. The firm turned to art deco forms for smokers' table sets, with chrome figures of dancers and swimmers. One table lighter cum cigarette box sometimes turns up in the contents of dolls' houses – it is modelled in the form of a very convincing cocktail bar, a desirable piece of smokers' *kitsch*.

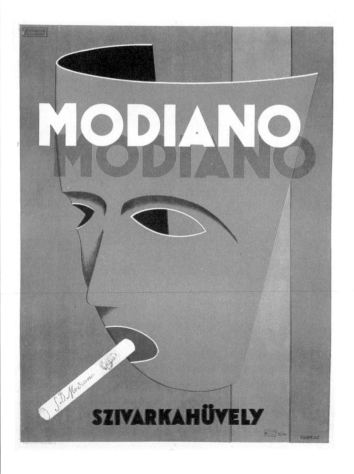

Below. A bold and effective poster for Hungarian Modiano cigarettes, something of a smoking-collector's rarity designed by Istvan Farkas about 1920.

Right. Job's cigarette papers are advertised in this poster of 1912 by Leonetto Cappiello, an Italian-born artist who created posters in Paris for 40 years, mostly in this century. His image conjures up opulence and exclusiveness.

Below. A tin dating from before World War Two which contained Sarony's cigarettes. The lid is designed as a game of roulette. The tin appears in a version some 11 inches (28cm) long and in another version just over half the size.

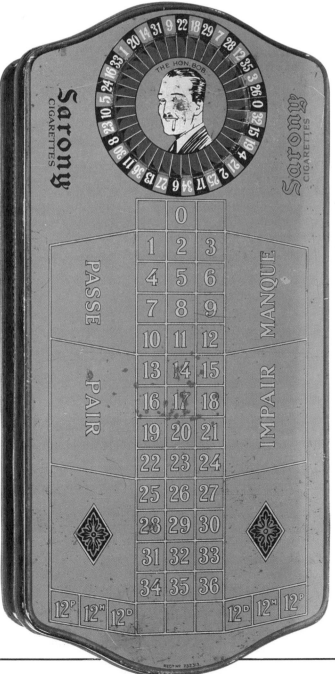

Novelty reigned again after the war, but not until times became less austere in the 1950s. A collected item is the Dunhill Aquarium, a table lighter in hand-carved Perspex which appears to contain miniature fish and water plants. It is found with a silver-plated top or with touches of gold fittings. There is also the Aviary in which miniature tropical birds seem to be captured. The Aviary did not match the sales success of the Aquarium; relatively few were made, thus underwriting its present-day rarity value. Novelties came to the end of their era when British purchase tax laws taxed them as 'models', and the age of the modern slimline dawned.

American lighters have a rich background. Shortly after Japan was opened to American and European trade in the 1850s, Japanese craftsmen started making tiny and precise adaptations of the flintlock mechanism for egg-shaped pocket lighters. These were among the first Japanese exports and acquiring them is a passion with some American collectors today.

The first American-made fluid and flint lighter is believed to have been the Koopman Magic Pocket Lamp, patented in 1889. It was an automatic, instantaneous firemaker. When a knob on the side was pressed the lid flew back and a spark ignited a wick. The fuel was alcohol. Grains of a synthetic flint composition were spaced around a paper disc which revolved against a sharp steel point to strike the spark. A packet of replaceable discs was provided with each lighter. Several lighters in the shape of pocket watches came out in the United States during the 1890s. In 1907 there was patented an ingenious American lighter of a type that was still being made in recent years by the New Method Company of Bradford, Pennsylvania – tomorrow's antiques in current use today. Working on the principle of catalysis, the lighter has a cylindrical wick wet with high-grade alcohol. When a particle of sponge platinum (the catalyst) is introduced into the chamber containing the wick, the thin film of pure oxygen which always surrounds platinum combines with the alcohol vapour to produce flame which lights the wick.

During the last fifty years, pocket and table lighters have been produced in hundreds of fascinating shapes, and nowhere more so than in the United States. They have an obvious appeal to collectors. Clubs and swop meets for enthusiasts of smoking paraphernalia proliferate, and hundreds of specialist dealers have set up shop to cater for the passion. Pipe collectors are legion. Cigarette and cigar lighters have a similar following of *aficionados*. The author is reliably informed that Anthony Donofrio put his barber shop in Hackensack on the collectors' map of New Jersey by stocking its shelves with a large and splendid hoard of cigarette lighters, the source of much wonder and pleasure to his patrons.

Cigarette cards are dealt with elsewhere in this book, as are posters and other advertising ephemera dealing with tobacco. There are thousands of different types of cigar label (and box), which attract their own following of collectors. The delights of cigarette packets, of which this century has provided a multitude of designs, are expressed enthusiastically in the words of Sam A. Cousley, writing for the American magazine of collecting, *Spinning Wheel*: '... the colourful cardboard type which held Turkish Trophies, Hassans, Helmars, and Egyptian Deities of the early 1900s; Melachrinos, Makaroffs, Moguls, English Ovals, and London Lifes of World War I years; and the 50-pack tins and 20-pack paper wrappers of such well-known smokes of the 1920s as Omars, Fatimas, Lucky Strikes, Camels, and Chesterfields.' Nor can we forget the old green Woodbine and Players packets of Britain and the wartime Victory V rations. Will tomorrow's collectors of smoking memorabilia judge dates from the progressive severity of health-department warnings on the packet and advertising?

Ashtrays have progressed through every successive decorative art style of the twentieth century. Take your choice from the bar-counter tin variety to the highly-valued glass products of Gallé and the millionaire's 'stocking-fillers' bought at Tyffany's. Match, or vesta, cases bring big money at British silver auctions when hallmarked by the masters of Birmingham. Enamelled art deco versions, often bearing a saucy design, are always sure of a ready sale. And there is a keen following for what Sam Cousley describes as cigarette-smokers' 'vest pocket roll-your-own devices'. These 'utilised grain tobacco such as Bull Durham and Duke's Mixture, and Riz la Croix papers. They were widely advertised for smokers who preferred "home-mades" to "tailor-mades", but did not "possess the manual dexterity to twist their own", even with two hands. Any western cowboy, of course, could roll beautiful smokes with one hand while galloping his cayuse across the prairie.'

Twentieth-century tobacco jars and humidors, cigarette and cigar cases, boxes and holders, cigar cutters and piercers, smokers' cabinets, tobacconists' rasps and other tools, even cigarette-dispensing machines, are all finding their way into modern collections. A splendid example of a cigar cutter, intended for use on the tobacconist's counter, is a glass fixture supplied in America during the early half of this century by the manufacturers of Muriel mild-blend Havana cigars. Inside are rotating knives powered by clockwork; a key is attached at the back for winding. By placing the end of the cigar in a hole on top of the machine, the knife is activated, cutting the tip off the cigar. Above the hole is a printed warning emphasizing the fact that smoking can damage your health in more ways than one: 'Do Not Stick Finger Into Cutter'.

At its least expensive level, collecting smoking memorabilia can consist of amassing free book matches. It can rise into the region of six figures, however, when considering the decorative, life-size figures which stood outside tobacco and snuff shops to signify the nature of their business. In Britain the highland

Below. A rather quaint smoker's accessory of the 1930s, in the era when the symbol of the motor car was very much a part of the fashionable whirl. The cigarette box was an important "prop" of the social scene and often mirrored Art Deco forms.

Bottom. A selection of Dunhill *Unique* lighters from 1925 to 1930. Alfred Dunhill invented this lighter using a Colman's mustard tin for the prototype. It was one of the first lighters that could be operated with one hand.

Right. A collection of meerschaum pipes, some of which go back into the realm of true antiques (meerschaum is a type of white clay particularly suitable for use as the bowls of pipes). Animal forms, such as the horse, dog, rhinoceros and elephant, are particularly attractive to collectors. Late Victorian images of royalty and politicians and American pipes of the early twentieth century representing presidents are fast appreciating in value. A variation on the pipe is the smaller, cheroot-holder which is also commonly found in meerschaum.

Scottish soldier was popular; there also and in Continental Europe were sometimes to be found large models of black-amoors, smoking pipes and wearing headdresses of tobacco leaves; America, of course, had its famous cigar-store Indians. These belong generally to the realm of true antiques – although a modern, skilfully carved reproduction would still be an indulgence of a wealthy collector.

The department of ephemera offers sheet music covers on smoking themes: song titles such as *No Smoking Allowed*, *The Cigar Divan*, the *Hookah Polka*; and from France: *Ma Pipe et Ma Femme*, *Ma Cigarette* and *Vive Le Tabac* (My Pipe and My Wife, My Cigarette, Long Live Tobacco). It also offers tracts both in favour of and against smoking. In our time, perhaps, smoking may become an obsolete or extremely rare fashion. Who knows? Certainly the ephemera of controversy – 'anti' publicity by government agencies and interested organizations, ripostes by the tobacco lobby – will be a part of collecting for tomorrow's students.

The more strident factions of the anti-smoking lobby have often been accused of hysterical invective and hyperbole. Even they, however, fail to match the acrid oratory of some campaigners of the past. 'Tobacco-drinking', as Philaretes, an English pamphleteer of 1601, termed smoking, had the effect of 'tasting and savouring much of the loathsome fume and duskish smoake which riseth and steemeth up to the braine by the roof and pallate of the mouth, first sent thither through the Tabacco pipe full charged with tabacco dust, and afterward scorched and incinerated by the extreme heate of the parching fire'. An eminent contemporary, King James I, published his *Counterblaste to Tobacco* in which he described smoking as, 'A custom lothsome to the eye, hatefull to the Nose, harmefull to the braine, dangerous to the Lungs, and in the blacke stinking fume therof, neerest resembling the horrible Stigian smoke of the pit that is bottomelesse.'

In the interests of historical balance, however, any collection of smoking memorabilia should include a record of the views of the great French playwright, Molière (1622-73): 'There's nothing like tobacco; it is the passion of all decent men; a man who lives without tobacco does not deserve to live.'

Smoking: Collector rating	
Scope and variety	7
Investment potential	C
Price range	From free book matches to six figures for a cigar-store Indian

SPORT

Right. Framed with other American baseball memorabilia is the Casey Stengel Baseball Hall of Fame ring, presented to the great star in 1966. The ring is gold, with a silver baseball set on a black onyx panel. Stengel's dynamic baseball career spanned a period of 63 years. Phillips in New York sold the ring for $18,700 (£12,400) in 1987.

A Wall Street securities dealer is working out his bidding strategy for a baffy, an Australian lawyer and a South African entrepreneur have both set their sights on a cleek, a Japanese computer tycoon has a yen for a gutty, and the agent of a Scottish dealer is weighing his chances of going home with a feathery. There are trouble-irons, hole-makers, rubberies, Colonels and dimples. Every branch of collecting cloaks itself in the mysteries of jargon. Golfing memorabilia seems to have more than most. The scene is the Phillips saleroom at Chester, which has a specialization in golf collectables. Despite the deep freeze of January 1987, golf devotees have converged on this north of England city from five continents to pay hard cash for the detritus of history's golf matches.

The afternoon sees some remarkable strokes, none more bold than the world record £5,000, or nearly $8,000, paid by the Scot's agent for a Victorian feathery golf ball, a tiny sphere of stitched leather into which William Gourlay, ball-maker, compressed enough chicken feathers to fill a top hat. Some old hands are amazed. An underbidder, Mort Olman, of The Old Golf Shop, Cincinnati, America's top dealer in the subject, remarks: 'I paid £1,700 [$2,500] for one last year and that was too much. Today's price was just plain crazy.' In the *Liverpool Echo* columnist Walter Huntley declares he is baffled: 'Of course, it's a very special golf ball, a 19th century Gourlay

feathery, which probably means as much to you as it does to me. Whoever bought it is obviously never going to use it on the links. I mean, imagine losing it in the rough the first time out!' Even the Phillips golf specialist, Robert Gowland (a former captain of Middlesex Colts who describes himself now as 'an occasional weekend golfer who happily plays off at 13'), admits: 'We were confident that the world record would be broken but this price is fantastic – absolutely unbelievable.'

The unbelievable tends to become the routine in golf sales. Certain clubs have reached almost the record price of the feathery. The 'amazed' Mort Olman has himself often been in the role of the 'amazer', paying, for example, nearly £17,000/ $25,000 for *Golfiana*, a tiny book of golfing poems, at a sale in Glasgow on the eve of Scotland's Open Golf Championship. The book's capture delighted Olman. 'This is the first one ever to come to sale. A real rarity,' he chuckled. 'Mind you, I didn't buy it for myself – not for that kind of money.' Big bids at golf auctions are often handled by agents acting for anonymous clients. One gathers the impression of a coterie of shy, mysterious addicts amassing treasure hoards of golfing memorabilia, and never blabbing about their collections at the nineteenth hole.

They have an eclectic shopping list. Baffy spoons are mid-nineteenth century applewood clubs used for lofting. There

Left. A rare pair of 19th century
Staffordshire figures of cricketers –
believed to be William Caffyn and
George Parr – depicting batsman and
bowler. Many other sporting types are
found in Staffordshire ornaments.

Below. A pencil and watercolour
original done for the magazine *Vanity
Fair* by Sir Leslie Ward, known as
'Spy'. It depicts a sterling character
whom the artist dubbed 'The Demon
Bowler'. A cricket enthusiast paid
$2,400/$3,600 in 1985.

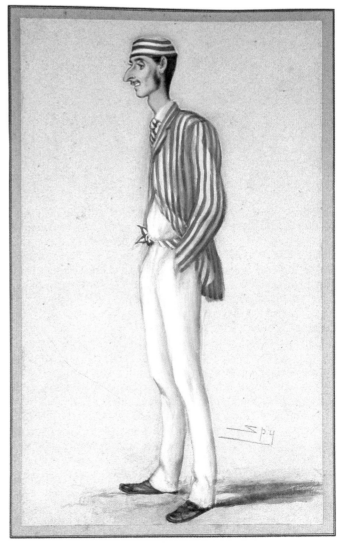

are cleeks, or driving irons, of 1880-90. Trouble-irons were made to the golfer's specifications and were used to extricate the player from a difficult position. The feathery was superseded by the gutty ball, composed of moulded gutta-percha, which flew better because of improved aerodynamics. Rubber-core, dimple and Colonel balls are all variations of type. A hole-maker is just that, an instrument which was part of the equipment of the Keeper of the Green, sporting a mahogany handle, wrought-iron shaft and a metal cylinder for hole-boring.

In addition to balls, clubs, books and pictures, golfing memorabilia embraces many other items. Metalware includes trophies, mugs, lighters, ashtrays, cigarette cases, tankards, desk sets, photo frames, spoons, brooches, watches, tiepins, medals and statuettes – all bearing emblems of the game. Similarly, ceramics and glass recall golf in a variety of guises and functions. The same is true, of course, for relics of cricket, tennis, horse-racing and, to a lesser extent, football and baseball. And in each sport, twentieth-century artefacts are scoring well in the salerooms.

Cricket collectables attract buyers from every part of the world where it is played. Sales devoted to this subject – or even sports memorabilia generally – were unknown before the closing years of the 1970s when Phillips in London pioneered this collecting connection. Cricket prices have now steadied to a gradual and reliable plane of appreciation after some early, dramatic ups and downs. One anecdote is worth retelling because it reflects a common trend in newly discovered fields of collecting.

There is a London public house in 'newspaper land' where it isn't cricket to mention W.G. Grace, the hallowed nineteenth-century giant of the game. After the first auction of cricketana, the news reached mine host through that afternoon's newspapers and radio that a humble cast-iron pub table – of the sort made prior to the turn of the century and for many years afterwards – had sold for the then remarkable price of nearly £300/$450. It owed its high price to the fact that it bore the facial effigy of W.G.

Top. Golfing ceramics, from left to right: a Doulton Lambeth stoneware jug; a modern Continental porcelain bowl, the centre showing a painted figure of a golfer; a Spode pottery mug.

Right. A group of cigarette cards, 'Golf Terms', issued in 1900 by Clarke's cigarette company of Liverpool and London. Sample 'terms': 'A scratch player' – golfer looking for the ball scratches his head; 'An uneven match' – small man and large, formidable nagging wife. Gems like these sometimes turn up in job-lots of less valuable cigarette cards.

Far right. Pottery figures of a soccer player with a ball at his feet and a goalkeeper in mid-action date from the 1920s-30s and were made in Czechoslovakia. After trailing a long way behind golf, cricket and even tennis collectables, soccer has finally come into its own as a specialized area of collecting with much to offer.

on each of the iron knees of the table legs: pub tables usually sport a female face there. On receiving the news, the pub landlord quickly realized that he had at least a dozen potential money-makers standing around his bar. They were quickly whisked upstairs and at opening time customers were met by an array of kitchen and makeshift tables. Even through years of patronage, most regulars hadn't noticed W.G., anyway, and those who had – and were aware of the auction news – were met with stony rebuttals if they made offers to buy.

Alas, however, for the landlord if he entertained hopes of getting rich. The saleroom can be an unpredictable field and the game of collecting sporting memorabilia can produce a very tricky wicket. When a similar W.G. Grace pub table appeared in the next cricket sale some months later, the price fell by half.

For mine host, there are certain lessons to be learned from this experience. In a newly found and rapidly moving collecting field, an auction price is by no means always a barometer of value or a guide to what a similar item might fetch next time. The first-time buyer of the pub table was a former Ceylon cricketer who had played against England and who wanted the memento a little more desperately than his underbidder. Neither man was present at the second sale. Secondly, in cricket and other sporting collectables, or for that matter any comparatively new

scene, the rarity of an object cannot be defined until it has been pulled out of the shadows and exposed to collector interest. One 'rare' item appearing in the headlines can bring out many more. If a dozen 'rare' tables turn up in one pub, how many dozens more are there in pubs across the village greens of England?

Several magazine and newspaper accounts of the vogue in cricket collectables talked, in those early seasons, about an apparent dearth in variety considering the enormous popularity of the game in the English world over the last two centuries. The time is long past for these pundits to reassess their views. Cricket memorabilia ranges from porcelain to ephemera, from furniture to silver, and includes books, textiles, bronzes, marble, advertising items and, of course, cricket bats themselves (buying autographed bats at auction need not be an expensive operation: they often cost less than a new bat in a sports shop). When a sport specialist is researching the lots making up a sale, he or she will tell you that the preparations involve discussions with practically every departmental specialist in the auction house, showing all too clearly that the great game covers most of the known branches of art and antiques.

Cricket bidders are by far the healthiest looking people who regularly attend the London salerooms – sunbronzed to a man. Like any other branch of collecting, they have their 'mad collector' stories – like the addict who paid more than £4,000/$6,000 for an incomplete run of *Wisden* cricket annuals, merely to obtain two editions which he was missing from his otherwise complete set back home on his library shelves. There are also the hopeless cases who call their homes *Silly Mid-On*, *The Crease* and other names borrowed from cricket field vernacular.

Tennis has now come into its own, with many decorative items such as jewellery or ornaments surpassing the value levels achieved by similar pieces with a cricket theme. Fishing and shooting have their followers, with special sections of sporting sales being devoted to these subjects.

'Fan' memorabilia is pouring out at a phenomenal rate for the millions of sports followers. When Yankee Stadium in New York City began renovations in 1973, there was such a large demand for souvenirs that the company in charge of the works sold lockers, uniforms, seats, ticket drums and other equipment on a departmental store basis. Pictures of famous baseball players who had appeared there were sold for from £100 to £230 ($150-$350). Fans scrambled for blown-up photographs such as one of Don Larson's last pitch in his 1956 World Series win over the Brooklyn Dodgers, or one of Hank Bauer sliding home in the 1953 series. On the final day of the 1973 season at the stadium, each member of the audience present to see the Yankees play the Detroit Tigers was presented with a long-playing phonograph record especially made for the day, entitled *Great Moments at Yankee Stadium*. These records are far from rare, since there were 32,238 fans there on that day (they watched the Yankees go down by 8 to 5).

Baseball bats manufactured with facsimile signatures of famous hitters are a common find in collecting circles. Beginners should be wary of these. Even an old bat may be signed in facsimile. The A.G. Spalding & Brothers catalogue for 1912 lists such bats for sale at $1 each; they bear the signatures of Larry Doyle, Harry H. Davis, Frank W. Schulte and other 'greats'.

Among the handsomest of baseball souvenirs are the top-quality items produced as presentation gifts. There is an elaborate bronze ashtray in the form of Shea Stadium, New York, issued for presentation at the 1964 dedication of the field. Members of the winning World Series teams receive a souvenir, usually a ring nowadays. The ring awarded to the 1969 'Miracle' New York Mets was heavily embossed, with a view of Shea. The gold, silver and black onyx ring presented to Casey Stengel in 1966 when he was inducted into the Baseball Hall of Fame at Cooperstown, New York (opened 1939), came up for auction at Phillips New York in 1987 among many other baseball mementoes. It sold for nearly £12,600/$19,000.

Fans at the auction were faced with a wide range of baseball memorabilia. A group of 12 lithographed paper baseball players, circa 1887, were in the £200-£350/$300-$500 class. A baseball sporting 'Babe' Ruth's signature and those of team-mates in the 1943 Yankees season scored £730/$1,100 (in fact, signed balls were more common than signed bats). There was an unusual radio, some 9 inches (22cm) high, modelled in the form of a baseball (£600/$900). Paintings and cartoons mirrored the sport in jokes and team-rousing chauvinism. For the armchair player, there was a coin-operated 'Hit a Homer' baseball game – '5 balls for 1c' – with a painted glass front and a lithographed diamond and stadium background; a snip at £330/$500.

Truly American is the sport of collecting decoy ducks, carved figures, usually in the form of a waterfowl or shorebird, used to lure live birds within shooting range. The Atlantic coast from Massachusetts to the Carolinas, and the inland region between St Louis and Chicago are the two principal areas where the birds were created. They differ from region to region, from carver to

carver, even from factory to factory (for mechanically produced decoys are recognized collector fodder, too). Consider the fact that there are about twenty species of native US ducks (and the drake and duck have different plumage), and many species of geese and other birds, and you begin to realize what a huge variety of decoy decorative art is theoretically available.

The most celebrated collection of bird decoys was that of William J. Mackey, Jr, author of the standard *American Bird Decoys*. At the time of his death in 1972 he had somewhere near 3,000 bird decoys. When his flock was dispersed in a series of auctions, the price of £7,000/$10,500 was obtained for a Hudsonian curlew carved by William Bowman. Values today have soared way out of sight of those 1972 levels.

For sheer volume of collecting, however, the palm must be awarded to the American enthusiasts of sports cards. These have been issued for nearly a century with cigarettes, newspapers, marbles, soft drinks, foods and chewing gum. Especially chewing gum. The statistics are impressive. In 1972 when an estimated one billion cards were issued, the Topps Chewing Gum Company of Brooklyn alone accounted for 250 million baseball cards. Collectors hate tricks such as that played on them by one gum-producing company in the 1940s: it skip-numbered its card sets (1, 2, 3, 6, 7, 9, etc) so that children aiming for complete sets would go on buying its bubble gum, forever seeking non-existent cards. Such tricks apart, it is not unusual for a present-day collector to have half a million cards – which emphasizes the truism that availability, like rarity, can sometimes add sauce to collecting.

Sport: Collector rating

Scope and variety	9
Investment potential	A
Price range	£20/$40 to six figures

TEDDY BEARS

Above. Teddy bears trace their lineage back to 1902. In bear terms, therefore, this anonymous specimen is only in the prime of middle age and therefore cannot hope to command the prices achieved by the veterans. Collectors look for telltale signs of re-stitching and re-stuffing, replaced pads and reconditioned growlers.

No teddy bear is strictly antique until at least the year 2002. Some early bear toys, possibly; teddies, no. While yet some years away from their centenary, teddy bears are being researched, catalogued, traded, and displayed in collections, both private and museum, with the solemnity accorded to fine antiques. A short time ago few, if any, entered the salerooms. People feeling the pinch would part with the family silver, a *Stag at Bay*, even grannie's trousseau, but the resident bear was rarely sent packing. Now bears are coming out of the woods in their hundreds, to be sold to the highest bidder. Their days as a protected species were numbered once the saleroom limelight fell fully upon them in the 1980s. On the international range, where American hunters dominate with dollar firepower, the rare veterans began to make £200/$300 apiece, then double that amount, and next they were into four figures. In the space of three years the highest recorded price soared from around £1,000 to £5,500 ($1,500 to $8,000). 'What! For a *teddy*?' people would ask – and rush upstairs to rummage in the attic.

Go backstage in the collectors' department of any major fine art auction house where, on shelves tiered to the ceiling, snooty French fashion dolls rub shoulders with googly-eyed American cuties, and horned phonographs are jumbled with ancient typewriters and busts of Queen Victoria – and you will find row upon row of grumpy-looking teddies awaiting the hammer.

The oldest can be little more than 80. In 1902 the American President, Theodore (Teddy) Roosevelt, was involved in a 'referee' capacity in a boundary dispute between Mississippi and Louisiana. He was cartooned by Clifford Berryman in the *Washington Star* as a hunter (a role he followed passionately), refusing to shoot an appealing, button-eyed bear cub, which represented the easy political option, a soft way out.

An enterprising Brooklyn toymaker, Morris Michtom, founder of the Ideal Toy Corporation of America, produced a cuddly toy in brown plush and, one story goes, obtained permission from the faintly bemused president to call it after him. Permission or not, Michtom displayed the toy and the cartoon together with the slogan 'Teddy's Bear', a name that later changed to *teddy bear*. The most famous, the most prolific toy was born. Today, there are reputed to be 140 million bears in America. In Britain 65 homes out of every 100 are said to have a resident teddy. There are bear clubs, meets, fairs. And picnics. President Reagan and Pope John Paul have declined to lend out their bears to these showy events; Mrs Thatcher, on the other hand, has allowed her bear Humphrey to grace a good cause; Princess Anne has also lent out her teddy.

The source of much of the teddy bear mania can be traced to a toy factory at Giengen, near Ulm in Germany. The Steiff family had a thriving business there making stuffed toys at the time of the Roosevelt affair. Margarete Steiff, a resourceful, indefatigable worker despite being confined to a wheelchair because of polio, saw a copy of the cartoon. She exhibited her own make of bears at the Leipzig Fair in 1903: an American buyer ordered 3,000. Steiff bears are today the most highly prized by collectors, especially by those in the United States. Among them are the aristocratic, world-record breakers.

The most desirable bear in collector terms is not the rounded, fluffy fellow that dominates the modern toyshop market. Early Steiffs are ungainly bears with long limbs and paws, pointed noses, piercing shoe-button eyes and a hump on the back. The hump was modelled on the grizzly, say some collectors. This is

Left. With early tin toys for company, these two teddy bears represent England (on the left) and Germany. The German bear is from the Steiff factory and although he is only about half the size of the English one he is worth about £500/$750, well over twice the price of the larger animal. Steiffs are consistently the leaders in the saleroom stakes.

Below left. An unusual mink teddy bear of modern manufacture. Despite being mink, however, he cannot emulate the prices of the battered, threadbare octogenarians.

Below. A good Steiff bear of the early years, practically guaranteed to top four figures if he enters auction. Vast amounts of Steiff animals were exported from Germany to the United States.

unlikely: it was merely where the stuffing of straw was finished off in the early days. After Margarete Steiff's death in 1909 improved techniques eliminated this characteristic feature.

Steiff just couldn't make enough bears to satisfy demand: 12,000 in 1904, nearly one million three years later. The plush for the German teddies (at first called 'Friend Petz' in their homeland) traditionally came from British manufacturers in Yorkshire, and it wasn't long before Britain was producing its own bears.

British and American bears had flatter features, more rounded bodies and limbs. They gradually moved away from the angular look of the Teutonic Teds, some of which had snarling mouths with rows of frightening wooden teeth. In 1909, with the bear craze sweeping America, you could buy just about everything either made into a teddy or decorated with a teddy: teddy bear tea sets, party games, penny banks, postcards, paper dolls, balloons, clothing, blankets, rugs, and so on. The Fast Black Skirt Company produced an 'Electric Bright Eye' teddy whose eyes lit up white on red when a paw was shaken. Strauss made a 'self-whistling' species. A rare collectors' item is the 'Bear-Baby' from Louis S. Schiffer of New York, in 1914: its head had a teddy bear face on one side and the bisque face of a baby doll on the other. In World War One Britain's Harwin and Company supplied the juvenile war effort with soldier, sailor and airman bears and a teddy dressed as a nurse.

Collectors argue about the sex of teddies: the consensus is that they are, generally male. It is interesting to note that in the first decade of the century the bears were widely advertised as a suitable toy for boys, corresponding to the doll for girls. However, manufacturers soon found that little girls were abandoning their dolls in favour of the teddy bear. An attempt to

push Barbara Bears in the inter-war years just did not catch on.

What is it that puts a price on an old bear's head? Mainly, age and rarity. Condition counts, of course, though a mint teddy bear is a scarce individual. Saleroom cataloguers sometimes use the description 'well loved'. At other times, the faults are more explicitly expressed: '... plush worn on belly, thigh and head; moth holes in feet; distressed paws showing stuffing; re-stitched back of neck; growler defective ...'. Bear-spotters are wary of replaced pads and eye buttons, repaired stitching, signs of re-stuffing or the lack of adequate stuffing, overworn plush. Judging the fitness of a bear has become a minor science, which is hardly surprising considering that even some models of the 1930s are well into three figure values, and that some 1950s and 1960s bears have begun to shine in the saleroom charts.

With the prospect of five-figure auction prices at stake, the fakers have moved in. Steiff's 'hallmark' is known as the *Knopf im Ohr*, or button in the ear: a tiny hexagonal metal trademark disc that was lightly attached inside one ear. Anyone attempting to make a bogus Bruin into a 'genuine' Steiff is tempted to obtain or fake this button and stitch it in the ear. Paradoxically, the existence of this button should be the first 'check' sign to an expert: children's fingers tended to pluck out these discs and few Steiffs have retained them down the years. Imposters have a tough time getting through a specialist's scrutiny.

Joan Dunk is a middle-aged London lady who began amassing her 300-plus collection in 1952. 'On my front door is a knocker with the letters HRETB,' she says. 'Some friends gave it to me. It means Home for Retired and Elderly Teddy Bears. I started picking them up when I saw people destroying them. I never liked dolls. Teddy bears are different. As collectables they're lovables – I mean, you can't cuddle postage stamps.'

Above. A friendly Steiff specimen obligingly shows us all the characteristics of an old and valuable bear: ungainly limbs, long pads on the paws, and a hump on the back where the early makers were unable to finish off the stuffing neatly.

Far left, top. This picnic consists of bears from the Steiff factory, with the exception of the jaunty soldier character which is an early mechanical novelty from the German firm of Schuco. They were photographed in 1986 shortly before the two largest bears made (left to right) £2,200/$3,300 and £3,080/$4,620 at auction.

Far left. The pale plush teddy bear dates from around the end of World War One and is probably English. The teddy bear industry built up gradually in Britain after a period in which cloth for German bears had been supplied by factories in Yorkshire.

Teddy bears: Collector rating

Scope and variety	6
Investment potential	B
Price range	£20/$40 to five figures

THEATRE

Scarecrow just flopped down in a heap on the floor and took his ease; what did a bit of dust matter to a costume that was meant to look like a rag bag anyway? Lion simply had to swish his tail out of the way to sit down and sip his coffee through his whiskers. But Tin Man found it *very* difficult, clanking and rattling as he tried to make himself more comfortable. 'Careful,' shouted the director, Ron Knee. 'That costume could be a collectors' item in a few years' time.'

We were sitting backstage at the Whitehall Theatre in Whitehall, London, in the coffee break during fittings and rehearsal for the Christmas show *Wizard of Oz*. Ron Knee had invited this author round to talk about one of his passions – keeping alive the live theatre by collecting and preserving the memories of shows gone by. Plays and players have their part, but also the tinsel and glitter of musicals and pantomime, that very British of Christmas institutions, a never-ending encore.

'A few years ago at a Hollywood sale they sold the shoes that Judy Garland wore along the Yellow Brick Road in the film of *Oz*. I wish I'd bought them,' said Knee wistfully. 'Take Tin Man's suit, for example. Look at it. It's a work of art. Made up literally of tin cans, 57 varieties. Now that could end up in a collection, though it's doubtful. You see, props tend to be too big or bulky to store or display for most collectors, so we concentrate on things like playbills, programmes, music scores, pictures, postcards and all that.' He pointed upwards to the flies at the biggest prop in the show, a gigantic balloon in which Dorothy would return from Oz. 'That's what I call a real collectors' piece. But who on earth has got room for it?'

Costume collecting is a tricky area, he reckons. There is little to be found dating from before the nineteenth century simply because in the old days there was no uniformity of style or period in the dressing of productions: actors provided their own costumes. Even when costumes were specially made for shows, they were, understandably, seldom made to last. Nevertheless, costumes designed by the 'greats' such as Erté – magnificent, richly decorated extravaganzas – are the stars of a theatrical collection, and are priced accordingly.

That the quality of theatrical costume has improved immeasurably was proved when Phillips sold stock of Britain's National Theatre, on the stage in London in 1986. Most were beautifully fashioned clothes of excellent, durable materials – durable because many of them have to suffice for more than one production and at other times they pay for themselves by being hired out to theatrical companies all over Britain. Preliminaries for the sale went on in a series of brightly-lit, white-painted tunnels underneath the rail commuters' platforms of Waterloo Station. Here in these make-believe vaults are the ghosts of 100,000 heroes, heroines, supporting roles and spear-carriers. Hiawatha was prepared for a strange ritual undreamt of by Longfellow; Cinderella and the Ugly Sisters were spruced up for their night of nights; Macbeth rehearsed an unscripted walk-on; and '17 assorted sheep', Don Quixote's tilting fodder, were herded for transfer to new pastures. Their lot was auction. Selected costumes from National Theatre productions going back to the 1960s were destined to be sold to raise funds for theatre projects. The range of buyers – the intervention of a

Far left. Only one hundred copies were produced of this 1895 poster by Lautrec for May Milton's show-business tour of America. The poster was apparently never used. These facts – added to the Lautrec cachet – make it eminently collectable material for present-day enthusiasts of the theatre.

Left. A magnificent poster by Alphonse Mucha advertising both the book *Princess Hyacinth* and a Czech performance of a ballet pantomime of the same name. Some specialists regard this as among the very finest work produced by Mucha. He designed the poster in 1911.

Right. Alphonse Mucha created this masterpiece for Sarah Bernhardt's American tour of January-July 1896. The foremost lithographer in the United States, Strobridge, had the honour of reproducing the poster for *Gismonda* from Mucha's original. Bernhardt had a sound business head and she is reputed to have made money from buying up stocks of Mucha posters produced for her performances and re-selling them.

handful of theatre companies and museums notwithstanding – showed that the collecting of theatrical ephemera is a thriving pastime.

Going, going were wigs from Cinderella and any amount of flunkies' finery; Maggie Smith's printed chiffon gown from *Othello*; suede cloth galore and grizzly-bear, otter and exotic bird suits from *Hiawatha*; ecclesiastical robes from *Edward II*; even Santa suits. Margaret Whiting, head of costume hire with 25 years' experience in the theatre, was enthusiastic: 'Feel these costermongers' suits ... lovely fabric. Make-believe eighteenth-century gents' costumes – they earn their keep ten times over in hire to theatre companies. We've put some perks in the sale for the Hooray Henries – jazzy uniforms, Ruritanian jackets, they love 'em for dressing up. Shepherdesses, cygnets, mice ... we've got the lot.'

A dedicated collector of the thespian art is John Kennedy Melling, who has written a treatise on his passion, *Discovering Theatre Ephemera*. He divides the subject into two dozen separate sections including autographs, costumes, postcards, cigarette cards, props, playbills and gramophone records. His scope embraces theatre, music hall, pantomime, circus, opera, ballet, puppets, films and television. He explains: 'The most obvious items are programmes and playbills or posters – originally the same thing, for the first programmes were small posters which had been flyposted around the town with beating drum to advertise the strolling players. In the nineteenth century there were complaints of pirate programmes sold outside theatres. Playbills are frail and should be kept in plastic envelopes.'

'Post no bills.' 'Stick no bills.' 'Billposters will be prosecuted.' In the modern age the cautions are, on the whole, respected – with perhaps the singular exception of pirate advertisers who spread the news of pop-music gigs. At the turn of the century, however, walls and hoardings were alive with *anybody's* announcements – the soap and cosmetic makers, the lamp-oil purveyors, the bicycle manufacturers, and the producers of theatre. Playbills, collectors' items all, listed the minutiae of every scene change and credited every Tom, Dick and Harry who took part, down to the ostler who led and fed the donkey in *Aida*.

Barnum and Bailey excelled in playbill hyperbole. Apart from their famous circus events, grand theatre was the essence of such spectacles as *Nero, or the Destruction of Rome*. After reading the following, you might think that there was no need actually to attend the performance:

'NERO ... the tale becomes one of terror, tyranny, revelry, wild unrestrained prodigality and splendour ending, finally, in an untimely death. These are the material events on which the plot and story are built, and to successfully and truthfully depict all the incidents, street scenes, court revelries, midnight orgies,

METROPOLITAN OPERA
LINCOLN CENTER

OPENING SEPTEMBER 1966

Left. Marc Chagall was commissioned to design this poster for the Metropolitan Opera, Lincoln Center, New York, 'opening September 1966'. The poster, printed in France, successfuly projects the performers in a setting of the rooftops of New York City.

And on that note, let us open a few programmes of the London Coliseum of 1939, for productions such as *French Without Tears* and *Gas Light*. A glance at the advertisements tells us that afternoon teas served in the saloons and auditorium were eightpence inclusive, supper at Pinoli's in Wardour Street cost three shillings, and a 14-day cruise to Tangier was priced at 24 guineas. For those of totally decimalized minds or transatlantic nationality, let it suffice to say that these figures are not considerable. Memories, overtures and beginners, please ...

fetes, festivals, ceremonies, combats, contests, loves, hates, conspiracies, arsenic episodes, tragic results, passions, lives, pursuits, pleasures and occupations of the Heathen, Barbaric and Christian peoples, all inhabitants of Rome in those days, has required no end of thought, labour time, money and every conceivable accessory.'

By the beginning of the twentieth century, however, such verbosity and the playbills that were its vehicle were becoming rarities. The decorative poster had taken over. The final examples of the playbill era, dating from the first decade of this century, are fit to rank among tomorrow's antiques.

In the end, nobody can tell you *how* to collect theatrical bygones. They just happen, though once you have set yourself up as a collector you will hunt out bookshops and other dealers who may have a sideline or mainline specialization in the stage. Occasionally, too, auction houses sell items or collections with a theatrical flavour. Theatrical designs at such venues will usually appear in sales of fine art. Items such as old toy theatres (and, sometimes, even the modern, skillfully crafted reproductions), theatrical photographs and bundles of old programmes tend to be included in general collectors' sales. On the whole, they are not expensive. The works of the top designers will command large sums at auction, but things like theatre programmes are generally priced only in the tens of pounds or dollars for multiple bundles. The game is not so much about making money, but saving memories. As John Kennedy Melling puts it, 'Whatever you collect, remember Noel Coward's remark that the only true souvenirs are memories. Theatre ephemera never lack atmosphere and memory.'

D'ALBERT'S

CIRCASSIAN POLKA.

Far left. The opera glasses are by Tiffany and Company and date from the turn of the century when theatre-going was perforce a dress-up affair. They have eighteenth-century courtship scenes painted on the enamel decoration. Accessories of theatre-going, ranging from objects of virtue such as these opera-glasses to the programmes of performances, are all part of theatre collecting.

Far left, below. A popular line in collecting from the late nineteenth and early twentieth centuries in the huge variety of sheet music covers. They range in price from single figures to over £100/$150. D'Albert's *Circassian Polka* makes a stirring appeal with its mountain brigand.

Left. Fanciful bird's head masks used in a British National Theatre production of *Hiawatha*. They were part of a large sale of surplus National Theatre costumes which brought museum curators, collectors and theatre groups flocking to stock up in 1985.

Left. A beautifully embroidered and decorated cloak, worn by Sir John Gielgud while playing Prospero in a National Theatre production. It was one of the costumes disposed of during the 1985 sale to raise funds for the NT. Contrary to popular belief, many theatre costumes are made of the most excellent materials.

Theatre: Collector rating

Scope and variety	7
Investment potential	D
Price range	A few pounds/dollars to £10,000/$15,000

TILES

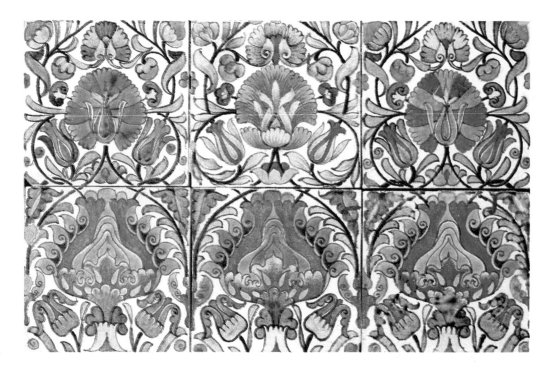

Right. For many modern tile collectors the standards are set by the accomplished late nineteenth century work of William de Morgan. This set of six de Morgan tiles is painted in the Persian manner with stylized flowers and foliage. For such a panel, a collector can expect to pay several hundred pounds or the equivalent in dollars.

Taking into consideration the marvellous range of modern tiles available and the excellence of innovative design of many of them, a casual observer might think the trade in vintage tiles was being neglected. This is not so. It is doing better then ever. The fact is that in tiles we have a branch of interior decoration in which the old mixes perfectly with the new. Setting old tiles in a background of modern examples is one of the attractions. It combines the convenience of a ready supply with the joy of collecting.

A few years ago an English couple paused from shopping in the bustling market town of Vera in south-east Spain to have a drink in a cavernous old cafe. The walls of the bar were clothed in a hideous new sheathing of shiny plastic representing wood panelling. The owner seemed very proud of his new decor. 'Just look at this,' whispered the Englishwoman in an aside, pointing to a gap between two rolls of plastic wallpaper where the ancient undulations of the wall had defeated the decorator's skills. The crack was wide enough to reveal that some lovely old tiles lay behind the 'wood panelling'.

Several sherries later, the landlord admitted that, yes, he had taken some of the old tiles down (although he had papered over most of them), and grudgingly agreed that the couple could have a look at them. In the way of Andalusian dealings it took three days of negotiation and an ocean of sherry to persuade mine host to sell the stock of tiles he had ripped from the walls in the name of 'progress'. They were art deco examples of flimsily dressed ladies flying through the stars, complementing panels of floral patterns. As these very words are being written, inspiration is provided by sight of those same tiles: those two predators were the author and his wife. The deco acquisition lines a dining room alcove in their Spanish village house, and part of a wall in their London home – in each case blending in perfect harmony with modern decorative tiles around them and nearby.

And what a wealth of variety is available among modern tiles. Real marble costs dearly, the vehicle for the talents of Italian, Sicilian and Portuguese designers; marble combined with hand-painted scenes of birds or baskets of flowers is not for any old wall. Reconstituted marble tiles are suitable for fireplace surrounds. Once, the vogue was for square tiles; it has now moved on to rectangular shapes, presumably to make rooms look taller. Choose between a scarlet poppy design which covers eight tiles (and any combination of floral flights of fancy) or hand-painted imitations of tiles to be found in the Blue Mosque of Istanbul. An enterprising Italian offers a seascape with figures in bathing dress and a golden beach as long as your wall will allow. One designer employs a team of artists who will copy original Victorian tiles. Another paints *trompe l'oeil* designs to order. The customer can also have tiles painted to match a fabric. The market for special commissions (some one-off antiques of tomorrow?) is as active as the ready-to-buy-sector.

The collectors' field from the nineteenth century onwards is immense. The most common remark of newcomers to Paddy Frost's tile trove in the heart of Chelsea, London, is: 'I never knew so many types of tile existed.' Many Americans beat a path to see her in Antiquarius antique market in the busy King's Road, SW3 (Paddy Frost Antiques, telephone 01-852-2203), where she stocks hundreds of old tiles ranging from singles at a few pounds to 12-piece sets and panels at prices in three figures. In the market generally the cost would rise well into four figures and more for the ultra-rare 'museum quality' ensembles.

Most people buy her tiles as collector pieces, to be displayed as such. But tiles can *work* too, she says. 'You can put them behind the sink, round the stove, use them as work surfaces. I've had people buy them to cover entire walls, inset among modern tiles like patchwork, use as trivet tops, place-mats and table centrepieces. One customer spent a lot of money on a large quantity of fine decorative tiles and horrified me when she said she was going to put them on the kitchen floor. My first reaction was: don't do that. Back she came after a few months and showed me a photo; they looked lovely. All I could say was,

Centre. Satyrs range through a woodland scene, hunting stags with dogs, in these Art Deco architectural tiles dating from about 1930; a delightful vignette that would make an attractive focus in a display.

Bottom. More William de Morgan: an early tile panel consisting of 16 squares, each one painted with flowers, buds and entwined scrolling foliage. A panel such as this – classed in the £1,000/$1,500 price area – will marry happily with modern tiles if the latter are carefully chosen. The choice in the collectors' field from the end of the nineteenth century onwards is immense.

Below. One of Minton's tile representations of 'The Seven Ages of Man', from the Kensington Gore studios, an example of gifted pictorial work, animated, colourful and reaching the heart of many collectors. Think in terms of £200/$300 or more.

"Tread carefully." A lady from South Africa bought a large number of fine old tiles and announced that she was going to lay them on the floor of her entrance porch.'

Delft has its following, with the Dutch eager to buy back their own, and the Japanese showing keen interest. Paddy Frost says she can sell art nouveau and art deco tiles 'just about as fast as I can find them'. There is a big surge in demand from Americans. English picture tiles, of which there was a large explosion in the 1880s, are popular, with Minton Shakespearian scenes and Wedgwood months of the year finding ready buyers. Flower panels of the 1890s are big sellers for kitchens and bathrooms. William de Morgan designs are "in a class of their own", his brilliant enamel colours and lustre tiles reaching well into three figures.

People leave standing requests to find tiles missing from their sets. A Welshman comes along regularly and asks: 'Has he turned up yet?'. *He* is Abraham Lincoln from a 'photographic' tile set. Paddy, a New Zealander, spent ten years seeking for her own collection the odd one out from a portrait set of four Maoris. It turned up when a general dealer from the north of England presented himself at her shop and asked: 'Do you want to buy a Red Indian?' She has known first-time buyers be so thrilled by a beautiful de Morgan or a seventeenth-century Delft that they have asked: 'Can you get me three dozen more the same?' Finding old tiles isn't as easy as just picking up the telephone and putting in an order, she explains; but it's more fun.

Tiles: Collector rating	
Scope and variety	10
Investment potential	C-D new; B old
Price range	A few pounds or dollars to many thousands

TINS

The original contents of tins range from candy to razor blades, but no commodity came containerized in a larger variety of charms than the British biscuit. The American cookie had its moments, but so wide and varied is the choice of British biscuits tins that the most dedicated American collectors of tins have their sights set across the Atlantic. British biscuit tins bring far higher prices under the hammer in New York than they do in London. The United Kingdom could justifiably complain about the tin drain.

The British housewife buying biscuits in the early decades of this century was presented with a fantasy of choice. It wasn't so much having to decide on cracknels or macaroons, crackers or ratafias, Captain's or creams. If junior wanted a fire engine to play with, Macfarlane, Lang was the answer. Carr's pushed out the lifeboat. Peek, Frean was romantic with scenes from great love stories encasing its products. And inventive Huntley and Palmer took the biscuit with grandfather clocks, handbags and a 'library' of finely bound volumes. The biscuit tin extravaganza was at its height.

Biscuit tin designs rarely gave a clue as to content. An exception was Crawford's lithographed biscuit emporium with the owner seen serving customers through the window; and, later, a 'Bicky House' money box. The motive of these tin come-ons was blatant: there was enormous incentive to eat up the contents quickly so that junior could get to play with the tin. These marketing gimmicks of the biscuit manufacturers – which flourished from the 1880s to the late 1930s, with their golden era between 1900 and 1915 – are a collectors' legacy in these days of plastic packaging. They were, however, strictly utilitarian.

In order to keep fresh and crisp, the biscuit, as every cook knows, must have a lower humidity than that of the flour used in

Below left. From the 1930s has come this tin which was made to contain Dutch cigars. It proves that the biscuit kings did not have a monopoly of colourful exteriors, even if they led in novelty shapes.

Below right. In the same era, Italy produced this tin for Tre Teste razor blades. The cost of tinplate and the advance of plastic and treated-paper packaging have sounded the knell for novelty tins.

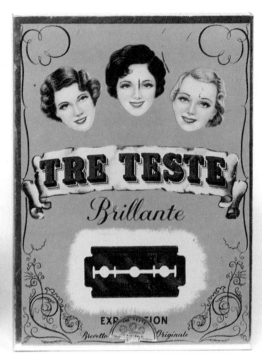

its making. To ensure this it must be cooked twice – hence *bis-cuit*, the French for twice-cooked. It follows that damp is the enemy of the biscuit; therefore, when the biscuit industry began to gather momentum in the first half of the nineteenth century, the manufacture of storage tins grew apace.

It was a genius in the London firm formed by James Peek and George Frean who in 1865 invented a way of making biscuits which dispensed with the traditional 'docker holes', found in some biscuits even today. Without these tiny pin-holes, the old biscuit would have blown up to small-football size in the baking – all shell and no middle. The old biscuits (even with holes) were as hard as bricks and needed good teeth. The new ones were short and palatable.

However, the name that everyone associates with the pioneering of biscuits (and, eventually with the most exciting biscuit tins) was Huntley and Palmer. Famous Reading Gaol, a biscuit-throw from the company's birthplace, was universally known in nineteenth-century underworld slang as the 'Biscuit Factory'; 'take the Huntley and Palmer' replaced the phrase 'take the biscuit', meaning to win a prize. Ireland produced William Jacob and the first cream cracker. Carr's of Carlisle flooded Britain with alphabet biscuits. In Glasgow Mr Lang took his nephew, Mr Macfarlane, into business and in mid-century the firm had switched the names round because the result sounded better. Mr McVitie and Mr Price, in the Edinburgh area, not only became famous in biscuits but secured the contract for royal wedding cakes. Another Scottish firm, Crawford's, founded in Leith in 1813, had by the end of the century a vast fleet of bicycle-borne salesmen peddling biscuits in fancy tins north and south of the border.

The mid-century tins bore stick-on labels. The first printed

tin on record came from Huntley and Palmer in 1867. Transfer printing was used widely until the invention of offset litho in 1875, which opened the way to printing on curved surfaces. Tins blossomed in a multitude of forms – bells, cannons, clocks, furniture, buildings, vehicles.

The British Empire was built on biscuit tins. The American Henry Morton Stanley, searching for Dr Livingstone in Africa, bribed hostile tribes with them. An expedition to Tibet traded empty tins for sheep milk. Hunters kept their cartridges dry and the bereaved stored the ashes of their loved ones in them. Missionaries in Uganda kept their Bibles in Huntley and Palmer tins to save them from white ants. When Queen Victoria's son-in-law, Prince Henry of Battenberg, died in the tropics he was shipped back to England pickled in a tank made from biscuit tins.

Examples of pre-1940 biscuit tins can still be found for a few pounds in Britain. They are worth approximately four times as much in the United States. The rarer, more exciting subjects – such as a Jacob's coronation coach of 1936 – leap into four figures on the American collector market when in mint condition. An incredible number of 40,000 designs were produced. A major auction in New York is considered fairly 'comprehensive' if it can muster 150-200 of these types. Obsessive collectors enshrine their biscuit tins in display cases, but some make them work on the kitchen shelves, storing tea, coffee, spices, flour … and even biscuits.

The American Can Company produced attractive tins in the first decade of this century. Particularly coveted is its tin for cinnamon, modelled in the shape of a cash register, and heading for a £330/$500 value at the close of the 1980s. Commemorative tins abound, with the largest number being devoted to royal and presidential events and anniversaries; wars and campaigns are also common. These commemoratives, stretching up to the

present day, are among the most inexpensive tins to collect. Chocolate, tea, coffee, cocoa, spices, cosmetics, razor blades and gramophone needles are among a wide range of products which have their tins, and their followers. All tin collectors demand items in prime condition. A rare tin, scratched, rusty or dented, will not enhance a collection; an ordinary tin in pristine condition will. Italy and Spain have made an attractive contribution of olive oil tins. America has the world's richest variety of beer and soft-drink cans. After Andy Warhol's artistic homage to Campbell's, there may be flourishing, unheeded, a race of soup-can collectors. Who knows?

Tins: Collector rating

Scope and variety	8
Investment potential	B for top quality
Price range	$50 to $1,000 plus in the USA
	£10 to £300 plus in Britain

Far left, top. A souvenir of Queen Elizabeth's coronation in 1953, meant to last as a tea container. And an unusual shape from Topsy Toffee – 'Good for kiddies. And good for you.' Collecting tins need not be an expensive pastime and offers hopeful investment prospects.

Far left. From the inter-wars era comes this biscuit tin formed in the guise of a 'bronze' bell. Biscuits tins were shaped in a multitude of ways. At the end of World War One some were modelled as tanks in camouflaged paint. Liners, coronation coaches, buses, airplanes were also made by the market-conscious biscuit manufacturers.

Above. The British firm of McVitie and Price issued this biscuit tin in 1933, a Louis-style, serpentine chest of drawers (6 inches, 15cm high). British biscuit tins bring much higher prices in the USA than they do in their home country. American collectors are attracted by their eclectic variety.

TIN TOYS

Above. Germany dominated the collector field of tin toys with its superbly crafted and finished models of ships, vehicles, planes and, of course, trains. This selection – which would make a respectable nucleus of any collection – dates from the early part of the century to the 1930s. Submarines were particularly popular in Germany, and are a specialized branch of modern collecting.

If you wish to see one of the world's greatest, specialized collections of antiques of tomorrow, enhanced by a setting of sensational appeal, go to the *Forbes* Magazine Galleries at 60 Fifth Avenue, New York, where the better part of a fleet of 500 toy boats is harboured, give or take the 40 or so that might be 'at sea', at any one time, on touring exhibition in the United States. Boats are an extensive and important part of tin toys, and the vast majority of those in the Forbes family fleet are of tin, the finest and largest collection in existence. The vessels represent the cream of production from the tin factories of principally Germany – with some splendid American contributions – between the 1890s and the 1940s.

The visitor finds liners and battleships realistically 'floating' in *trompe l'òeuil* environments where no water actually exists. A carousel of leisurely sternwheelers circles lush meadows to the accompaniment of Dixie music. Submarines go about their deadly business apparently deep in a green, half-lighted ocean where the stricken *Lusitania* rests for ever on the sea bed, and the only sound is the echoing ping-ping of Asdic signals. Bath toys swim on a 'soapy' sea of glass marbles filling a vintage tub that was rescued from an emporium of posh decorator-antiques along Fifth Avenue.

The collection and its imaginative setting (the latter brilliantly conceived and executed by the New York design team of Peter Purpura and Gary Kisner) owe their being to the collecting zeal and expertise of the magazine owner,

Malcolm Forbes, and his second son, Robert. The appeal of the exhibits to young and old alike results from the invention and skills of the tinplate toy manufacturers, Märklin, Bing, Fleischmann, Carette, Arnold, Radiguet, Ives, Orkin and others.

The vast majority of tinplate toys, being of twentieth century manufacture, fall into the ambit of tomorrow's antiques. Model trains are dealt with in their own chapter. Many of the finest tin toys represent transport – sea, road and air. The last two subjects, in particular, continue to inspire the production of exciting toys which are worthy of collecting.

No one is more knowledgeable or has written more on tin toys than David Pressland, a British veterinary surgeon and a collector of renown. He was one of the first to see the tremendous collector potential in the output of tin from Japan in the post-war period, at a time when many others equated imports from the Orient with the cheap and shoddy.

Pressland, author of *The Art of the Tin Toy*, observes: 'Shortly after the war [World War Two] the Japanese cast aside the mantle of imitation and assumed that of innovation, rapidly achieving a position of dominance in the world's tin-toy industry with a brashness of colour, a peculiar oriental ingenuity of action, a tinny quality that was all their own – "tin toys" and "Japan" were now synonymous. Like German toys of an earlier age, Japanese toys of the 1950s and 1960s reflected in miniature man's latest technical and scientific achievements. New cars, planes and novelty toys were produced in great profusion. The use of clockwork gradually declined as more and more new toys were fitted with cheap friction motors or battery-operated electric motors. Some of the more sophisticated Japanese tin cars were fitted with a simple pre-programmed radio-controlled unit ...

'The single most important new influence on the toy makers, however, particularly in Japan and Russia, was the space-exploration programme that began in earnest in 1958 with the orbiting of the first *sputnik*. This and the subsequent series of manned space flights charged the toy-makers' imaginations, and innumerable tinplate space rockets,

Above. He's called 'Lilliput', he stands 7 inches (18cm) in height, and he comes from Japan. Among robots he is an early specimen, dating from the 1930s, therefore earning a price-tag of several hundred pounds.

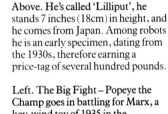

Left. The Big Fight – Popeye the Champ goes in battling for Marx, a key-wind toy of 1935 in the £1,300/$2,000 class. American Marx shone in frivolous novelty toys far removed from the serious products of Bing and other renowned German makers of tinplate juvenilia.

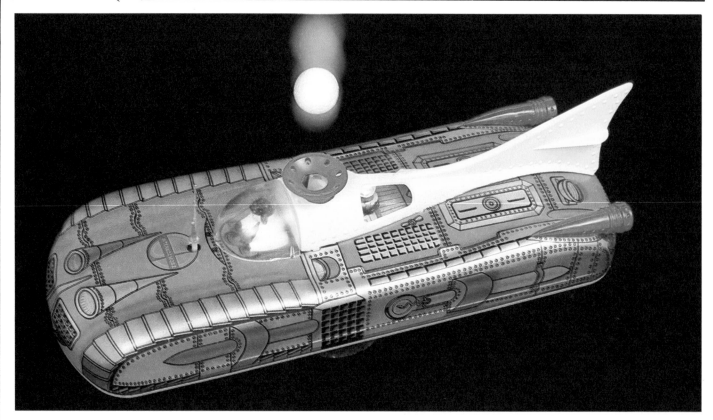

Above. The cosmonauts take over: from Hungary comes this ingenious tin vehicle, fast making inroads in the capitalistic West with its dramatic action *sputnik*. At the press of a button, the *sputnik* hovers 'in orbit' on a jet of air.

Below. At present anchored with the *Forbes* Magazine battle fleet on Fifth Avenue, New York, is this tin warship by the German maker Carette. It has clockwork insides, and planes to search for the enemy (17 inches, 42cm in length). Truly a twentieth-century wonder of its day.

Above right. Modern tinplate toys from several countries in all their colourful, 'tinny' glory. To collectors they are irrestistible *en masse* like this.

sputniks, spacecraft and moon-landing vehicles appeared in the shops. These were usually battery-operated, and often had refinements such as flashing lights and sound effects. [A Hungarian-made space vehicle in the collection of John Strange, designer of this book, projects into the air a free-flying, spherical 'space capsule' supported on a column of warm air.] Each new achievement in man's conquest of space was recreated in miniature, although the rapid sequence of these achievements inevitably doomed the lifespan of each toy to one or two seasons.

'So remarkable has been the Japanese achievements that I cannot help feeling that a generation hence, the art of the best Japanese tin toys of the 1950s and 1960s will be almost as greatly appreciated as that of the pre-1914 German toys is at present, especially as it may well represent the swansong of the "Age of the Tin Toy".'

The pre-1914 period of German production is, of course, regarded as the 'golden era' by tin-toy collectors. The products of Bing and Märklin (see Model Trains on page 120) epitomize the standard of quality achieved by the toy factories. Bing was renowned for its fine locomotives, plus the excellence of detail and the skill with which luxurious fittings were reproduced in the manufacture of its toy motor cars. Märklin's trains and railways covered the world; its ships were feats of miniature engineering, down to the smallest detail of rope ladders in cast lead – yet they retained an essentially toy-like look.

They had a host of competitors, many of whom were founded in the Nuremberg area of south Germany, where the toymakers flourished on old regional traditions of pewtering and clock-making. Lehmann earned a name for tin novelty toys such as ostrich-drawn carriages and parasol-shaded tricycles, powered by clockwork. Carette had a more solemn approach, yet was capable of supplying its clockwork boats with a frivolous, funnel-fitting key designed as a two-dimensional plume of smoke (Bing, too, used the gimmick: good ideas were freely appropriated throughout the industry). Distler founded its toys of transport on a tradition of

penny tin novelties. Fleischmann graduated from bathtub floaters to a wide range of large boats in the 1930s and is well known today for its model railways. Hausser and Lineol produced intricately fitted horse-drawn field kitchens and ambulance carts of World War One, spendidly engineered motorized transport of the Nazi era; Hausser, as Elastolin, and Lineol under its own name have legions of worshippers who collected their composition troops (see Toy Soldiers on page 178). Tipp and Co launched fleets of motorized transport with working headlamps and searchlights, tanks that sparked, and squadrons of aircraft, some of which dropped exploding bombs fired by amorce caps.

The American tinplate toy industry also had its origins in a clock-making area, at Bristol, Connecticut. Manufacture soon spread to Philadelphia and New York. At the end of the nineteenth century American toymakers were producing nearly 80 million tinplate toys a year in a boom stimulated by the development (in 1895) of lithographic processes which enabled colours to be directly printed on to the metal surface. This was obviously much cheaper than hand-painting each model. The firm of Edward Ives, which had started production in 1868 and had achieved an early best-seller with a mechanical boat-rower, was a leader in the market. Legions of young Americans could testify to the claim that 'Ives toys make happy boys'. Many of the American toys were based on the expertise of immigrant workers from Germany and France, and the industry benefited from the slow recovery of German output after World War One. American toymakers formed an association which insisted on the imposition of steep protective duties on imported German goods.

One of the major producers of clockwork toys in the early twentieth century was Ferdinand Strauss, a firm that was eventually taken over by Marx. Louis Marx, born in 1894, became a millionaire in his twenties thanks to his genius for inventing and marketing amusing and cheap tin toys: The Mouse Orchestra, a zany quartet around a tinny piano, Popeye The Champ in a boxing ring and many other

Right. A Lehmann limousine with electric lights, four opening doors and a chauffeur separated from the passenger seats by a partition. Cars like this (which is 13 inches, 32cm in length) were the basic, middle-range products of Germany's toy invasions of Britain and America between the wars.

Right. A Märklin Standard Oil tanker truck, powered by clockwork and guided by electric headlamps.

Below. Boxed and in pristine condition, the 'Motor Car Constructor' from Meccano gave you the choice of making a tourer, as shown here, or a racing car. The construction set came complete with driver and lights. Frank Hornby, who was to achieve Hornby O-gauge railway fame, patented his Meccano constructor outfits in 1901; they were a tremendous success through several generations.

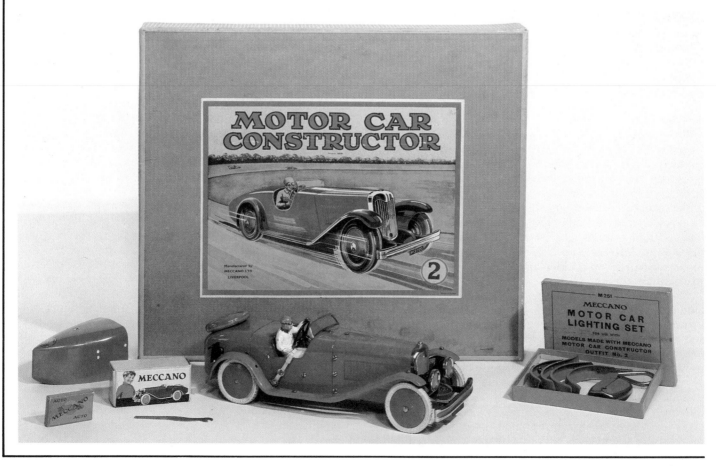

Left. A strange tin toy of modern date, with its origins somewhere East of Suez. It shows signs of being hand-painted. The post-war years, from the 1950s to the present day, have witnessed a big switch in tinplate manufacture from the West to the East, with Japan emerging as the world leader.

Marxisms of the 1930s drew their inspiration from the movies. Despite the fact that there is a huge amount of Marx material around in the present day, it is fast appreciating in value and is probably the most popular collector field in the middle-range price echelon.

In Britain, William Britain (the father of William, the inventor of the famous hollow-cast Britain's toy soldier) had been making tin novelties since mid-Victorian days. Cheerful carousels, dancing bears and drunken Scotsmen modestly sustained the family fortunes before the advent of the lead battalions in 1893. Then in 1901, Frank Hornby, who was to achieve Hornby O-gauge railway fame, patented the Meccano system of construction outfits. On the whole, however, tinplate toys were not a British forte. Chad Valley motor vehicles from the early part of the century are collected, as are the products of Brimtoy, which later amalgamated with Wells to form the firm known as Wells Brimtoy. Lines Brothers, which owned toy-making factories from 1858, registered the Tri-Ang trademark in 1927 and the Minic mark was used on excellent clockwork tin cars in the 1930s. When discussing metal transport toys, Great Britain's claim to collector interest lies in the Dinky Toy and Matchbox successes dealt with in the chapter on Toy Vehicles of diecast and other manufacture on page 192.

French tinplate production tended to polarize. At one end of the range, there were cheap, somewhat ephemeral 'tinny' novelties and poorly made cars for the mass market; at the other end, there were superbly produced replica models aimed at the rich by the firms of Andra Citroën and JEP. During a large part of the 1920s and 1930s these two companies were bitter competitors in a war of accuracy, in which Citroën, with its opening doors and exquisitely modelled fitments, had the edge. Citroën models are the aristocrats of toy motor car collections. Their following is keenest in France and neighbouring continental countries.

Serendipity is stimulus to a collector. Robert Forbes has made 'finds' for his toy boat fleet in unexpected quarters. A 31-inch (75cm) Märklin submarine of 1920, now in the *Forbes* collection, was recovered from a lake on the Long Island estate of Henry Clay Frick, the railroad tycoon, by the chauffeur's young son (ponds are a principal reason why toy boats are rare). Other successful sightings have come from South America, where there is a strong German trading tradition. From an East Coast attic came a Märklin battleship, the *Posen*, which was brought home from Germany by a World War One Doughboy in the American Rainbow Division. Robert triumphantly hijacked his long-sought Märklin *Lusitania* for £16,500/$25,000 at an auction. But he derives as much pleasure from having picked up a little tin riverboat at a country antique shop in New Jersey for $5 – 'In the space of about ten years, its value has gone up to around $1,000,' he says.

Tin toys: Collector rating

Scope and variety	9
Investment potential	A
Price range	£10/$20 to well into five figures

TOY SOLDIERS OLD

Above. The steel helmets and khaki uniforms of this Britain's unit of the Royal Horse Artillery make it a rare set. Mostly the RHA figures came in dress uniform. Steel helmeted realism in 1940 was little appreciated by the juvenile customers, and few sets were made.

Below. The boxes of toy soldier sets are a collecting subject on their own, the targets of eager barter-and-buy. The label on this wooden box is typical of the way German makers packaged their goods for the London market.

Since the dawn of the 1970s no category of saleroom item has appreciated more consistently and steadily than old toy soldiers. Come recession, currency fluctuations, ups and downs of Wall Street, fads and fancies in the fine art world, wars, politics and any other potential influence on the collecting market, they have resolutely marched on to higher and yet higher values.

How *old* is an old toy soldier? The overwhelming majority of those which are fought over at international auctions are far from being antique in the true sense of the term. The earliest commercially-made toy soldiers – the tin, almost two-dimensional 'flats' of the Nuremberg pewterers in south Germany – date back to the late eighteenth century, but only a minute proportion of these 'earlies', and few other flats or 'solids' pre-dating 1890, come into the main collector arena. An estimated 75 per cent of toy-soldier collectors throughout the world concentrate on the armies of William Britain and his heirs, and he did not launch his British invention of hollow-cast lead figures into the market until 1893. By the late 1960s the use of lead for toy soldiers had ceased. Given the firm's domination of the collector market, therefore, seven decades of relatively modern history form the main catchment period for toy-soldier collecting.

With the demise of lead production, there came an almost immediate collector boom for the obsolete toys. Prices rose rapidly, so rapidly that the collectors looked around for other, and possibly less expensive, means of satisfying their acquisitive appetites. A breed of 'new old toy soldiers' was born. These figures, almost universally solid, are made in the traditional look and 'feel' of the old toy soldiers; some are even cast from Britain's shapes. It is a cottage industry peopled by a few small firms, but mainly by one-man outfits,

usually collectors themselves. Already some of the new figures are rising in the saleroom charts. These soldiers, together with intricately-detailed 'connoisseur' figures and modern dioramas (realistic scenes utilizing groups of figures), are dealt with in the next chapter. Before that, you are invited to review the pensioned-off old warriors of toy soldiering's golden years.

Lead soldiers epitomize the 'just-fancy-that' school of saleroom lore. People are amazed that old penny toys, tucked away and forgotten when the children grew up, can sometimes fetch as much at auction as the family silver. Furthermore, many a family that has no silver to sell or enjoy may conceivably have lead soldiers hidden away in the attic. The rise and rise of the steadfast toy soldier over the last two decades can be seen in the constantly changing world record prices for sets of figures. Significantly, all the following record prices of their time were paid for Britain's soldiers, and the buyers were American (hence the prices are quoted principally in dollars). All the milestones were established at Phillips, which pioneered specialized soldier sales and holds more than any other auction house.

At the start of the 1970s, it was rare for a set to go much over $100 in America, or £50 in Britain. Around this figure, a box of eight Montenegrin infantry, introduced by Britain's to salute a gallant ally of World War One, went into toy soldier history. British nostalgics may note that a little over one shilling would have bought it when new. The following few years saw a steep increase in interest, particularly among American collectors. In 1977 the film star Douglas Fairbanks Junior shipped his collection of Britains to London for sale. 'I have no place to keep it these days,' he told this author, from his New York apartment. His rare band of the red-coated

Above. A fighting square of Britain's Highlanders from the *Forbes* army, based in Tangier, Morocco, prepares to do battle in the African sands. Collectors who wish to emulate the display should ensure the sand is thoroughly dry; damp is the mortal enemy of the lead soldier.

Below. Possibly the rarest of Britain's soldiers: a trooper of the British Camel Corps. He could be obtained (together with eight regimental comrades) only by buying a giant display box packed with infantry, cavalry and artillery, issued in the first decade of this century.

Above. Heyde of Dresden was one of the German manufacturers with designs on the British Empire. It encroached on India with this magnificent tableau of a tiger hunt, peopled by its solid, but naively animated figures. (*Forbes collection.*)

Below. Flat figures by a Nuremberg maker represent a Prussian (grounded) and an Austrian in combat. They are 30mm scale. The tiny tableau is part of an extensive, 7,500-figure diorama of the battle of Leuthen, 1757, in the *Forbes* Museum of Military Miniatures.

Royal Marine Light Infantry set a record for any set of toy soldiers at £800, or $1,400 at the prevailing rate, a figure which made the wire services throughout the English-speaking world. Why was the set so rare? It was issued in 1938 and the following year war came; production at Britain's factory was soon to be interrupted for the war effort. The line never appeared in post-war catalogues, therefore only a limited number of sets were made. The band went to a new home in Chicago.

In the following year the record rose to $1,750 for a horse-drawn supply unit of the Boer War, issued in extremely small numbers in the khaki and slouch-hatted uniform of the Imperial City Volunteers. This record fell with a bang in 1980 when Malcolm Forbes paid $8,000 for a 660-man formation of the London Scottish Regiment, converted from Britain's figures into a 1916 battalion on the Somme in France; it went into the *Forbes* Magazine Museum of Military Miniatures in Tangier, Morocco. In May of 1984, however, a Texan lawyer could lay claim to paying the highest per-figure sum when he captured a set of nine Royal Fusiliers for $5,400, or $600 per man. Later the same year, a 13-piece set of the Royal Horse Artillery, boxed and mint, soared to $9,000 (nearly $700 per piece), with a similar set breaking the $10,500 barrier a few months later, in 1985. This 1940-issue of the RHA, with its gun, limber, horse team and outriders, is rare because the men are not in the usual ceremonial blue and gold, but in khaki – and they are wearing *steel helmets*. At the time of its issue, production was interrupted by the war and, anyway, the set was something of a marketing flop: little boys preferred brightly dressed soldiers to those wearing drab khaki, therefore only a relatively few sets were made. The extremely unusual feature of steel helmets underwrites the unit's scarcity value. That is the sort of classic case history that honed collectors esteem for an item.

At Christmas time 1986, the New York salerooms established a world record of $12,000 for another set of the Boer War supply column. But the triumph was short lived. Within a month, London was hitting back with the 'great unobtainable' of toy soldier collections. Among the hundreds and hundreds of boxed sets of soldiers, beautifully labelled and encased in shiny crimson paper, which Britain's marketed, there were occasional large display sets. The largest was set number 131 (practically all the firm's issues had a number, beginning with the Life Guards at number one). It was first marketed in 1905 at 90 shillings (£4.50 or approximately $18 in those days) as a 275-piece super-presentation box for the little boy who had everything. Very few of these sets were made: those that were tended to be gift sets presented to royalty visiting Britain's exhibitions up to about 1925. In the giant three-layered wooden box there were infantry, cavalry, bandsmen, artillery, sailors and nine extremely rare figures of the British Camel Corps. Customers could obtain the British Camel Corps only by buying the huge box. So rare are they that a single figure in prime condition is estimated to be worth about $750 today.

Now, at the beginning of 1987, one of these giant boxes had come on the market for the first time. Although 'well played with', the contents of the box included 251 of the original pieces (including the nine Camel Corps), made up by extras to a complement of 281. The box had been passed down through three generations after purchase from Britain's factory in London in 1908. The vendor, Tony Fowler, a 62-year-old retired general manager of a greetings card firm, said ruefully: 'My sister and I used to play with the soldiers, and I had a cannon which did some terrible damage – which

accounts for some of the casualties. Little did I realize when a head went off that I was throwing away £20 or £30 a time.' Most of the contents were in good condition, however. At auction, the box created a new world record for any one set at $17,000, paid by a collector in Ohio.

There was a cautionary footnote to the sale. At some stage in the life of the box, a well-meaning parent covered it in flowered wallpaper, presumably to hide the dilapidations of time. Toy-soldier experts consider that this may have knocked a cool $2,000 off its collector value. Lesson to be learned: an original box matters; the existence of the box can often add $30-$50 to the value of a Britain's set of eight infantry or five cavalry. And repainting or retouching detracts from the value of an old soldier in the view of most collectors. A war-scarred veteran showing his wounds is usually worth more than one who has been freshened up. Integrity is all.

Besides Britain's figures, which have a fast-growing bibliography of their own, there is a wide field of toy soldiers from which to choose.

The tin flats of Germany, beautifully engraved and painted, survived commercially until well into the twentieth century and have had a revival in several Continental production centres. Flats of the period between the 1890s and the late 1930s are undoubtedly underpriced. They have little following in Britain and America compared with the enthusiasm for Britain's and other full-round figures. Attractive 20-piece sets, exquisitely painted, and bedded in straw packing within their original oval boxes of thin, split pine, can often be bought for the price of a single mid-range Britain's soldier. Any old flats – that is, prior to 1940 – have to be a reasonable investment at current market prices.

In the nineteenth century, Lucotte and Mignot in France turned out glittering cohorts of French Imperial troops in solid lead alloy, and they are among the aristocrats of collections. Mignot soldiers are still produced today. The French, being the French, were not keen on making the enemy, so the collector who concentrates on these figures has to settle for parades rather than battles. The sky is the limit for a good Lucotte mounted general of the First Empire. Despite their value, however, there is not much evidence of faking. Collectors learn to distinguish between old and modern

Below. A Wehrmacht soldier made by Elastolin makes a ceremonial appearance. Elastolin and Lineol were the premier German makers of composition figures and reached their peak of output and originality in the 1930s and early 1940s. Their sawdust, glue and linseed oil armies are remarkable for their realism.

Above. The Britain's model fort, manned by the firm's soldiers, folds flat when not in action. Although it is made only of stiff card, it is a very expensive collectors' piece, worth many hundreds of pounds. The reason is simple: the fort was on sale in the 1930s and relatively few examples have survived nursery siege warfare.

Far right. Indian lancers attack bandits in a jungle village, a stirring Imperial exploit seen through Heyde's German eyes. The houses and trees help place this prized collectors' item apart from the other sets. *(Forbes collection.)*

Right. Heyde figures of Germany represent British stretcher-bearers going about their duty in the late nineteenth century. Most makers in Germany, France, Britain and the USA included some medics among their fighting troops. They provided doctors and nurses as well as medical orderlies with the wounded.

Below. A rare Britain's post-war unit, the Bahamas Police Band, marches up to the gate of a geographically misplaced German castle. Although they are by no means thick on the ground, toy forts are comparatively inexpensive to acquire. Specialists say they are underpriced and one of the best buys in the toy soldier world.

Mignots; the latter, which are as finely detailed as their forebears, have revealingly glossy paint compared with the dullish bloom of the old-timers.

The Germans were the most inventive of the toy soldier makers. The solid figures of Georg Heyde, a firm which vanished in the Dresden bombing of 1945, climb trees, put up signalling wire, shoe horses, bandage each other, and gather round camp fires smoking pipes and quaffing schnapps. Large sets in good condition run well into four figures, and there are many British and American collectors of Heyde: the company pushed its market frontiers into the English-speaking world, therefore there are numerous sets representing the armies of Britain and the United States. An unstable alloy used in their manufacture makes these solid German figures susceptible to a lead disease brought on by damp. Like all lead-based figures, they should be housed in a non-damp atmosphere at even temperature, and kept away from direct sunlight and harsh electric light which ruins their paintwork. When stored, the soldiers fare best layered in acid-free tissue paper.

Some of the finest German handiwork and realism is to be found among the composition soldiers of Elastolin and Lineol, and the tinplate, wheeled hardware that went with these troops of sawdust, linseed oil and glue. The heyday of the German composition armies was in the 1930s and early 1940s, although they were manufactured from the early years of the century. Despite the ravages of the war and its aftermath, large numbers of Elastolin and Lineol soldiers have survived. Some of the rarest examples are portrait figures of Hitler, Goering and other leaders of the Nazi Party. Composition soldiers fare badly in a damp atmosphere; if the surroundings are too dry or too warm, however, the wire skeletons will react and the composition body will crack.

America was not well served for toy soldiers. The better-class market relied on imports of German and French solids and the hollow-casts of Britain's and other UK makers. However, in the 1930s the United States developed a uniquely American toy soldier. It was sold mainly in the five-and-dime stores, especially those of F.W. Woolworth, and became known as the dimestore soldier. The figures were rugged, practically unbreakable, but crudely modelled compared with their European counterparts. They had a lifespan that reached the threshold of the 1970s and played a special part in the boyhood of several generations of Americans. Today, high prices are paid by collectors for dimestore rarities: their very 'ordinariness' during their selling years probably meant that vast quantities were thrown away or otherwise destroyed as their owners grew up. Two companies are highest in collector regard: Barclay, named after a street in West Hoboken, New Jersey, where the firm was founded in 1924; and Manoil, started by two brothers of that name in Manhattan in 1928. A third firm, Grey Iron, of Mount Joy, Pennsylvania, made some of the world's most unimaginative, but probably the most durable, toy soldiers – in cast iron.

An American toy-soldier collector and appraiser, Henry I. Kurtz, says: 'Like their British, French and German cousins, the Barclay, Manoil and Grey Iron troops have gone to the Valhalla reserved for toys that have faithfully performed their playtime duties. Now they are valued by collectors and remembered with pleasure by former five-and-dime customers who, as youngsters, would pluck them out of the bins at five cents apiece.'

Old toy soldiers: Collector rating

Scope and variety	9
Investment potential	A
Price range	From £5/$10 for individual pieces to £20,000/$30,000 or more for the rarest, mint sets

TOY SOLDIERS NEW

Below. Napoleon exists in effigy more than any other toy-soldier general. Washington, Wellington, Alexander the Great – they have all been cast in lead. Kings and queens have had their day. This model of Charles and Diana, the Prince and Princess of Wales, was made by Blenheim, had a very short manufacturing life, and became a collectors' item.

Throughout the year 1983 every movement of the Mahdi's Dervishes was being plotted in obsessive detail in a ledger in London. Peter Johnson, the author of this book, and his wife Anne were involved in a new stage of their curatorship of the *Forbes* Magazine Museum of Military Miniatures, which is housed in the majestic Palais Mendoub at Tangier, Morocco. They were about to recreate the River Nile in a splendid and spacious new gallery of the museum, overlooking Tangier port and the Straits of Gibraltar.

The river and its immediate hinterland were the least of their problems. Glass sheets placed over a blue-painted base supplied the 'water'; sand, transported from the beach beneath the cliffs at the foot of the Palais gardens, provided the Sudan. The fleet of 12 river boats, with skeleton crews of British bluejackets and Tommies, had been airfreighted from the United States after being fashioned by a master re-creator of toy soldiers, Harold Pestana, who is otherwise Professor of Geology at Colby College, Maine. Now, for the *mise en scène*, hundreds of British, Egyptian and Sudanese troops and a Royal Navy contingent had to be recruited at sales of lead soldiers and from traders. Above all, there was a desperate need to raise an army of Mahdist tribesmen, a toy soldier commodity not noted for its abundance at auctions.

Steady purchases of old Britain figures fleshed out the ranks of the Anglo-Egyptian force (which eventually became an amalgam of the 1884 Gordon relief expedition and the Kitchener advance to Khartoum in 1898). There was a period of several months during which the curators vouched that not a Dervish moved in London without their knowing about and capturing him. Models by Continental makers were snapped up at auction. Britain's Arabs were acquired by the score. But the main supply of Mahdists, given the paucity of old toy figures of this type, had to come from the ranks of the new wave of modellers – those who produced modern figures fashioned in the style of yesterday, the makers of 'old new toy soldiers'. Jock Couts's shop, Under Two Flags, in central London, was trawled empty of running Dervishes and flag-carrying, mounted emirs, bearing his own imprint and those of Bulldog and Marktime. Other modern makes were found in the auction rooms, among job-lots of soldiers: Ducal and Trophy. Telexes to the *Forbes* headquarters in New York raised fresh bands of camel-mounted Dervishes and sword-waving tribesmen on foot, supplied by Brigade Miniatures. The same company also came up with some delightfully animated Egyptian infantry, to complement Britain's rather static troops of the Khedive.

Early in 1984, the polyglot armies were placed in position around and centring on Harold Pestana's impressive, but still toy-like, flotilla of gunboats which he had scaled to 2-inch 54mm toy-soldier ratios. The new toy soldiers marry excellently with the old. Britain's Mountain Artillery units rub shoulders with Camel Corps from the Brigade Miniatures stable, and 'fuzzy-wuzzies' of the 1980s mix easily with white-garbed Arabs of the 1930s. For the curators of the world's largest and most comprehensive collection of toy soldiers – nearly 100,000 at the latest count – the 'new old toy soldier' had come of age.

The 'father' of the new toy soldier is, indisputably, Shamus Wade of Britain, whose Nostalgia series of unusual units of the British Empire from 1850 to 1910, now discontinued, has

Left. A magnificent participant of the battle of Crecy, 1346. It formed part of a collection of figures recalling the age of chivalry which was owned by Commander Frederick Ping. From 1963 to 1977 he managed – and enriched by conversion and re-animation – the moulds of Richard Courtenay, celebrated for his lifelike knights.

Left. Typical of the interesting new avenues of toy soldiery opened up by small, independent collector-makers from the 1970s onwards are these Soldiers, masterminded by Jed Hailey, a leading English collector. (*Forbes collection.*)

Below left. Dioramas are a growing aspect of modern model-soldier production, often the work of amateurs seeking to enrich the display qualities of their armies. This professionally-constructed scene represents the British army fighting hard against the Zulu tide at Isandhlwana in 1879 when six companies of the 24th Foot were completely wiped out (*Forbes collection.*)

Right. Blenheim, a small British company, designed these, part of a larger group representing both sides in the American War of Independence, 1776, for the Princeton Battlefield Area Preservation Society. A few sets were allowed on the collector market and became highly prized. (*Forbes collection.*)

Right Post-war animation in the last of the lead toys before the nursery became a plastic and die-cast world of spacemen and their fantastic hardware. Where's that tiger? Elephant-borne hunters track through the jungles of obsolescence (*Forbes collection.*)

an exalted status in collector regard. His approach to modelling is a rare one, best summed up in his own words: 'Of course, research is not just uniform details. Just as important is the type of man, who they were, what they did, physique, complexion etc. Most model soldiers seem to be made from the outside in, i.e. endless research is done to get the uniform right, then a standard figure of a man is fitted into it. With Nostalgia, it is the other way round. First the man is discovered, then the uniform is added.' Thus his Indian Mutiny veterans, which were paraded at the Delhi Durbar of 1903 and are exemplified in the *Forbes* collection, not only march with martial pride but with the unmistakable aura of old age; his Fanti woman carrier, baby on back, looks as though she *belongs* to Africa; and many a white officer towers in physical height over his colonial troops. The makers of the new toy soldiers are far too numerous to list here. Britain's itself, still in business as a thriving toy company, ranks among them with its growing range of skilfully modelled diecast figures, the accent being on ceremonial and pageantry; Britain's early plastic sets, especially the Eyes Right series, make handsome money at auction alongside their lead forebears from the same stable. Many of the new makers have outlets through specialized modelling and toy-soldier shops and some through the better department stores in leading cities of Britain and the United States. A constant update on their output is maintained in the *Old Toy Soldier Newsletter*, where new issues are reviewed for collectors. The illustrated magazine, the world's best on the subject of toy soldiers generally, is published bi-monthly from 209 North Lombard, Oak Park, Illinois, 60302, USA (telephone 312 383 6625). A random dip into the magazine reveals welcoming reviews for newcomers: a series of 60 standard bearers of the French Revolution issued by Mignot of Paris to celebrate the bicentennial of the revolution in 1989; a vignette of Captain William Peel and five naval ratings, heroes of the Indian Mutiny 1857, by Star Soldiers of Center Line, Michigan; and HMS *Mosquito*, a delightful stern-wheel river boat from Jock Couts at Under Two Flags in London.

Head and shoulders above most of the 'connoisseur' models produced for those who demand the finest detail and accuracy are the knights from the age of chivalry modelled in Britain under the Courtenay banner and by the late Frederick Ping. The cream of their output, masterpieces of animation and heraldic splendour, were reaching towards the magic figure of $1,000 per mounted figure in the latter years of the 1980s. They will stand the test of time as classic pieces of miniature modelling in the years to come.

Dioramas, three-dimensional 'pictures' of model soldiers going about their business or at play, are a specialized area of the collecting field. They have a very personal appeal, and a diorama that is attractive to its creator does not always strike a chord in the hearts of other collectors. Small dioramas abound at auction and their prices tend to be less than buoyant. The finest dioramas have been created to special commissions, among them the superlative works of Edward Suren, who has contributed some magnificent tableaux to the *Forbes* collection.

Typical of the chequered market fortunes that can await dioramas was the fate of a gigantic Battle of Waterloo made up of 20,000 warring troops and 8,000 horses. A team of modelmakers spent 285,000 man-hours constructing the model which employed 1-inch/20mm plastic figures. The process from the beginning of research to completion took 14 years. More than 150 eyewitness accounts of the battle were studied. The makers, a professional modelmaking firm in the

Left. A Napoleonic standard-bearer of the third regiment of *Voltigeurs de Ligne*, an example of the excellent work to be found in Mignot soldiers emanating today from Paris. The models are worthy heirs to the great French toy-soldier tradition established by Lucotte and Mignot. (*Forbes collection.*)

west of England, had the diorama on public display for three years. Pressing financial problems forced Waterloo to the auction block. It was hoped that it would raise £15,000, but on the first occasion it was offered it failed to sell. With its terrain and its *son et lumière* equipment, it was just too vast for most collectors to take on. The Battle of Waterloo was fought once more in the auction room – and this time the victor was the Royal Green Jackets regimental museum at Winchester, which clinched the matter with a £4,000 bid. The affair of the diorama proved an obvious truism about toy-soldier collecting: small is beautiful.

New toy soldiers: Collector rating

Scope and variety	9
Investment potential	C
Price range	£6/$10 to three figures; more for connoisseur models

TOY TOWN & COUNTRY

Many of the buoyant prices at lead-soldier sales on both sides of the Atlantic are not for lead soldiers at all. One focus of attention has moved away from military miniatures to the range of civilian models and accessories made in lead and other metals, the toy town and country scene. It is a specialized field, essentially an offshoot of the toy-soldier industry rather than a part of diecast toy vehicle production with which the next chapter deals. Toy town and country choice covers a wide spectrum of subjects and activities: leisure, farm and barnyard, zoos, circuses, gardening, sports, the fire brigade and the Salvation Army, among many. War has nothing to do with it – except for the fact that the toy soldier geniuses, such as William Britain and Georg Heyde, made some of the most delightful and inventive 'civvy' toys on the market.

In 1923 the editor of *The Toy and Fancy Goods Trader* congratulated Britain's for 'a triumph which from a spectacular point of view eclipsed anything which they have yet done'. The rave phrases rolled from his pen – 'acme of perfection … all our expectations fell short of the real thing … beautiful … comment is unnecessary …' He was welcoming the arrival in major marketing terms of Britain's toy farms at the British Industries Fair of that year. Previously the exhibit had

Below. Mignot, being French, seldom produced a set of soldiers without a flag-bearer. Therefore, even when it made a civilian group, the Paris fire brigade, the smartly uniformed firemen were accompanied by a standard-bearer. This modern set comes from the old moulds. (*Forbes collection.*)

featured the firm's wildly successful toy armies. In 1923, however, the company had sprung a surprise on their customers by devoting half the display at the annual shop-window event to a landscape scene representing a village and farm.

It was peopled and stocked by the new Home Farm pieces which were to sell in millions and millions, a delightful and huge variety of lead figures that have now become collector items (many of the farms pour out of the London factory of Britain's to this day in *plastic* torrents).

There were, to quote the trade journal, 'cows, sheep, chickens and every denizen of the farmyard, a lake with ducks and swáns, while dotted here and there about the village were to be seen all the familiar figures of country life: a parson, a ploughman, a policeman, the shepherd, and the Weary Willie all found their place in the picture'. The Weary Willie who caught the editor's eye is not specifically identified, but the role was soon to be filled by Britain's Village Idiot, the rarest farm figure of them all today. Numbered 587 in the catalogue, and destined to become a villager with a price on his head of £100/$150 or more in prime health, the idiot was a remarkable model, smocked and rustic-hatted, shod in heavy boots, his cross-eyed face beaming and his chunky body with a movable arm which could raise a straw to his mouth. It is said that when Britain's showed one of its first farm and village sets to King George V and Queen Mary, one of them remarked on his absence with the words, 'But where is the village idiot? Surely no English village is complete without its village idiot.' Britain's remedied the omission, and the figure appeared in the catalogues at least up to the outbreak of World War Two. Thereafter he was dropped – better taste having prevailed – thus adding to his rarity value. The price of a Village Idiot makes him the target of fakers. Collectors know him by 'feel', weight and the bloom of the old paint.

The Village Idiot represents a facet of the enormous variety of Britain's farm pieces. It was one reason for the range's big success. The firm recognized this in its catalogue: 'The Model Home Farm has the additional advantage, that whilst the smallest box of models is a complete toy in itself, any further purchases, whether bought by the piece or in boxes, are fully complementary to previous collections, whether large or small.'

Britain's started numbering its farm pieces at 501. These numbers, it should be remembered, *never* appear on the figure itself, whether it be soldier, farmworker, animal or even Mickey Mouse, but are the catalogue reference numbers, which also appear on the end-labels of boxes of sets and in some examples on the box lid itself. The first figure was the farmer, with a stick held in his right hand. The arm was movable, being looped on to a projection on the shoulder. This typical Britain's feature, which gave their soldiers so much attraction for generations of small boys, was widely used for a farm population engaged in a multitude of tasks. Farmers' wives followed, one type having a furled umbrella held in her movable arm. Apart from all types of farm animal (including Spiteful Cat with arched back), there are lead-alloy trees, hedges, gates, buildings, carts, trucks, tractors, haystacks and corn sheaves. Much of the farm series

Below. A rare set by the British make, Charben; number 519, Hikers' Camp, with its original box. It came out at the height of the 1930s enthusiasm for taking to the countryside with boots, haversack and tent. This is a coveted item now worth several hundred pounds. (*Forbes collection.*)

Bottom. This busy scene shows German society parading in their fashions for a military steeplechase at the turn of the century. Several of the officers would be familiar to soldier collectors, as they turn up in more warlike sets. A charming and expensive group – well into four-figures.

Below. The ubiquitous dimestore figures of the United States were not confined entirely to military subjects. Here, Christmas is celebrated in a charming novelty scene by the firm of Barclay, better know to American boys for its machine-gunning, bomb-throwing Doughboys and GIs.

Bottom. Heyde at its most inventive. The great toy-figure factory, based in Dresden, Germany, failed to survive World War One. At the peak of production early this century, it made some splendid 'toy town' tableaux, including this zoo for the English-speaking market. (*Forbes collection.*)

Bottom right. The Salvation Army – a civilian line from Britain's that has created world price records when it has appeared at auctions of lead figures. In its day it was a poor-seller among little boys, however, which accounts for its comparative scarcity as output was limited.

was miniaturized in Britain's Lilliput range which matched the OO and HO model railways. There are collectors who specialize in the Lilliput world where a piglet is no bigger than a grain of rice and two carts fit snugly in a matchbox.

Other collectors bypass the farms in favour of lions and tigers, chimps' tea parties, trapeze artists and dancing elephants, the inhabitants of Britain's zoo and circus. Britain's made foxhunting sets to go with the farms, a whole range of famous football teams, gnomes in various sizes, and a cohort of Disney characters, the best-sellers among these being Snow White and the Seven Dwarfs. Perhaps one of the most attractive lines is a garden, made up of metal flower beds to be planted with different blooms, rockery, balustrades, crazy paving, greenhouses, pergolas, trees and lily ponds. From the farm series you can borrow for your garden an old man and woman sitting on a bench. Miniature gates swing on hinges and a gardener pushes a tiny mower across cork lawns. A good garden ensemble (it has no limits: the customer could always add to it) ranks in value today with that of some of the rare toy soldier sets.

The move away from war memories in the 1920s paved the way for other makers in Europe to produce civilian lead toys in large numbers. Long before this era, however, Heyde of Germany, renowned for its 'animated' soldiers, had produced some superb non-military sets. In the author's collection is a Heyde representation of the Wagner *Ring* cycle, a very rare set depicting Siegfried going through his ordeals. There are dragons and flames of lead, grottoes of composition material, the hero in half a dozen poses. Heyde's zoos, too, were little wonderlands complete with animals, cages, turnstiles and family customers. Germany's Elastolin specialized in very realistic, large-scale zoo animals in composition; they are considerably underpriced in today's market. From France, Mignot has given us a frenetically active fire brigade, driving horse tenders, hosing the flames and climbing rescue ladders.

In the United States a folksy heritage of figures has been left by the dimestore soldier makers (see 'Toy Soldiers – Old' on page 178). Manoil brought out a line of civilians under the label, 'The Happy Farm', which featured 40 types of country folk. Farmers sow grain, harvest with a scythe and pitch hay. Women churn butter, cook, wash laundry and perform other domestic chores. There are also bricklayers, hod carriers, carpenters and blacksmiths. Barclay's winter scene was a sure seller at Christmas time among successive generations of Americans. Grey Iron, whose soldier production was somewhat undistinguished, earns a place in collectors' hearts for its range called 'The American Family', chunky figures bordering on the primitive, which seem to recall the era of pulp comics of the Thirties through the war years. One set, 'The American Family on the Beach', is a collectors' target,

Below. A Britain's hunt in full cry over toy countryside. Spot the fox.

with its props of a stretch of boardwalk, a lifeboat and a cabana: shades of Coney Island and Atlantic City.

Collecting toy town and country is for explorers. Gems turn up at collectors' swap meets, in the stock of general antique dealers, at specialized toy-soldier shops and in auctions devoted to soldiers. Antique markets are a rewarding ground, for the reason that many general dealers who come across the more naive, primitive looking pieces fail to recognize their value. It is not unknown for a Barclay skater or a Britain's Village Idiot to turn up in a box of 'junk' or a job-lot at a country auction. Britain's Salvation Army figures, first issued before World War One, had little appeal to boys (although they were bought by Salvationists), so relatively few were manufactured. The first Salvation Army bands to appear at auction went for staggering prices, but then others began to appear from attics and toyboxes. The price dropped, but a large, mint band can still play to a tune of thousands of dollars, rather than hundreds, if it is accompanied by a group of officers including a woman carrying the magazine *War Cry*.

Toy town and country: Collector rating

Scope and variety	9
Investment potential	B-C
Price range	£2/$5 to the higher four figures

TOY VEHICLES

Right. Complete with its colourfully labelled original box is this set of Dinky Toys series number 24, a pre-war treasure that is avidly sought and reverently collected. This group has come slight signs of metal fatigue, common to some models of the time.

'If only I'd saved my old Dinky Toys!' The cry goes up as the Oxo van and the Holland Coachcraft streamliner realize hundreds at auction. Remember those Buddy 'L' heavyweights that went to make Mustang fighter planes for the war effort? The Ives toys that were considered as just so much scrap iron? The Matchbox and Mattel 'moderns' we consigned to the jumble sale? If only we'd kept *everything*.

On both sides of the Atlantic the collector boom in iron, steel, diecast and slush-moulded vehicles and other toys is largely nourished by what was thrown away in earlier generations. The resulting scarcity of certain items provides the stimulus of the chase. Collecting, however, is full of paradoxes. An American collector of cast-iron toy vehicles (a speciality of the United States), a New England doctor who uses the pen name of C.B.C. Lee, observes: 'It is the very combination of the relative scarcity *and multiplicity* of the older toys, plus the preference of collectors for cast iron over diecast zinc alloy and plastic, that makes pre World War Two toys the most attractive to collectors.' Collectors need that multiplicity of choice as much as they need the spur to go on seeking the almost unobtainable.

Lee's criterion for collecting standards and values is simple: 'Condition is important. Paint-wear can drop the

value to half, and broken or missing parts can drop it to nearly nothing. Repairing can occasionally partially rescue an exceptionally rare piece, but more often depresses the value. Reproductions are appearing on the market, and will also tend to depress the values of the real thing. As with anything else in a free market, cost is largely a matter of supply and demand, both of which can wax and wane cyclicly. Let the buyer beware.'

There are two favourites for the title of the first manufacturer of model cars: the Weeden Manufacturing Company of Bedford, Massachusetts, and Carlisle and Finch of Cincinnati, both of which produced vehicles before 1900. Cast-iron toys were made in America just after the Civil War and they reached their zenith by the beginning of the twentieth century. With the arrival of the motor car, nineteenth-century makers of cast iron toys who continued in production included the firms of Hubley, Dent, Wilkins and Kenton. Others, notably Arcade, A.C. Williams and Champion, successfuly made their mark during the first three decades of the new century. The automobile's development inspired the toy industry to feats of miniature engineering. The Hubley Packard was a complex assembly of nearly twenty parts, with opening front doors, hinged hood, seats

and driver. Many of the toys of the pre World War Two decades are today valued in thousands. But Lee has a cautionary word to add. In *Collecting Toys*, Richard O'Brien's series of American price guides, he wrote about Arcade's rare and valuable Brinks armoured truck: 'If someone found a case of 12 Brinks trucks in an old warehouse, he might sell the first for $3,000, but would have trouble getting $500 for the twelfth one.' Those words were written for the guide's 1980 edition, so some multiplication of amounts would now have to be made – but the message remains the same.

At first, all the production of Hubley (founded in 1894) was in cast iron. By the late 1930s, however, the firm had gone heavily into diecast zinc alloy, a method of making toys which had developed out of the linotype casting technique used by printers. In the war Hubley produced 5 million bomb fuses, then geared up to toys again. Students of multiplicity note that in 1952 the company produced 9,763,610 toys plus a further 11,184,878 that were exclusively cap pistols. Massive bulk, rather than massive numbers, was the hallmark of Buddy 'L', another leading American toy vehicle maker. Buddy 'L' vehicles of high-quality heavy steel were first made in 1921 and were named after the young son of Fred Lundahl, the company's owner. 'Impressive indeed – those mighty steel

Buddy "Ls" that rode high, wide and handsome through the Depression era', one admirer and collector has enthused about the firm's fleet of large trucks, fire engines, earth-movers and construction vehicles. The costs of transportation and materials forced the company to seek a lighter metal during the 1930s, but Buddy 'Ls' last to this day, indestructible dinosaurs of the toy world, sadly often rusted and repainted (two factors which considerably lower their collector value).

What is claimed to be the first zinc alloy diecast vehicle was the Model T Ford produced by the Dowst company of Chicago in 1914. Two years earlier the firm had launched a range of dolls' furniture under the label of Tootsietoy, named after Tootsie Dowst, the boss's daughter. The name stuck and Tootsietoy vehicles flooded the market over succeeding decades. Collectors love their uncompromisingly toy-like appearance. Tootsietoy, incidentally, earned kudos for being chosen to supply the little metal players' symbols used in the de luxe edition of the game Monopoly.

In Britain, toy-soldier firms such as William Britain and John Hill and Company (Johillco) began to make toy vehicles, but they used the slush-moulding lead technique applied to their battalions of figures. Great Britain had to wait

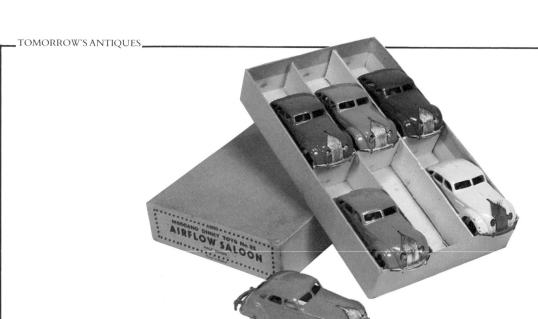

Left. A rare Dinky Toy trade pack of six Airflow Saloons in different colours. This series 32 was introduced in January 1935. The original price was ninepence per vehicle.

Below. From the collection of a distinguished American collector, Dr. Clinton B. Seeley, of Andover, Massachusetts: a rare cast-iron Mack 'Lubrite Gasoline' truck from the Arcade factory. It measures 13.5 inches in length (32cm)

Right. A rare Arcade cast-iron Buick coupe, complete with driver. This model dates from 1927, and is also from the Seeley collection. A car made for hefty motoring in the nursery.

until the 1930s before diecasting became an accepted process for toymaking.

In 1933 Meccano, under Frank Hornby, announced its first diecast cars. The firm's famous Dinky Toys arrived on the market the following year, and were an immediate success. Dinky Toy collectors are legion. They revere the pre-war production and are willing to pay several hundred pounds for a rare early model, such as a Pickford's delivery van of the middle 1930s, or thousands for a mint boxed set of airplanes or other vehicles. Collectors when being offered early examples examine the vehicles carefully under a microscope for telltale hair-cracks which are the first signs of metal fatigue. Its presence can catastrophically affect the value of an otherwise coveted rarity.

The 1950s saw a number of British companies prospering and challenging the virtual monopoly that Meccano enjoyed with Dinky Toys: Crescent, Lone Star, Charbens, Bembros,

Above. Part of the basic pre-war fleet of the inimitable Dinky Toy production line: a model 36d Rover Saloon with tinplate figure. This is an expensive collectable when in first-rate condition. This example sold in London for £550/$775 in 1986.

Left. An extremely rare Ives cast-iron two-seater runabout with unusual clockwork mechanism, the vehicle has the original driver and functioning tiller steering – the pride and joy of the Seeley collection. Length 6.5 inches, (16cm).

Scamold, Merlin, Spot-On and Chad Valley. Fast-rising stars on the scene were Lesney Products with its sensational Matchbox series of models, and the Corgi toys of Mettoy. Model cars were being produced both to play with and to collect. The customers demanded more and more refinements such as doors which opened and the most delicately detailed finishes. Mattel's Hot Wheels, flying along thanks to low-friction axles, arrived to revolutionize the model car industry. In the fierce competition, fortunes were made and, firms went to the wall. The onset of obsoleteness, as ever, spurred collecting zeal. The immense numbers and types of diecast toy vehicles which have been made throughout the world – a reserve which is added to immeasurably every day – make this field of tomorrow's antiques one of the most dynamic and interesting for collectors.

Toy vehicles: Collector rating

Scope and variety	9
Investment potential	A-B for rarities
Price range	£2/$5 to many thousands

VALENTINES

CANOODLING.

A PRETTY sight it is to see,
Two hearts bound up in unity!
But though the thing is doubtless sweet,
It doesn't quite become the street!

This good advice, I'll give to you,—
Whene'er you want to bill and coo,
Repress your soft, and fond delight,
At least, while in the public sight!

This creature is willing to marry,
Can you resist the temptation?
Why ladies do you so tarry?
His match is not in the nation.
Take him & mould him as you please,
What all refuse! aint he the cheese?

Above. An American 'black' Valentine of the late nineteenth century. It was popular to send these cheeky missives, poking fun or even roundly insulting the recipient. As there was little incentive to keep such a Valentine, relatively few have survived – hence their collector appeal today.

Above right. Another American Valentine of the same ilk. Men – especially entrenched bachelors – received their share of Valentine abuse. This quaint specimen has a desirable 'mechanical' feature: the man raises his top hat when a paper lever is manipulated.

Valentine, the patron saint of lovers, inspired sweethearts to indulge in a yearly exchange of gifts from the Middle Ages onwards. He is still producing antiques of tomorrow. Valentine cards of the Twenties and Thirties, many of them with intricate mechanical novelties of the pop-up or moving-part variety, have long been keenly sought by collectors on both sides of the Atlantic. The last great Valentine-sending era came briefly in the 1950s before rising postage stamp costs put too high a price on love by mail; some musical-box Valentines of this period are destined to be regarded as gems of their time. The clock has moved on. And, paradoxically, the 1980s' vogue for sending loving greetings through the personal advertisement columns of morning newspapers on 14 February has had the effect of partly re-fuelling the greetings card industry. True collectors of Valentines see as much validity (if not value) in a modern comic classic as in an early Victorian lacy example.

It was towards the close of the eighteenth century that lovers began to exchange poetic messages on or around 14 February, instead of sending small gifts, such as gloves, posies of flowers or trinkets, which had been customary. (St Valentine, the Christian martyr renowned for his chastity, was beheaded on 14 February in the year 270, although some authorities attribute the age-old customs to the pagan celebration of portents of spring).

People copied popular verses, and these early messages

Left. Hearts, flowers and sentimentality, the essence of the true Valentine. This type of card was a popular line at the turn of the century and well into successive decades: it is a stand-up Valentine, which gives a three-dimensional effect. The staple stuff of collecting.

Below. From a slightly earlier era, this Valentine is decorated with gilt embossed and paper lace. Hand-coloured flowers and cloth leaves surround the lady's face.

tended to be on quarto sheets of paper, rather than 'cards' as we know them today. One of the pioneer commercially-produced Valentines is in the British Museum – published in 1789 by J. Wallis of Ludgate Street, London. It bears a red heart and the verse, 'Believe my love's without disguise/So let's marry and be wise.'

Subsequently, romance received a fillip, not least from developments in lithography, which paved the way for commercial production and opened the floodgates for a wide variety of Valentines that were to replace the elegant, copper-engraved and hand-coloured missives of the late eighteenth century. Mail services were advancing, too. Postal improvements in Britain in 1815 boosted the custom of sending Valentines, and by 1835 the Post Office was recording an extra 60,000 mailings on 13 February. Similarly, Cupid welcomed the coming of the penny post with open arms in the 1840s. Ready made envelopes, another postal revolution, came into use in mid-century when De La Rue perfected an envelope-making machine that was one of the wonders of the Great Exhibition of 1851 in London. Valentines, many of which had remained folded quarto size, became smaller to fit the new envelopes. In both America and Europe during the next three decades people took eagerly to the novelty of comparatively cheap postal rates to send loving messages just before St Valentine's day. Their

scribbles left their mark on history.

One collectors' item crossed the Atlantic at least three times in the mid-1980s, thanks to specialized Valentine auctions. It is a hand-coloured print of young lovers, with a verse beginning, 'When thou art near, the sweetest joys still sweeter seem...', addressed to Mrs Johnson at 114 Prospect Street, Milwaukee, Minnesota, and cancelled 'Feb. 12 Richmond 1861'. Its modern travels hiked its value from £13/$20 to more than £20/$30. Another Valentine is treasured even more highly because of a young lady's cry form the heart. It was penned beneath two Victorian penny-red stamps on the envelope, which was addressed to a Mr J.L. Knight, Bookstall, Rye Lane, Peckham, London, in 1872: 'Run Postman Run – my own true love is waiting'. History does not tell us whether Mr Knight became her Mr Right.

Valentines from this time exist in great variety. Decorations of tinsel, pressed flowers, ferns, real lace, feathers and even paste jewellery can be found. Examples with delicate, coloured-paper cut-outs have realized three figures at auction. There are greetings in the shape of gloves, a throwback to the custom of exchanging gifts. From the last 20 years of the century come a wealth of satin and net, and cards which open out concertina fashion as three-dimensional stand-ups.

Mechanical Valentines of the day are very popular with

Below. Exquisitely crafted as a home-made operation by an American woman in the mid-nineteenth century, this personal offering foreshadowed a huge flood of factory-produced Valentines. It is made out of layered paper.

Right. A selection of Valentines, prepared by a collector, each with its own mount to protect and display it, an ideal way of preserving a collection. Such touches are the hallmark of a true, serious and dedicateed collector and are to be applauded.

collectors. They depend on finger power and contain hinged panels, arms that move to raise hats or umbrellas, doors that open to reveal a church, levers to be pulled to activate a swing, clothes that peel off to show saucy underwear. Perhaps the archetypal 'mechanical' example of the Valentine at its most romantic and lacy is the beehive type, which can command a figure in the low hundreds of pounds or dollars for a rare version: pull a tiny piece of string and it raises a beehive-shaped spiral of paper, revealing a tender message, a couple of love birds or a sylvan scene. Another novelty is a currency note or postal order drawn on the Bank of Love.

Modern swains penning lines for the small-ad columns on Valentine's morn might well take inspiration from their forebears, although at some cost in wordage. A best-selling pamphlet of mid-Victorian days puts forward this verse as the sort of thing do-it-yourself Valentines should be writing to the objects of their affection: 'Ah! wert thou but the graceful vine, and I the tendril true, Around thy graceful stem I'd twine, and fondly cling to you.'

Ready made, printed cards abounded by this time, but there was a big market for such booklets as the sixpenny 'Ladies' Polite Valentine Writer', published by Dean and Company which supplied stanzas for all seasons of the heart – from what to do about unrequited love to how to repel an unwanted suitor. Collectors love these Valentine handbooks and they sell in London for up to £100 each and $200 in the United States.

A nineteenth century booklet, 'Cupid's Annual Charter', provides verses to be aimed at all manner of targets: a faithless lover ('Mark, perjured swain…'), an old maid ('Your wrinkled face, and looks so sour/Repel all thoughts of love…'), a miser, a prude, and many more. Many Valentine handbooks and cards pay attention to luring potential husbands from the bottle ('But then, good Sir, mistake me not,/I own I do not like a sot…'), and to converting crusty old bachelors:

'With your dog, your can and pipe,
You seem to pass your life;.
And though at least you're fifty-five,
You do not take a wife.
Reflect in time, 'tis not too late,
Change Jowler for a bride,
'Tis better far to have a mate,
Than a puppy at your side.'

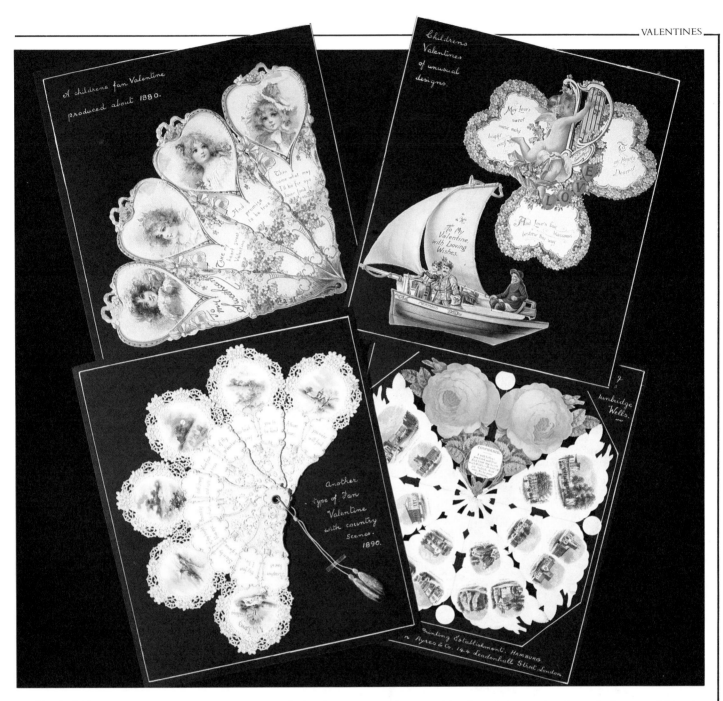

A childrens fan Valentine produced about 1880.

Childrens Valentines of unusual designs.

Another type of fan Valentine with country scenes. 1890.

Cheeky Valentines with derogatory messages pack the shelves of greetings card stores today, but insults on St Valentine's day are nothing new. In the latter part of the last century Americans and Britons excelled themselves in sending scurrilous messages. 'Black' Valentines, a far cry from the lovey-dovey variety, are at the top of many a collector's list. They were mailed to recipients who were accused of being spiteful, vain, flirtatious, miserly, ugly and scandalous. Each message of abuse was accompanied by a grotesquely unflattering drawing of a woman or man. These derogatory cards are today relatively rare and valuable (up to £100/$150 each) for the simple reason that not many of the recipients would have been inclined to keep them for posterity.

From various international collections we know, for example, that an unfortunate widow in Boston, Massachusetts, received a disrespectful caricature of herself as a crone, accompanied by a somewhat optimistic message: 'Your black, my Dear, becomes you well, But soon you'll hear the Wedding Bell!' A lady obviously renowned for gossiping was admonished: 'Your scandal's Like a barbed dart, But mind, base girl, 'tis my design, If other falsehoods you impart, For to expose you, Valentine.'

And a rakish dandy, given more to love of moonshine than matrimony, was solemnly warned at the end of a verse: 'For take my word, a tippler loose I'll never for a Partner choose.'

The reason why people could, in theory, mail such messages with impunity lay in the traditional custom of sending Valentines anonymously. As Charles Dickens intones through the character of Sam Weller in *Pickwick Papers*, 'Never sign a Walentine with your own name'. Thus relatively few Valentines have the personalized, unique cachet enjoyed by signed postcards of old. This is what makes the original envelopes such a valuable property: just as they might have revealed to the recipient some clues about the identity of the anonymous sender, so the envelopes provide interesting information for the collector and historian.

Valentines: Collector rating

Scope and variety	8
Investment potential	C
Price range	£2/$3, to £500/$750

WAR EPHEMERA

Below. Sixpenny sheet music that snatched a laugh or two from the horrors of World War Two. Ephemera such as this can often be found in rummage sales. It is as much a part of the wartime scene as more serious memorabilia.

Bottom. Typical of the mass of literature that was showered over Britain in World War One was this leaflet aimed at the pockets of the people of Lincolnshire. Leaflets were also dropped on the enemy as a propaganda weapon. As peace came, leaflet-drops were put to work for travelling circuses and other shows.

At the main London salerooms of Phillips in a certain week of April 1983 an ex-libris bookplate engraved with the name of Adolf Hitler was politely but firmly turned away as a probable forgery. A fake Nazi flag was given the same treatment. Sotheby's declined a bunch of Christmas cards bearing the Fuehrer's facsimile signature. Christie's was coolly uninterested in photographs of the Berlin bunker and documents purporting to be awards for long service to the Nazi party. In the wake of revelations that the much-trumpeted 'Hitler diaries' were nothing more than clever fakes, the Third Reich was having a bad week.

The diaries had been a news publishing enterprise and no auction house was involved in the affair. But the publicity with which they were heralded had inspired a procession of would-be vendors carrying Nazi-related letters, albums and more bizarre objects to the saleroom doors. Among this stream of German material – far above the usual volume of 'input' thanks to the talk of the millions allegedly paid for the diaries – was the normal proportion of forgeries that the experts have come to expect with Third Reich material. (Perhaps, too, the saleroom specialists were doubly on their guard at this particular time.)

One fact that emerged from the upturn of Nazi memorabilia is that Hitler himself was something of an expert 'forger'. He had to sign so many documents that he resorted to the mechanical writer, a device that reproduces a credible signature from a matrix. 'Hitler's genuine signature on even the most mundane document can mean a few hundred pounds or dollars at auction. On a citation for a particularly grand Iron Cross the sum goes up to thousands,' said one specialist. 'But to impress the party faithful, Hitler drew on the technical skills of the Third Reich to produce excellent facsimile signatures, and these appear on hundreds, possibly thousands of documents that are relatively worthless. In addition, deliberate forgeries of Hitler memorabilia abound. We don't normally see all that many at the auction rooms, but they change hands all the time in the street markets, inspired by the prices being fetched for genuine memorabilia of the period.'

Tony Oliver, a British collector of war memorabilia whose expertise and experience is often tapped when special auctions are being prepared, explains the economics of the bogus: 'Two pennants may appear and they are said to have been for Goering's car; they are discovered to be modern American reproductions – a difference of, say, $3,000 and $60 in value. A Knight's Cross of the Iron Cross, believed by the owner to have been Goering's, is a genuine decoration, but *not* Goering's; it means $300-$500 instead of many thousands. Similarly, an unscrupulous person, beating a path to the door of a known collector, might add an engraving of a coveted regimental insignia to a silver-plated chalice to try to lift its value from $100 to $1,000.'

However, it is the ephemera of war, rather than the hardware, which is the main target of fakers, probably because documents are easier, and certainly cheaper, to reproduce than objects. Paper abounds in war. For every man put into the field there is a mountain of paper. Observers of war have frequently remarked on the huge amounts of letters, documents, diaries, photographs that litter the field along with the dead and debris. (Melton Prior, special artist in the

Left. Adolf Hitler produced this picture of a Bavarian village scene in bodycolour and pastel during his days before coming to power. At the end of the war it was taken from the proposed Nazi Party museum site at Linz in Austria. Thirty years after Hitler's death, it sold at auction for £4,600/$7,000, more on its historic connection than on its artistic merit.

Below. London Hospital, 1914 – a painting by Sir John Lavery, signed, and inscribed in the artist's handwriting, 'Presented by the artist to the Ulster Division Fete, 1917.' It has been exhibited at several municipal art galleries thgroughout Britain.

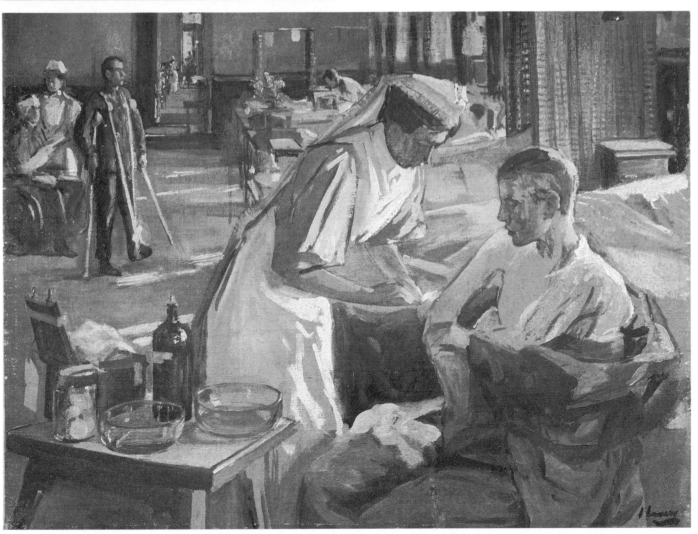

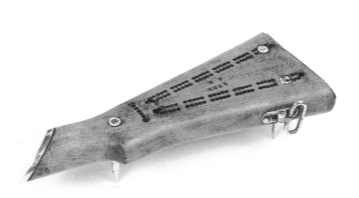

Above. This cribbage board is made from the stock of a World War One rifle and is inscribed '1914 R.F.'. The legs are made from 3 bullets and the pegs are concealed in the end of the stock where the equipment for cleaning the rifle was originally housed.

Below. Symbol of wartime grit and grin-and-bear-it. A civilian ration book for the period of 1945-46, similar to those which had been used throughout the duration of hostilities.

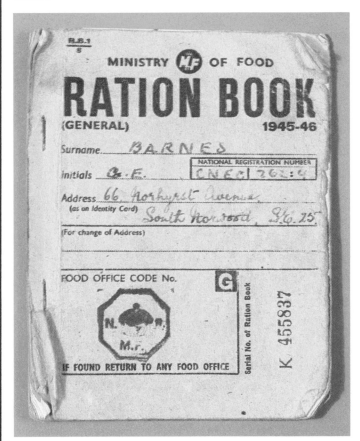

Zulu War: 'Amidst the various articles belonging to them [the British dead of Isandhlwana] which were scattered over the field of carnage were letters from wives … portraits of those dear to them, and other homely things, remembrances of the dearest occasions.' Archibald Forbes, war correspondent: 'I chanced on many sad relics and letters from home, photographs, journals, blood-stained books, packs of cards … Colonel Glynn found a letter from himself to Lieutenant Melvill, dated the day before the fight.')

Sometimes the immediate provenance of a war item is the soundest clue to its authenticity. Much material from the theatres of Europe and the Pacific in World War Two is sold at auction by the soldiers who brought it home with them. If an apparently interesting piece of historic memorabilia comes with a first-hand account of how, where and when it was obtained, it stands a good chance of passing the initial stage of the credibility test.

At other times provenance has to rely on second-hand testimony. A postcard-sized watercolour, said to have been painted by Adolf Hitler and used by him to pay for food when he was hard up in Munich in 1913-14, comes into the auction house. The view is of the Maximilinaeum, now the Bavarian parliament house, in pen and sepia ink wash, signed with Hitler's initials and dated 1914. The picture is accompanied by a letter from a well known Hitler expert living in Munich in the 1960s, stating that the watercolour came from the picture collection of Frau Helen Schwaiger, a waitress who received payment in Hitler's works for food she served him in a Munich restaurant. Stylistically, the picture could be Hitler's; the initials appear genuine. At auction, the watercolour fails to sell. Perhaps the reserve price is too high. Perhaps potential buyers feel unsatisfied on balance of probabilities. In the same sale, other Hitler watercolours of the same period do well, some of them making $7,000 each, a price based more on the artist's notoriety than on his skills.

In 1985 a cache of documents and photographs of the Hitler era was discovered in a Canadian attic where it had lain unopened for forty years. A crate containing some 3,000 items was inspected by a family living in Golden, British Columbia. It had been brought home at the end of the war by Frederick Schiesse, who had been an intelligence officer with the Canadian forces in Europe. At that time he gave his family one brief look at the documents and then packed them away. Schiesse died in August 1984. His family called in Phillips from London. The cache formed 115 lots of a special sale of war memorabilia: it included a mass of historic documentation from the files of Hitler's deputy, Martin Bormann. The introverted nature of Bormann, his closeness to Hitler, and his mysterious disappearance from the ruins of Berlin in 1945 made the material of special interest, and it sold for many thousands of pounds at auction.

The Third Reich takes up a large part of collectors' attention because the war memorabilia which it has left is exceptionally well documented and its 'hardware' is composed of exceptionally well-made objects, often in materials of intrinsic value. But that is by no means the whole story.

Among soldiers' possessions which have become collectors' items are copies of the British army's 'Small Book' from the days of the redcoats, a kind of soldier's guide containing regulations and information, and details of his service and pay. Some still turn up in their original protective metal cases. Paybooks from the middle and late nineteenth century, and its turn, are fairly common, particularly of the Boer War. World War One paybooks also appear in numbers, among them German examples. Officers' commissions, leave passes,

Left. The tin hat and air raid precautions – facts of British life in World War Two. The photograph shows a group of the Home Guard – 'Dad's Army' – recruited for defence purposes.

Below. The three silver badges are examples of badges worn by the sweethearts of men serving in the Royal Air Force during World War Two. They are seen here with the actual navigator's tunic badge.

discharge papers, and metal identification tags of World War Two are collected, although there are no many of them that they have as yet little value unless they have a special association.

When British troops were at war in the Sudan in the very late 1880s a few officers took with them their new toy, the Kodak camera. Edward Douglas Loch, a Grenadier Guards officer, was one of these Kodak pioneers. His collection of 160 photographs, largely concentrating on the movement of troops and supplies along the River Nile, is now in the National Army Museum of London, a valuable record of the campaign. There is also a collection by an anonymous brother officer who took a more personal view of the campaigning, capturing touches of humour such as shots of three Cameron Highlanders balanced precariously on a camel, and an adjutant hiding bashfully behind a fly whisk. Such material is the stuff of soldiers' ephemera, rather than the dramatic battle scenes.

Bruce Bairnsfather, a British officer serving in France in World War One, became the most famous comic artist of the war (his subsequent drawing tours included spells with the American Doughboys) through the cartoons of frontline life which were published by Bystander magazine. Old Bill, sharing a shell-hole with a younger soldier, remarks: 'Well, if you knows of a better 'ole, go to it!' The collectors juggle with 'telephone numbers' when discussing what the original of this cartoon might fetch on the market today. That apart, there is much Bairnsfather material to be collected. He was a prolific artist, and there are many original watercolours around. Then there are his *Bystander* collections of cartoons, the *Fragments* series, postcards, books, theatre programmes, advertising ephemera, as well as a huge and varied range of

1917 chinaware on which his cartoons were transfer-printed. Some Bairnsfather material goes on to span World War Two.

The original Bairnsfather art work of a well known and loved Old Bill cartoon will outsell an original Hitler watercolour. And so it should – it belongs to the warmer memories of wartime comradeship and 'togetherness'. Wartime ephemera collecting embraces a British ration book and clothing coupons that tell of times when cuisine was a triumph of ingenuity and fashion was make and mend. It includes signed photographs of Churchill and FDR. A 1940s advertisement for Craven A cigarettes (British readers, please note, ½d for 10); how-to-survive manuals issued by the Air Raid Precautions organizations; music covers of songs of the day such as 'Till the Lights of London Shine Again' and a cheery number called 'Adolf', showing a Tommy giving Hitler six of the best on his backside; American wartime bubble-gum cards by the ton: these are the ephemera of war on the home front. And what am I offered for lot 252: a small hand-cranked gramophone said to have been used by RAF pilots while waiting to 'scramble' at Hawkinge fighter station in the Battle of Britain – on it, still, a scratchy but playable original 78 of Vera Lynn, singing 'We'll Meet Again'?

War ephemera: Collector rating

Scope and variety	8
Investment potential	B
Price range	£10/$15 to five figures

WAR HARDWARE

Sergeant Shoichi Yokoi, wartime veteran of the Japanese army, would be surprised to find what people collect. Sergeant Yokoi did not make much of a name for himself in World War Two. In fact, it was not until nearly thirty years after the end of the war that he became known at all – when he emerged from a cave on Lubang island in the Philippines, where he had been hiding from the Americans in the belief that the war was still going on. Sergeant Yokoi might have been amazed to discover, even in 1974 when he gave himself up to international fame, that the trappings with which the Imperial Japanese army went to war now had a place hanging on collectors' walls and encased in museum cabinets.

For collectors of wartime mementoes there is a large choice, ranging from cigarette cards of the day to planes and tanks. Paul Raymond, the London theatre and nightclub impressario who amassed one of the biggest private collections in the world, covered the whole range in his collecting. Here was World War Two under the roof of the Whitehall Theatre in the centre of London, a display that Raymond called the London War Museum. After two years, however, he had to surrender to a Westminster City Council ruling that the building must be used for live theatre rather than exhibition. The embargo led in June 1985 to the biggest war sale in history, with the auctioneer Andrew Hilton sitting uniquely in the 'rostrum' of an American armoured half-track in front of the sentinel effigy of General Patton.

Items ranged from wartime clothing coupons to a Spitfire, suspended in the gods. Under the hammer went Churchill (a signed photograph and other memorabilia) and effigies of other wartime leaders and generals; tracked vehicles, motorcycles and desert scout cars; British 25-pounder and Oerlikon guns, German and Allied machine-guns and an

Below. At the end of World War Two many Allied soldiers brought home with them superb scale toys of German military vehicles such as these, made variously by Tippco, Lineol and Hausser (of Elastolin soldier fame). German technical excellence and ingenuity went into the making of these fine models, which are lavishly fitted with intricate working parts, and manned by composition members of the Wehrmacht.

Left. Throughout the world there is a proliferation of clubs of enthusiasts who collect World War Two fighting vehicles of the Allies and the Axis powers. The members will sometimes spend years refurbishing and re-equipping an armoured half-track or a rare motorcycle combination. This is some of the veteran transport that has now achieved museum status.

Below. A Heinkel 111 similar to those which led Hitler's bombing squadrons. This example took part in the *Battle of Britain* motion picture. Its provenance includes spells in the Spanish air force and display at Britain's Historic Air Museum, Southend. It was purchased by show-business impressario Paul Raymond for his London War Museum at the Whitehall Theatre, and later found a new owner when the museum closed in 1985.

American Arctic sled; a searchlight, staff cars, and a scooter used by the airborne troops at Arnhem.

There were enough life-size uniformed models of British, German, Italian and Japanese troops for a collector's parade – lot 84, Kamikaze pilot, 'sold to the gentleman standing by his side'. And planes: a Mustang in the colours of a USAAF squadron based at Leiston, Suffolk, in 1944-5; a Messerschmitt 109 in desert colours; a German Fieseler Storch reconnaissance aircraft in Afrika Korps livery. Housed in storage was a German Heinkel 111 bomber. A sinister looking group of Hitler and his henchmen were mostly bought by an anonymous Swiss bidder who had an agent at the sale. The Hitlerites paid the day's highest prices for effigies of wartime leaders, prompting the observation from Tony Oliver, a leading collector of war memorabilia: 'Notoriety seems to have a premium. To date, only three motor cars have ever gone above a million dollars each: Al Capone's, Bonny and Clyde's, and Hitler's.' Among the famous and the infamous, however, a British Land Army girl and a humble air-raid warden found bidders. At the coffee bar, collectors' talk was of relative values: 'Back home I can buy Tommies' steel helmets at $8 each, GIs' at $25, and the Wehrmacht's at $75.' 'I think Rommel was a steal at $600, uniform and all.'

Behind the big auctions of war memorabilia is a complicated infrastructure of specialization. The highest, most expensive level is that of actual warplanes: a Spitfire in flying condition will head towards the $1 million ceiling within the next few years, the experts predict. Genuine flying veterans of World War Two can only get scarcer. Then come the wheeled transport worshippers who recondition, repair and

Below. Going, going...gone into the history of evil. Members of the Nazi hierarchy are fronted by Adolf Hitler in this group of effigies, dressed in uniforms of their time, which came under the hammer at the sale of the London War Museum. The successful bidder for most of them was an anonymous Continental collector. Churchill, Roosevelt and Stalin and distinguished military leaders such as Patton, Montgomery and Rommel also joined the ranks of collectors' acquisitions.

Below right. Suspended in time in the heart of London: a German Feiseler Storch observation aircraft of wartime vintage awaits bidders above a collection of staff cars and Allied Jeeps. In the near distance is a Spitfire Mark IX. The engine of this famous aircraft is missing, but many collectors place most importance on the integrity of the frame and fabric; an old engine usually has to be replaced or completely reconditioned to achieve flying capability.

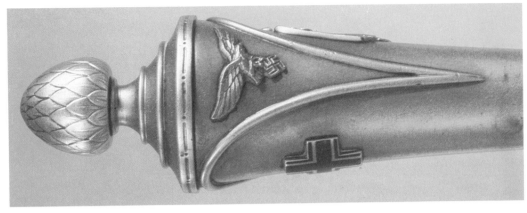

Left. Erhard Milch, Luftwaffe deputy to Goering, owned this silver-topped baton. He surrendered it to a British Commando hero, Brigadier Derek Mills-Roberts, in 1945. Mills-Roberts, who had just witnessed the results of horrific Nazi atrocities, was so incensed by Milch's arrogant 'Heil Hitler' and his disregard for the victims, that he broke the stick over the German field-marshal's head.

re-engine the vehicles of World War Two and the Korean war. There are specialized arms collectors, bayonet people, enthusiasts of badges and medals, and those who collect only uniforms. At some points the collecting fraternity becomes confused with the dealers in 'wartime surplus' material – webbing, haversacks and clothing used for everyday and leisure purposes – and their customers.

As wartime collecting spreads, the news percolates to the general public that those dust-gathering relics, brought home from a long-gone war, may be valuable, after all. There was the case of the only-too-real Hitler memento that closed the saleroom. An old lady from west London brought in a parcel and asked for the 'wartime souvenirs' department. A cataloguer who had been a former Royal Air Force armourer unwrapped the object and recognized it immediately as a wartime unexploded German incendiary bomb, still fused.

He called the police, who evacuated the building until army bomb-disposal men arrived. The woman, whose husband had been a fire-watcher in the Blitz, had found the bomb in the street, and had kept it on top of a wardrobe. It could, said the bomb disposal men, have gone off at any time in its 40-odd years on top of the wardrobe, or on its journey to the salerooms by Underground train. The lady was assured that the art market did not have much call for unexploded bombs.

War hardware: Collector rating

Scope and variety	9
Investment potential	C
Price range	From £5/$10 to six figures

WILD WEST

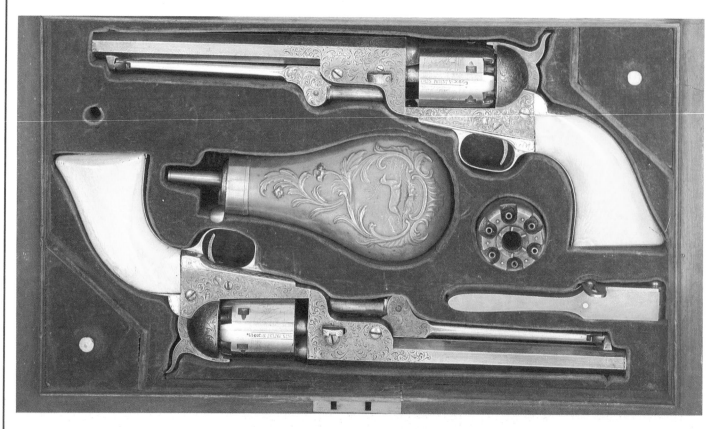

Above. Cased for presentation purposes, this pair of nineteenth-century Navy Colt pistols most probably were never fired in anger. The Colt collecting scene is complicated by the existence of large numbers of cleverly made reproductions that came from a Turkish factory in Constantinople even as the West was being won. Collectors of firearms in the United Sates form a large and specialized group among those interested in artefacts of the pioneering era.

A young American cavalry lieutenant who campaigned among the Cheyenne Indians on the Tongue River with Frederic Remington (1861-1909) has left this description of the artist: 'We first became aware of his existence in camp by the unusual spectacle of a fat citizen dismounting from a tall troop horse at the head of a column of cavalry. The horse was glad to get rid of him, for he could not have trained down to two hundred pounds in less than a month of cross-country riding on a hot trail.' Remington, so continued the account, shook the lieutenant's hand vigorously. 'Sorry to meet you, Mr Sydenham,' he said. 'I don't like second-lieutenants – never did. Captains are my style of people – they lend me horses.'

Horses were part of the being of Remington, who is probably the most widely collected artist of the American Western scene. He wanted his epitaph to read: 'He knew the horse.' As Remington progressed from illustrator to painter, he complained: 'People won't stand for my painting sunsets … got me pigeon-holed in their minds, you see; want horses, cowboys, and West things – won't believe me if I paint anything else.'

The lieutenant who saw Remington in his essential, hard-riding, travelling role as illustrator revealed something of the artist's technique of drawing from memory: 'No pencils, no notebook, no "Kodak" – nothing indeed but his big blue eyes rolling around at everything and into all sorts of queer places.' Everything Remington saw he noted in his brain and later translated it into dramatic action for high-paying magazines such as *Harper's Illustrated Weekly*. The statistics of his artistic output were as big as the man. Among his 2,739 pictures were illustrations for 142 books, of

Below. The daddy of the American long gun and a respected antique forebear of all the firearms on the new frontier. This flintlock Kentucky rifle dates from around 1800. It has a sighted octagonal barrel inlaid with a silver plaque inscribed S. Lauck. It sold in London in 1983 for £20,000/$30,000; intervening years have probably doubled its value.

Bottom. A late nineteenth-century buckskin vest from the Sioux nation of American Plains Indians. The buckskin-fringed garment is worked in beads and the back depicts two braves on horseback surmounted by crossed American flags. Plains Indian clothing, ceremonial objects and weapons are in the front rank of ethnographical collecting.

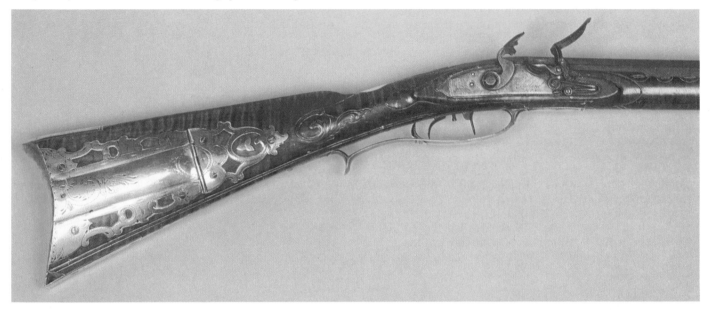

which 8 were his own. His first and most popular bronze, the famous *Bronco Buster*, was published first in an edition of 40 by the sand-casting method, and subsequently (after 1898) no fewer than 250 casts were made by the lost-wax process. Familiarity has not stopped it being a runaway success: one example sold for a record £95,000/$143,000 at Phillips in New York in April 1982, and it has gone on to reach sensational new heights since then.

Frederic Remington represented a school of artists who had little time for art galleries. Theirs was a world of a bed-roll pitched beneath the stars, a hurried sketch under fire on a hill top, and a tin plate of stringy meat shared with soldiers bivouacking in the rain. Perhaps he spoke for many of his breed of Western illustrators when, visiting an exhibition – a rare event for him – of impressionist paintings in the East, he said: 'Say, I've got two maiden aunts upstate who can *knit* better pictures than those.'

Remington and those who went before him, like the great Charles Russell and Albert Bierstadt, master of the towering landscape, have long been hailed as geniuses of the Western scene. A new generation of Western artists was to rise. Some considerable time after there was little of the West to pioneer, East Coast painters were still setting their eyes on the prairies, in the 1920s. One of the now most celebrated of those to go West was William Henry Dethlep Koerner (1878-1938) whose speciality was action-adventure subjects, and who had illustrated hundreds of serials for popular magazines as well as for Zane Grey's cowboy books. Koerner stands high in collector esteem today and his pictures are customarily well into five-figure values. His wish was to meet people who had lived during the tempestuous times of Billy the Kid, Wyatt

Earp and Buffalo Bill. His canvases capture the essence of the West and are full of historical authenticity. He accented his paintings by using as props original Indian artifacts and genuine nineteenth-century cowboy gear.

From the second generation of new Western illustrators come men such as Tom Lovell, Tom Ryan, Frank McCarthy and John Clymer. Such is the hold of the old West on modern imagination that specialized sales of American art (not excluding the photography of Indians by people like Adam Clark Vroman, F.A. Rinehart and Edward S. Curtis) are now leaders on the auction circuit from New York to Los Angeles, with some outbreaks of virulent bidding fever at showcase sales in places such as Denver, Houston and Dallas.

The North American Indian contributes some of the most exciting (and expensive) art to the ethnographical collecting scene, but the major part of this contribution belongs to the genre of true antiques. It is an abundant heritage, with as much difference between the art and artifacts of the woodlands Indians of the east and the fishing tribes of the north-west coast as there is between those of the northern plains nations and the desert peoples of the south-west. All is not in history, however. From the south-west, for example, many weavings, carvings and other handicrafts produced in the present day are worthy of inclusion in any survey of tomorrow's antiques.

Inuit sculpture, too, is a booming branch of modern art: the Canadian Eskimos are creating simple, powerful forms out of soft stone – green, black and grey soapstone. Their contemporary output stands alongside their art of the nineteenth century, which is also found in ivory and whalebone as well as soapstone. A watershed in the fortunes

Far left. This Colorado Indian subject is typical of the type of interesting Western watercolour that can still be found, with diligent exploration, in the middle-hundreds bracket. The artist is Charles Craig and an obscure date on the picture places it in either 1872 or 1892.

Below left. After a painting by Arthur Fitzwilliam Tait, this vignette, entitled *A Check – Keep Your distance*, is from a group of four hand-coloured, tinted lithographs published in 1852-1856 by N. Currier. The other three titles pre-empt Hollywood's version of the West: *The Prairie Hunter – One Rubbed Out*, *The Pursuit* and *The Last War Whoop*. Tait's Westerners struck gold in 1982 – £4,400/$6,600 for the four prints at auction.

Left. *The Last Stand:* Frederic Remington at his best in a characteristic shoot-out. 'I paint for boys, from ten to seventy,' was how he summed up his approach to art (National Archives, US Bureau of Public Roads).

Below. An oil painting of *A Council on the Mesa* by Frank Tenney Johnson (1874-1939), a mood picture capturing the the essence of the Apache on the trail. Western paintings are a very buoyant area of Americana.

of Inuit art was the organization by the Canadian Eskimo Arts Council of an exhibition called 'Masterworks 1971', which travelled to the British Museum, Le Grand Palais, The Hermitage in Leningrad, and the Philadelphia Museum of Art. Individual Eskimo artists, who had long languished in anonymity, began to be known to the metropolitan art-gallery clientele of the western world: Abraham Pov, Charley Inukpuk, Isa Smiler, Baranbas Akkanashoonark, Pudlo and Kaka.

The cowboy has gone, and with him the tools of his trade. He is remembered in story, on canvas, in bronze, and, above, all through the medium of celluloid. Hardened collectors are justifiably suspicious of handguns and Winchester repeaters that are touted around as the 'real thing'. There is more fakery than reality on the dangerous ranges and poorly mapped frontiers of collecting; it behoves the tenderfoot to be wary. The Colt revolver itself is the victim of forgery. After the success of the Navy Colt of 1851, a flood of Colt-type revolvers reached Britain and America in the nineteenth century from a factory in Constantinople. The Turkish 'Colts' were well made and eminently usable. A trader's cache must have been discovered in the early 1960s, for in mid-decade they began to appear in the dealers' trade with increasing frequency. In the late 1980s, an arms specialist estimated the going price of one of these Turkish Colts at about £100-£140/$150-$200 on the international market. At

that time, a true Navy Colt 1851, 'with a bit of finish', was valued at £650-£850$1,000-$1,300, and a mint example in its case at £2,000-£3,500/$3,000-$5,000.

When this book was at the beginning of the long, long trail that leads to publication, an early 1980s catalogue of a Phillips New York sale of Western art was one of hundreds of records and documents that came under perusal. The subject 'sitters' of some of the pictures therein tell part of the legend of the West: Buckskin Sam, Sitting Bull, Border Gunfighter, The Apache Devil, Bull Moose, The Dude, Chief Yellow Man, and John Wayne ... destined, every one of them, for the collector's corral.

Wild West: Collector rating

Scope and variety	7
Investment potential	A
Price range	£100/$200 to six figures

THE WORLD AROUND US

Right. Aristocrat of twentieth-century American furniture: an oak library table executed by George M. Niedecken for the E. P. Irving house at Decatur, Illinois, in a collaboration with the architect Frank Lloyd Wright. A superbly crafted piece of furniture for the record books.

Far right. Grandmother probably had one that was handed down from generation to generation before her: 'The Challenge' sewing machine of a type first registered by Joseph Harris of Bull Street, Birmingham, England, on February 12, 1871, and in service for many a decade since then.

Below. Deco delight of the early 1930s, destined to continue to be the target of collectors tomorrow. The octagonal mirrored top of this occasional table complements the glass rods on which it is supported.

The elegant oak library table illustrated here was designed for the twentieth century by George M. Niedecken. The style is American Prairie School. The inspiration was born of a marriage of talents – those of designer, Niedecken, and architect, Frank Lloyd Wright. The result is a masterpiece of furniture of our age, a piece that belongs near the pinnacle of any collection of tomorrow's antiques.

The library table was created for the E.P. Irving house at Decatur, Illinois, around 1910 and belonged to the Prairie School concept of 'total design' as epitomized by the work of Wright. Niedecken's designs in light oak complemented the celebrated architect's schemes of open interior planning. In December 1986, after a protracted but unsuccessful search for a purchaser who would be willing to maintain the house and its original furnishings, the collection was sold at auction by Phillips New York. The library table from Decatur changed hands at $20,000 (£13,000) and started life anew somewhere else in the United States.

Much of this century's furniture will stand the connoisseur's test of time. Prices for the works of France's Emile-Jacques Ruhlmann (1879-1933), who introduced the distinctive forms of Art Deco furniture, have long been rivalling those for the works of the earlier master cabinetmakers. His furniture uses exotic woods such as macassar ebony and amboyna, and is often found with inlay of silver, ivory and mother of pearl. It epitomizes the luxury furniture of the years before the Wall Street crash.

Furniture inspired by the Swiss architect, Le Corbusier, and that designed by the Hungarian Marcel Breuer, and the German Mies van der Rohe is already eagerly collected. Corbusier regarded a house as a machine for living, and his

Below. The irrepressible Charlie Chaplin. Among collectors of studio ceramics, he is one of the most popular Royal Doulton issues of the 1920s and 30s, sure of four figures at auction.

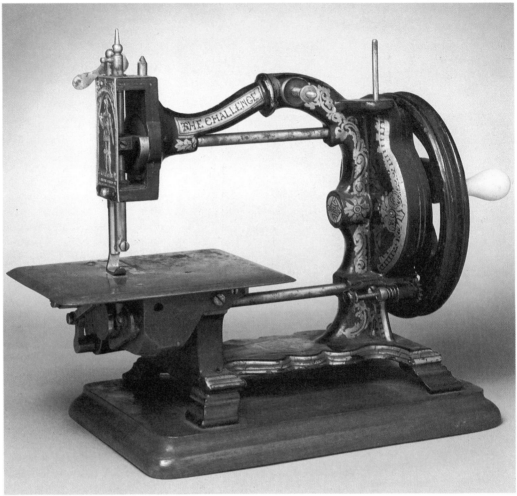

furniture represents the working parts. Breuer, head of the Bauhaus furniture department in 1925, designed the first tubular steel chair after being inspired by contemplating the handlebars of a bicycle; his pioneering cantilevered chair appeared in 1928. From Mies van der Rohe in 1929 came the *Barcelona* chair, consisting of a steel frame and a slung leather seat and back. The tulip chair of Eero Saarinen, a Finn working in America, was the first to employ fibre-glass. The diverse talents of Charles Rennie Mackintosh (see the clock which he made as a wedding present in 1917) and the Cotswolds School of furniture designers are drops in an ocean of British talent that has contributed to the antiques of tomorrow.

A Cotswolds son, pupil and mentor was the late Sir Gordon Russell, whose furniture spanned nearly seventy years of good design. His creations of the Twenties and Thirties became collectors' items in their own time. They attract top bidding when they appear in the salerooms. Awards and honours were deluged on the man who, while introducing new shapes in furnishings, had to contend with handwork purists who saw treason in his belief that hands and machines should be allies not foes. In 1979 the author spent a day talking furniture with him at his Cotswolds home in the west of England. What Sir Gordon, animated, enthusiastic and still making furniture at the age of 86, had to say then is important in the context of tomorrow's antiques.

He beamed through his round spectacles with almost schoolboyish delight when one told him of a friend who still has a much-admired nest of three tables bought at Heal's in London during the war, a product of the Russell-guided Utility furniture scheme. 'It always pleases me when people

tell me that,' he said. The past, present and future were all one in Sir Gordon's conception of good design. He praised the work of the traditional High Wycombe makers of Windsor chairs, the only existing range 'slotted in' to the wartime Utility framework because of its economical and practical qualities: 'If you've got ham bones near the surface like me, there's nothing for comfort like the beautifully shaped elm seat of an eighteenth century wheelback chair.' Practicality was important. 'Today the modern movement has run into the sand. They are trying to evolve shapes which have never been seen before. Chairs for instance. The result is you can't sit on them. Students could learn more by paying attention to what has been done before. After all, if you've got 1,000 years of tradition, you don't want to throw it into the ditch.'

Gordon Russell went to school at Chipping Campden in the Cotswolds about a year after C.R. Ashbee had moved his Guild of Handicrafts there from London. He was deeply influenced by the Cotswolds movement and when he returned from the 1914-18 war with a wound, the Military Cross, and a desire to 'set up a workshop to make decent furniture for ordinary people', the path was laid for one of the most brilliant furniture designers of our age. The rest – wartime Utility, the Council of Industrial Design, growing international renown – is history.

Although the 1940s Utility scheme, of which he was the prime architect, laid down irradicable lines of good design, beneficially affecting the course of furniture for several decades, and was a resounding success in its context of the war, Sir Gordon was firmly against official direction of taste in principle. But he just as firmly believed that people should be educated out of the old ways of accepting 'caricatures' of past

Left. Wristwatches have already become important features of the best jewellery sales, not only for their precious-metal intrinsic value but for their quality of manufacture and place in design history – especially those with an Art Deco flavour. Modern time-keeping shows its face in this selection of modern watches.

Below. From tiger and bear to pierrot and monarch, this display of Royal Doulton figures ranges in time from the 1920s up to modern history with a 1970s figure of Queen Elizabeth II on the extreme right of the middle row. Royal Doulton collectors and their societies have proliferated around the world in the present day.

styles; and the 'Chippendale' cocktail cabinet in laminated plastic was a favourite target of his scorn.

Had he been born earlier, and been able to work in furniture's golden age of the Georgians, what role would he have filled by choice? Without hesitation, he said: 'I would have liked a small country workshop, while still occasionally spending a bit of time in London – a great furniture centre, after all. Just 12 or 20 people. The sort of thing some people are determined to stamp out. They have the fatuous idea that size and speed are all and that it's socially irresponsible to buy something everyone can't have. I'm all in favour of an elegance that's going out of life.'

One suspects that Sir Gordon Russell would have summoned up approval, on design grounds, if no others, for that symbol of the 1940s and 1950s, the jukebox. It was practical. Moreover, it came in forms that were of its day and its function. The design was all it should be: loud, brash, attention-seeking, gaudy – especially the American Wurlitzer model which was the first (in 1974) to enter the saleroom charts above the four-figure level. In the 1950s a new Wurlitzer cost about £300 in Britain. The manufacturers kept changing the machines because the public wanted the latest model. Operating companies who supplied the music machines to leisure outlets found their warehouse stacked high with redundant models. 'We used to put hammers

Below. Art Deco, 1930. This chair is part of a sycamore drawing-room suite with reeded ebonized decoration, comprising cocktail cabinet, settee in pink dralon upholstery, two pairs of armchairs and standard lamp. Experts consider that suites such as this are underpriced compared to some Victorian furniture.

Right. *Tomorrow's Antiques* takes a curtain call with the assistance of Enrico Caruso, whose famous operatic features are reproduced in colourful caricature on a rare enamelled pendant of the 1920s/30s era by LaCloche Freres. Deco styles belong to some of the most popular areas of jewellery.

through them, but that was hard work,' says one former operator. 'We found it was easier to wheel them out to the hoist in the loft and push them out. They were built like tanks. It was the best way to break them up. We kept one intact, as a showpiece and to hire out to movie companies.'

Alongside jukeboxes as a modern collector craze is the vogue for buying old penny-in-the-slot view shows, fruit machines and pin tables – the hardware of the seaside pier. Some rare peepshows – *The Spanish Inquisition*, *The Haunted House*, *The Drunkard's Dream* – are almost rivalling the better juke boxes in value. A lifesize *Sioux Medicine Man* which accommodates the fruit machine in his huge chest has gone into a British enthusiast's collection at over £2,000/$3,000. In countries where the coinage has changed since the Fifties, a secondary trade in old coins is flourishing, but many collectors are converting their machines to take the present day money.

The frontiers of collecting are daily coming closer to our own times. Hardly an eyebrow is raised at collectors' sales when radio sets of as late as the 1950s appear. A 1930s British Bakelite receiver of circular form might fetch £100 in its home country, or over $200 in the United States. A novelty in radios can easily be double this value. Example: an unusual *papier-mâché* 1927 loudspeaker in the form of the British comic-strip characters Pip, Squeak and Wilfred, made for a child's bedside. And here is the television era under the hammer: 'An interesting Murphy 16-inch black and white television receiver, circa 1950, on a tubular stand.' An endless souce of information for radio and TV collectors is Gerald Wells, who, at his home in Dulwich, south-east London, has amassed a lifelong collection of more than 1,000 wireless sets, all in working order. He saves old radios from garbage dumps

and from dustbins, and even admits to having been arrested in his youth for submitting to his craving by *stealing* radios. His home is a museum. The condition from which he suffers, he says, is 'wirelessitis', a disease contracted even before birth when his mother must have received a shock from a nursery socket during installation of electricity in the house in 1929.

Modern art is already a boom area of collecting, as are the contemporary decorative arts. The ceramics of Clarice Cliff, Bernard Leach and Susie Cooper, among a host of twentieth century potters, are the targets of collectors – and forgers. Royal Doulton is something of a religion. Carnival glass is on a high in the United States. Clocks and watches, typewriters, sewing machines, woodworking tools, steam engines, garden furniture, fountain pens, lawn mowers, pocket calculators, transistor radios: they are either collected now, or will be collected as time hallows models with the aura of obsoleteness. What will posterity say of some of the gift-wrapped flotsam of the Eighties: novelty cups and saucers in the shape of crumpled balls of paper, vases made like dented plastic beakers, telephones shaped as tomatoes and bananas, sunglasses that confront the onlooker with a wildly winking hologram of an eye?

At the Castle Museum in York, replicas of the Victorian parlour and other domestic scenes are now accompanied by a British 1950s room setting and a 1981 kitchen. Three computers have made it to the museum. One of them, a Sinclair ZX80, already 'looks as though it came out of the Ark', says the curator.

Robots, too, are the victims of the disposable society. New models are fast elbowing yesterday's stars out of the market, into collectors' hands. Surely, we should find a shred of sympathy for a shambling newcomer of the late 1980s, named Dingbot and described in these terms by a toy magazine: 'This bump-and-go guy shuffles along, holding a map as if trying to find his way. Occasionally, he'll stop, turning his head back and forth while muttering some robot noises. He then wanders off, trying different directions.' Will someone kindly point him in the direction of tomorrow's antiques?

Alan Bonner 45 top. **Richard Carr** 10, 45 bottom. **Anthony J. Lambert** 144 top, 145. **Kirsty McLaren** 16 bottom, 17, 18, 31 left, 35 top, 49 top, 52 right, 63 bottom, 70, 71, 77, 80 top, 84, 85 right, 90, 111, 112, 113 bottom, 114, 115, 125 left, 174 top, 203. **Con Putbrace** 175, 177. **John Strange** 43.

The publishers wish to thank **Donay Antiques of Camden Passage, London, Graham Webb of Brighton** and **The Atkinson Collection** for their help and advice.

The illustration on page 77 came from stills issued to publicize films by the following companies:– **Columbia Pictures, EMI Film Distributors, United Artists Corporation Ltd, Warner Bros Pictures.**

Dunestyle Publishing Ltd. have endeavoured to observe the legal requirements with regard to the rights of the suppliers of photographic material.